Chapter One.

Better

Throughout the 1960s and 70s a staff contract with the BBC offered a job for life. If you had blown a raspberry at the Queen or heaved a custard pie at the Pope then you might have been asked to resign but quite frankly, I doubt it. The result of this tremendous job security was a flowering of inventive endeavour which became the envy of the broadcasting world. Creative men and women from all walks of life and of all eccentric mental conditions, jostled together in the indulgent hot house that was the British Broadcasting Corporation. They frequently produced programmes of remarkable quality. But the job security of the BBC had its downside too for it enabled artistic dimwits, technical incompetents and walking managerial disasters to thrive and prosper. I worked for the BBC for 31 years and it was my great good fortune to encounter a mixture of all them.

It was as a trainee assistant film editor, eighteen and straight from school that I joined the BBC film department in November 1965. I was to learn a great deal about the technicalities and niceties of film editing; I was to learn even more about just how useless it was possible to be and yet still achieve success in those golden days of the BBC.

Every Trainee Asst. Editor spent their first eleven months in a series of 'four week' attachments to different cutting rooms. It was a good system, the trainee became the third member of the traditional team of editor and assistant. You quickly got experience in a wide range of programmes and of course you got to work with a wide variety of Film Editors. Rumours quickly spread, around my intake of trainees, as to which editors were best avoided. Top of the list was one Teddy Ballstrobe, an extraordinary name for an extraordinary man. The reasons for his notoriety were many, varied and all revolting.

Teddy Ballstrobe was in his mid-fifties at that time. He always wore the same suit which looked as if it had been bought in the mid-forties and was one model up from the de-mob suit of legend. He was portly, bald and he sweated a lot. Under the neon lighting of the Ealing Studios canteen his face seemed to shine. It was in the canteen, one lunch time in my first month at the studios, that I met Teddy for the first time. He was carrying his lunch tray and looking for somewhere to sit.

"Oh God." said Ken, one of the editors I was sitting with, "Here comes bloody Teddy Ballstrobe, spread out everybody, make it look as if there's no room." But we were too late.

"Move over maties." beamed the shiny Teddy "Make room for a little 'un." I thought I heard some of the others actually groan. "I've got a really good new joke for you lot." said Teddy as he settled himself in.

"Teddy, we are still eating," Ken quickly interposed, "so we certainly don't want to hear any of your jokes. Besides, we have Anna with us." He gestured towards a young trainee who was lunching with him.

"Oh that's alright," Teddy insisted, "this is a clean one, it's not about sex, you'll like this one darlin, trust your uncle Teddy. " He leered at Anna and I was beginning to realise that he was not only an old bore, he was also an old letch.

"I said No, Teddy." Ken insisted, "Join us but no jokes, understood?"

"But this is a good'un. You don't mind a bit of fun do you love?" Teddy's ploy was hardly subtle, but it had the desired effect, as Anna had no wish to appear prudish. "Oh no," she said "I don't mind the odd risqué joke."

"Well I do," said Ken. "Because Teddy's jokes aren't risqué they are invariably disgusting."

"Oh I'm so sorry, Ken" said Teddy, "I didn't know you were God Squad."

"I'm not God Squad Teddy, as you well know; I just don't like your jokes, I have never liked your jokes. They are boring and they are disgusting, so just eat your lunch and give it a rest, OK?"

Things were becoming uncomfortable. The only person who seemed to be blissfully unaware of any tension in the atmosphere was, ironically, (I was soon to realise typically) Teddy himself.

"It is a really good joke." Teddy muttered after a pause, "and you needn't worry about the little lady, cos like I say, it isn't about sex."

"You mustn't worry about me anyway." said Anna unwisely. Ken just sighed. Teddy leaned back on his chair with the air of a man who was about to hold the assembled company agog with his scintillating powers of wit and repartee. "Right then here goes.'"his piggy eyes sparkled around the table as he paused for maximum effect....

"Well, there was this dirty great lump of shit, covered with flies."

He didn't get any further. Anna nearly choked on her coffee, the rest of us just fell about laughing. Teddy was completely bemused.

"What's wrong with you lot? That isn't the joke it's just the beginning."

We continued to fall about, Teddy grunted in confusion; irony was not his strong suit.

So that was my first encounter with Teddy Ballstrobe but, unfortunately, it was not to be my last for, only a week later, I discovered that my next monthly attachment was to Teddy's cutting room. Oh well, it was only for a month. Perhaps it wouldn't be too bad? As this was the start of my BBC career I was still naively enthusiastic and punctual so, on my first Monday with Teddy I arrived well ahead of time. I drew the cutting room keys from the front desk, opened up and switched on the equipment. Besides, I thought, I am only 'the trainee,' and with any luck Teddy's full time assistant will be ok. The thought had scarcely entered my mind when the phone rang. It was Phillip, Teddy's assistant. He was calling to say that he wouldn't be in for at least a week because he had the 'flu. I sat down in a mixture of panic and shock when I was snapped back to reality by a hideously familiar voice.

"What the fuck are you doing 'ere??"

It was the man himself.

"I'm a trainee, I'm attached to you for a month, my name's Mike."

"Oh Gawd, well anyway Phil always gets the key, that's his job, he's my assistant, not you."

"Sorry, I didn't think that it mattered."

"Well it does."

"Actually Phil just phoned to say that he's not coming in. He's got the 'flu."

"Oh Fuck." and with that Teddy Ballstrobe scuttled up the corridor towards the administration block.

"Welcome to the wonderful world of tele." It was Howard, the editor whose cutting room was next door to Teddy's. "What have you done to upset the great man so early in the day?"

"Well nothing, I hope. I'm a trainee and I just told Teddy that his assistant, Phil, had phoned in sick."

"Oh well, that would be enough. You see it is Phil who does all the work. Teddy just sits around all day reading the Daily Mirror. If he ever did know how to edit film, and that's open to question, he certainly forgot it all a long time ago."

"Looks like I'm in for a fun time then."

"Reckon so." The swing doors at the end of the corridor banged open as Teddy waddled back.

"Ah well best be getting on, " said Howard and he quickly disappeared back into his room.

Teddy had come back with the news, relayed to me with swear words in every phrase, that the 'front office' had no one available to cover for Phil's absence and that Teddy was to use me as his assistant for the time being. As he stood there sweating and swearing I noticed, for the first time, that he had a dent in his forehead. I tried not to stare at it but as it actually pulsed the angrier he became, it was very difficult to ignore.

"Suppose you are wondering about me 'ead." said Teddy in the first sentence for a while that hadn't contained the word 'fuck'. "I had an 'op on me brain a few years ago and they had to put a metal plate in."

I was tempted to ask if the metal plate had been put into to protect his brain or had simply replaced it altogether but I chickened out and said something *jejune* like, "Gosh how dreadful"

"Oh it's alright, they did a good job; I'm still one of the best editors in this fucking place. Anyway I'm off to the shops. You'd better get on with that lot." He gestured to a pile of film cans on the table and, before I could ask what I was supposed to do with them, he was gone. It was stupid of me to feel vulnerable but I did. This was the start of my second month at the studios and I was terrified of making a cock up. Had I been in the same situation six months later I would simply have put my feet up and read the paper until the lazy old bugger came back. As it was, I felt that I must do something, if only to prove that I was keen and efficient. I looked at the film cans. They were large 2000ft reels of 35mm tele recordings. In those pre-video tape days programmes were recorded by pointing a specialised film camera at a modified TV screen. Live pro-grammes were recorded as they were broadcast so that they could be repeated and, in the case of major dramas, were often recorded and edited, like film, even before their first broadcast. By looking at the labels on the cans in Teddy's room I realised that they were tele recordings of American Variety shows. I had no idea what was to be done with them but I noticed that they seemed to be in no particular order. I therefore decided to stack them in date order according to the labels on the cans. I didn't know what else to do.

It was about two hours later, about lunch time, the Teddy returned. I had, by then, sorted out the cans and stacked them on the film rack. I was cleaning the editing machine as he opened the door.

"What the fuck have you done?" he yelled.

"I've sorted the film cans out, like you said, they are in date order now."

"But Phil had got them into the order they were wanted for transmission so we could work on the urgent ones first."

"Well I'm sorry, but I didn't know that, did I?"

"Don't you get mouthy with me you stupid little git," Teddy shouted as the metal plate in his head went into turbo pulse. "Some fucking assistant you've turned out to be." and with that encouraging remark he waddled off to lunch. I spent most of the lunch hour desperately trying to find some list that Phil might have made which would enable me to put the cans back into the original order but I could find nothing at all. Just after lunch Howard from next door looked into the room. "I shouldn't worry too much, if I were you," he said "Teddy has gone home, he told the office that he must have got the same bug as Phil, so they've asked me to have you as my trainee for the month."

"Oh, that's great," I said, " but I think I've made the most awful cock up with Teddy's film cans."

"It can't be any worse than the cock up he would have made with them. Besides, always remember, It's only television, it's better than working."

So I had escaped a month of misery with Teddy Ballstrobe in cutting room S5 and ended up working in S4 with Howard Bilton, one of the most relaxed and talented editors at the Ealing Studios. He was also the youngest, having made it to editor aged 21!

It was four years later that, by an odd twist of fate, I was working again in cutting room S4 that the awful Teddy Ballstrobe met his Waterloo. As he got his come-uppance at the hands of a Wiley Scot, perhaps I should say that he met his Bannockburn but, whatever battle you choose, Teddy met it in spades.

As I said, four years had passed since my brief, unpleasant, encounter with Teddy and a lot of things had changed. For one thing I was now a recently promoted film editor; so I was safe from the likes of the ghastly T. Ballstrobe. The long suffering Phil was long gone, having taken up a job offer in BBC Bristol. He didn't particularly want to move out of London but anything was better than life with Teddy. That was, perhaps, the worst thing about the man. He always gave his assistants a miserable time; always humiliated them in front of production staff by blaming them for cock ups which were invariably his own. He also did his damnedest to make sure that his assistants never left him to work for anybody else. In this he was really cunning for he managed to convince the 'front office' that his assistant was a bit thick but never mind, a year or two with Uncle Teddy and the lad would probably learn enough to pull him through. The awful thing was that the managers seemed to believe him. Perhaps he had some cronies amongst them, for certainly all the other editors knew that Teddy was worse than useless. Another explanation could be that that the managers neither knew nor cared and saw Teddy as a pain in the arse who they just wanted to keep out of their hair. If this meant reducing a succession of assistants to depressive wrecks, so what? It kept Ballstrobe off their backs and that was all that mattered. Mind you, they had enough sense never to give Teddy a female assistant; his Chauvinism and wandering hands were too legendary for them to be that stupid.

I don't suppose that I was thinking very much about the problems of Teddy and his assistants on that day when I was to draw the cutting room keys for the first time as a fully-fledged film editor. It felt good to be back at the Ealing studios once again because during my apprenticeship I had worked at BBC premises all over West London, most recently at the Lime Grove Studios which was a dump, if ever there was one.. Now I was back at Ealing, with all its links to history of British cinema. Ealing where you could delude yourself that you were part of the heritage of film making and not just working for an off shoot of tatty television. As I walked down the corridor towards cutting room S4 I started to wonder about how I would get on with my new assistant. I had never met her and only knew that she was on a short term contract and had been working in America for some time. She had an odd name, Kikki Torville. I didn't have long to wonder as I had hardly got the door open when a very buxom young woman rushed in all of a flutter.

"Are you Mr. Crisp? I'm Kikki, I'm so sorry I'm late but the traffic was truly awful. Did you have to draw the key yourself? Oh I am sorry."

"You're not late at all, I was early and I'm Mike, please. Mr. Crisp makes me feel uncomfortable."

"Well you're the boss," Kikki said as she took off her coat and, in so doing, revealed that she was a very fashion conscious dresser. Her lamb's wool sweater was very expensive, very figure hugging and very revealing. I couldn't help but notice that Kikki had plenty to reveal.

"Do you want to start work at once or shall we go for a coffee? I could bring you one here, if you like?" she said as she checked her lipstick in her compact mirror. I thought that I was going to get on very well with Miss Torville.

"Let's go to the canteen for a coffee, then," I said. "I'm not even sure what it is we are going to be editing, yet."

"Oh it's a film about the artist Chagall. Frightfully intellectual I imagine. The director looked in last week when I was synching up the rushes. He seemed sweet enough, ever so vague, but then aren't they all? I told him not to bother coming in until Wednesday; I thought that you would like some time to settle in."

My God, I thought, "I wish I had been that assertive when I was an assistant." and by the time we had reached the canteen I was even more certain that Miss Torville was going to prove to be a first rate assistant..

When we reached the canteen Kikki insisted that I sit down while she fetched the coffees. I agreed, on the condition that I would get them at lunch time. I must confess that it felt good to sit at a table and wait for Kikki to bring my coffee over as it gave me a chance to enjoy the congratulations of various old friends, including a lot of the editors with whom I had worked as an assistant. Amongst them was Howard who teased me about having taken over his old room, next door to the dreaded Ballstrobe. Howard, the lucky devil, was now working in one of the superior cutting rooms which over looked Walpole Park, at the back of the studios. When Kikki re-joined us she had a friend with her. He was a rather odd looking lad. He was quite short with wild curly red hair; his teeth were not only protruding, they were crooked and his trousers were exceedingly baggy at the crotch. When he spoke there was no mistaking that he was a Scotsman, indeed he looked like the cartoon image of a wild highlander, such as you might see in a copy of the Beano. After a few minutes in his company all this was forgotten because his conversation was jolly and he was obviously very intelligent. Kikki introduced him.

"This is my friend, Johnny. He works in the room next to ours."

"With the dreaded Teddy?" I said.

"Yes, worse luck," John replied, "The trouble is I can't seem to get away from him. I've been up to the front office time and time again, to ask for a move, but they take no notice."

"The thing is that as long as Teddy has Jonny working with him he can cope and that is all the front office care about." Kikki added.

"I don't know why they employ him at all, " said Howard, "Perhaps he has friends in high places?"

Johnny glanced at his watch and downed the rest of his coffee, "Ah well I best go and open up." he said, without much enthusiasm.

When he had gone Kikki told me what an awful time Johnny was having and it seemed to me that Teddy Ballstrobe must have got even worse since I was last at the studios.

"That awful old man swears at him all the time and blames him for everything that goes wrong which is pretty rich coming from a man who couldn't cut his way out of a paper bag. It is such a shame because Johnny is such a good person; he might look as if he is just all teeth and bollocks, (why does he wear those awful trousers, darling?) but he really is a lovely chap." Praise from Kikki was praise indeed, I reckoned.

My first week with Kikki past pleasantly enough. The film we were working on was interesting and her impression of our director turned out to be accurate. His name was Peter and he was tall, docile and Canadian. He came on Wednesday, said that he was very happy with what we had cut so far and that, if it was alright with us, he would leave us alone for a week to get on with the rest of film. "Just give me a call if you need me," he drawled, as we all set off for home on Wednesday evening.

"That's the sort of director I like, " I said after Peter had left us.

"Me too, darling," said Kikki.

So we got into a comfortable routine with Peter coming in two or three times a week to see how our first cut was coming together. Part of that routine was visits from

Johnny from 'next door'. Whenever he could find an excuse to get away from Teddy he would scuttle into our room and have a moan. I couldn't blame him for we often heard Teddy swearing at him and telling any visiting production people that his assistant was a 'useless little C... God knows why they never said anything. I suppose they must have been afraid of him.

It was during one of Johnny's clandestine visits to our cutting room that Kikki came up with the thought that the only way to resolve the situation was for Teddy to be persuaded to ask for a replacement assistant. "But he'll never do that, " I said. "He needs Johnny to do all the editing for him."

"What if Johnny was to do something frightful?" She suggested.

"Well then, I guess, they'd sack me," said Johnny.

"There has to be a way," said Kikki.

Over the next few days, whenever the three of us met we discussed increasingly bizarre strategies to tame the dreaded Ballstrobe. In truth, most of them were just silly ideas to cheer Johnny up; fast acting laxatives or the traditional boxing glove on a spring, concealed in a film can. Kikki insisted that there was something you could put in coffee which turned the victim's urine purple but none of these schemes met the most important condition that no blame should seem to rest with Johnny. The eventual solution to the problem was to occur in the most unlikely way.

A few days later the three of us were out shopping in the lunch hour. We had gone into Bentall's drapery department as Kikki was looking for new curtains for her flat. She was a determined and exacting shopper so we spent ages walking up and down on the thickly carpeted floor of Ealing's most expensive department store. There was nothing that Kikki really liked and, as we were leaving, she got a static electric shock when her hand touched the brass banister rail.

"It's these damned shoes," she said. "I sometimes wish that I'd never bought them."

"The Nylon carpet in here doesn't help." I said.

"Maybe, but I've had several small shocks in the cutting room and that isn't even carpeted; No it's these shoes alright. To be honest,' she added, "I don't really understand how it is possible to build up a static charge in the cutting room."

"Oh it's bound to happen if you are wearing rubber soled shoes and winding a lot of film backwards and forwards," I said, somewhat relishing the role of the wise and experienced man of the movies.

"The shocks in the cutting room are never too bad because there is so much metal equipment about; you earth yourself before you can build up much of a charge. You'd been walking up and down in here for about half an hour before you touched that rail, that's why the shock was a bad one." I stopped my fascinating explanation of the early

16

theories of electricity because I had suddenly become aware of the most curious gurgling noises. To my alarm, I realised they were coming from Johnny.

"Oh orrr Oh.. That's it, that's bloody it!" Johnny was suddenly frantic with excitement.

"Alright darling," said a reassuring Kikki. "So now we know that's the reason. There's no need to throw a seizure."

"No, don't you see?" said Johnny. His eyes sparkled with an unusual fire and his red hair stood on end like the hackles of an excited dog.

"But what is there to see?" I said, rather lamely

"It's the way, the way I can escape Teddy". He started to chortle with such glee and force that his trousers, which never seemed very secure around his waist, seemed to be imminent danger of descent.

"It's so obvious; I'll come into work really early one day and wind thousands of feet of film through a cleaning cloth. I'll build up a charge enough to stun an elephant. Then when Teddy comes in, I'll go up to him and earth myself."

"But surely that won't work?" said Kikki, "you need to touch something metal.''

"But I will, I will." Johnny was now laughing in a decidedly unnerving manner.

"Well I don't understand." said Kikki.

"Think about it," Johnny replied, "There is only one editor in the world it would work for." With that he rushed out of the shop like an excited highland terrier.

"He must have finally cracked." There was a distinct note of concern in Kikki's voice. "Why could it only work for Teddy, what's so special about him?" There was a pause while we both thought. Then we turned to one another and said, in near unison,

"Teddy has a metal plate in his head!"

Both Kikki and I were relieved that for the next few days nothing untoward seemed to happen in the next door cutting room. Teddy and Johnny worked uneasily together with only the occasional curse from Teddy drifting through the wall back to us. I think we both secretly hoped that the idea in the department store had been abandoned like all the rest.

We didn't actually witness the appalling row which was finally to precipitate Johnny into to full static electrocution mode. This was because it took place in the dubbing theatre, the sound suite where all the elements which constitute the final sound track of a film are mixed together. Teddy and Johnny had gone there for the final 'dubs' of a series of twelve short animation films for children, on which they had been working. It had not been a complicated editing job. (Teddy was never allocated anything remotely difficult.) The series had been made for French television and the only editing required was to reduce the running time of each episode by a couple of minutes and replace the original French titles with English ones. The original French tracks of music and effects had been supplied so the sound mix was simply to replace the original French voice-over with an English one. All this was very straightforward stuff for the a professional team of editor and assistant and Teddy and Johnny had followed the usual procedure of editor (Teddy) making the picture alterations and then assistant (Johnny) fitting the new commentary to the picture. The trouble was that when they came to the dubbing theatre nothing fitted. The picture and the sound were miles out of synch with each other. Teddy, as ever, went berserk and called Johnny every kind of fool, twerp, fucking Scottish dwarf and incompetent little c... He generally created such an awful scene that Emma, the producer's secretary, who had only come to confirm the final timings, burst into hysterics and was off sick for ten days. She finally only regained her composure after a fortnight in Frinton with her aunt.

In the midst of all the shouting and swearing it was the sound mixer who worked out what the problem was. Teddy refused to admit any blame but it became quite obvious that he had added the new titles to the front of each episode after Johnnie had fitted the new commentary. He had then made no effort to alter the sound tracks to match. Even if couldn't be bothered to make the adjustments himself and had lumbered Johnny with the job, all

19

would have been well. The truth was that the old fool hadn't given it a thought. In the cutting room such adjustments are simple but, once in a dubbing theatre it can take ages to sort out synchronisation problems. Worst of all was that, by abusing and humiliating Johnny, Teddy had created such a dreadful atmosphere that it took four times longer to sort out the problem than otherwise might have been the case. The dubbing session was due to end at five thirty; eventually it ran on until past ten o'clock. Johnny set of home that night determined that it would not be long before he took his revenge.

It was in the canteen, next morning, that Kikki and I heard about the dreadful scenes that had taken place in the dubbing theatre the previous night. We had a friend, Terry, in the sound department and he gave us a graphic account. I remember thinking that it was a good job that we were ahead of schedule with our film as I felt pretty sure we were not going to get much work done that day. I felt even more certain when I looked out of the canteen window to see Johnny heading towards the cutting room block. I thought that there was something odd about the way he was walking. Then I noticed that he was wearing shoes that I had never seen him in before. They were shoes with very thick rubber soles. I gulped down my coffee and rushed after him. When I got to the cutting room I was relieved that there was no sign of Teddy but I was disturbed to find Johnny sitting at the electric rewind and winding a 2000ft reel of film through a Selvet cleaning cloth; an ideal way to charge yourself with static electricity.

"I've heard about last night," I said, "and it made my blood boil but surely you're not going ahead with your static shock plan?"

"I bloody well am," replied Johnny, through gritted teeth, "but don't worry, it won't be today because Teddy has taken the rest of the week off. That gives me the perfect opportunity to find out how much film I need to wind through to get well charged up."

"But aren't you afraid you might kill him?" It was Kikki, who had joined us.

"No chance." said Johnny, almost regretfully. "I've got a degree in electrical engineering, don't forget. He'll just get a good jolt and probably see his whole life flash before him."

"Oh my God, but in that case, he might die of boredom." said Kikki.

"Look, I know you both mean well," said Johnny, "but this is my fight so just let me get on with it, ok?"

So we did and for a couple of weeks, life went on much as normal. In fact, as we were reaching the end of our editing schedule on the Chagall film, Kikki and I were too busy to pay much attention to the odd curses and rows from next door. Perhaps, out of wishful thinking, we had pushed Jonny's fiendish scheme for revenge to the back of our minds, comforting ourselves with the thought that his experiments had, most probably, proved fruitless... Then one day, in the manner of a 'B 'movie script, we heard dialogue which chilled us to the marrow; it was Teddy's voice. "For Gawd's sake stop pissing around on that re-winder and come over here and give me a hand." I realised that I had heard the dull whine of the rewind machine continuously all through the morning. I just knew that the next few moments would be memorable.

I suppose it is all too easy for someone immersed in the world of film to liken dramatic events to famous moments of cinema but it is honestly true that for the following three minutes Kikki and I found ourselves taking part in a scenario usually reserved for a 'Tom and Jerry' cartoon. There was a moment's hush as the significance of Teddy's words sank in. We stopped and waited. Then it came; a crackle like the sound that a radio makes in a thunder storm. This was followed by a bellow of pain like nothing I had ever heard. It sounded as if the Loch Ness monster had just been harpooned. Then there was a crash as Teddy fell backwards into a pile of empty film cans. We had no time to wonder what we should do because at that moment our door burst open and Johnny rushed in. He dropped the latch and held himself against the door. It was a wise move, because if we had any fears, that Teddy might be dead or unconscious, they were immediately dispelled by a thunderous banging on our door. The cutting room doors at Ealing studios were heavy, solid, fireproof items but under Teddy's manic assault I seriously began to wonder how long ours would last out. It seemed to bend

and buckle under his torrent of thumps and great clouds of
dust blew in around the sides.

"You evil, murderous little c... You let me in! Let me in right now, do you hear? You let me in cos I'm going to tear your fucking head off!" Frightening as the situation was I couldn't help but think that only Teddy could be stupid enough to believe that the possibility of having his head torn off would encourage Johnny to open the door. "Don't think you're going to get away with this, you fucking Scottish dwarf. I'm going to the front office right now, Right Fucking Now. You hear? I'm not working with a fucking psychopath." He kicked the door three or four times more then we heard him blundering unsteadily up the corridor, cursing all the way.

"Well," said Johnny, "It worked. I saw a static spark leap from my finger straight on to his metal plate. It must have jumped about five inches."

Teddy stormed up the studio central road-way to the front office and, despite all objection from a clutch of protective secretaries in the outer office, he burst in on a meeting of the studio's top management team. They were not best pleased to have their self-important deliberations interrupted by a raving maniac. It was a supreme irony, and typical of management. All Teddy's previous lies concerning his assistants had been believed the truth he was telling, this time, seemed completely incredible. Mind you, it must have been hard to believe.

"Fucking psychopathic Scottish dwarf turned himself into a bleedin' human generator and earthed himself to me metal plate, the fucking metal plate in me brain. It was

fucking attempted murder; that's what it was and no mistake."

The secretaries in the outer office could hear everything
and told Kikki that Teddy's rant continued for about fifteen
minutes. He was eventually calmed by the offer of three
weeks special leave.

So Johnny's plan had worked. He was moved away from
Teddy and eventually became Howard's assistant. The
management did make a few enquiries about what had actually happened and they completely believed Johnny
when he said that he honestly didn't know why Teddy behaved like he did and that maybe he had forgotten to take
his pills that day. When Teddy came back from leave he
was put on 'light duties' until his retirement some ten
months later. God knows how his duties could have been
made any lighter, seeing as he hadn't done a hand's turn in
about fifteen years, but at least it provided the excuse for
him not to need an assistant.

Johnny eventually became a film editor and a very good
one. He has several Bafta awards to his credit. He recently
told me that at a party after one of the Bafta ceremonies
he was cornered by a keen young film student. On hearing
that Johnny had been working at the Ealing studios in the
late 1960's he was interested to know if Johnny had ever
heard the fantastic story of the bullying editor who had a
metal plate in his head and who had been electrocuted by
his exasperated assistant ."Surely the story is just one of
those film industry legends?" the student inquired. "Must

be," said Johnny. "Whoever heard of a film editor with metal plate in his head?"

Chapter Two.

Gentle Men and Malevolent Machines.

One of the most appealing features of the film world is the huge diversity of people who are attracted to it. At BBC Ealing in the 1960's a production might have a costume designer who had been educated at Roedean working alongside a makeup supervisor who was as common as muck (and of course vice versa !) Some cameramen and editors had worked their way up from being cinema projectionists, some had been officers in the forces. One Ealing cameraman was a cousin of the Queen and several had been petty criminals... some still were. It certainly was a heady mixture and very much a microcosm of society at large. After my early encounter with Teddy Ballstrobe I was, therefore, not surprised to meet Richard Coutts, or Dick as he preferred to be called. He was the exact opposite of Teddy Ballstrobe because Dick Coutts was a perfect gentlemen. I suppose he must have been in his late forties when I worked with him as a, recently qualified, assistant editor. He was, at that time, the chief film editor of tele recordings and specialised in working on programmes about great actors and acting, indeed anything theatrical. It was perfect casting because Dick himself cut quite a theatrical figure. He was tall, thin faced and wore heavy, expensive, horn rimmed spectacles. He had a short, sporty, overcoat with a fur collar set off with a jaunty, almost alpine hat. He often wore a waistcoat under his Harris Tweed jacket and, when he smoked, he used a long ebony cigarette holder which had solid gold trimmings. Though he could easily be mistaken for an actor, it would have been an old fashioned one, playing leads in Noel Coward comedies. Visually, he might have made a great Sherlock Holmes but vocally he was possibly too gentle for the part. The only thing that Dick Coutts had in common with Teddy Ballstrobe was his ability to be bemused by the technical equipment in the cutting room. In fairness it is perhaps worth stating that until the early 1970s British editing machinery was clumsy, badly engineered, junk.

Because Dick's work involved editing long tele recordings he had one of the better viewing machines in his room. This was a German 'Keller'. It could take 2000 feet of picture and sound and play the picture back on a large, bright, screen; the fact that the Keller had good sound and a bright picture made it a much better piece of kit than most of the other editing machines in the Ealing cutting rooms. However the Keller did have one terrible fault. It only happened once in a while but this made the problem all the more distressing when it occurred. You could edit for weeks on end, with the Keller Machine running the picture and magnetic sound track gently through its sprockets and rollers at normal speed, or up to four times speed, as you desired. There was no damage to either picture or sound and everything was controlled by some elegant buttons which fell easily under the editor's hand. Then one day, without warning, the machine would throw a fit. You would be watching the film as usual when, with the screech of a demon, the Keller would start to run the film through at 4000 miles per hour. The whole machine shook with rage and nothing would stop it. Furious pressing of the stop button had no effect whatsoever and by the time that the penny had dropped that the only way to halt the demented machine was to pull the plug out, it was too late. The Keller had wound the film through to the end of the reel, slicing it neatly up the middle in the process. The first time I witnessed this dramatic event was when I was assisting Dick Coutts as he edited a series entitled 'Great Acting'. This was a number of programmes which interviewed such luminaries as Lawrence Olivier, John Gielgud, Ralph Richardson and Edith Evans. The director was a very dapper and camp little man called Hal Taylor. Hal knew everybody who was anybody in the hierarchy of British theatre but, like so many theatricals working in television, he knew sod all about film technique. He was therefore completely happy to depend on Dick's editing skills.

Hal usually arrived in the cutting room at about 10.30, very civilised of him, and he would be wearing a mohair grey overcoat set off with a silk cravat and a gold pin. He never went anywhere without his Trilby hat and often kept it on all day. I think both Hal and Dick knew that they could easily edit one of the 'Great Acting' programmes together in a week; after all a 'talking head' interview is not the most demanding of formats, but Hal enjoyed fussing about the studios. He had scheduled four weeks editing for each of the six interviews so that kept him away from the Music and Arts department's bitching politics for a glorious 24 weeks! I suppose that is why he was so unconcerned when the editing equipment threw a fit and delayed operations for hours at a time.

The BBC felt obliged to 'buy British' whenever possible and that was the reason for the purchase of some of the worst editing machinery ever to curse a cutting room. The German Keller, the device Dick Coutts used, may have had a spasm every now and then but the Acmade, its British equivalent, was a pain in the arse every working minute. The picture was small and dim; the sound wowed so badly that editing music was almost impossible. Added to this, the machine was so badly engineered that it regularly chewed up both sound and picture. On rewind, it had the habit of causing the film to build up into a cone and then throwing it onto the floor. In one memorable case an Acmade actually managed to throw the film out of an open window.

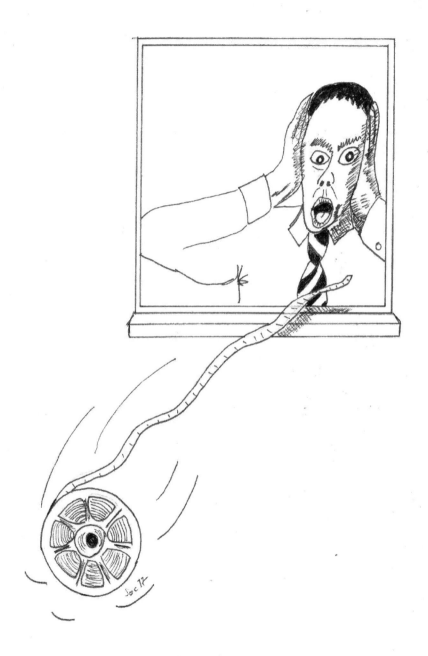

The programme so roughly abused was a tele recording, imported from the USA, of 'The Perry Como Show.' The show had been recorded live 'off air' so the American commercials had to be edited out before the show's UK transmission. The film had arrived at Heathrow airport at noon on the Saturday of transmission; it was due to be broadcast at 8pm but the programme planning department were across the logistics well enough, they thought. A dispatch rider was booked to pick up the film from Heathrow airport as soon as it had cleared customs and deliver it to Ealing Film Studios, where a film editor, on weekend overtime, would remove all the American advertisements and then forward the programme to TV Centre, in Shepherd's Bush, for transmission. It was a well-planned operation and all went smoothly until the editor pressed the rewind button on the Acmade. I mentioned, earlier, that at this point, the treacherous machine chose to throw the film out of the window, but there was one other important detail that I have so far omitted. The fact that the film landed in a puddle! Needless to say, the Perry Como show on BBC TV that night had to be seen to be believed. All desperate attempts to clean mud and grit from the film had been of little avail and, indeed, had only served to scratch the film still further so that Mr. Como seemed to be performing behind malevolent coils of animated barbed wire. The fact that no one wrote in to complain either meant that, either the show was less popular than the BBC mandarins imagined or, more probably, that viewers simply thought it was 'interference'. Television reception in the early 1960's was never entirely reliable.

There was, therefore, a sense of dread in the cutting room when Dick's Keller machine was taken away for repair and an Acmade was wheeled in to replace it. I think Hal thought that Dick and I were being needlessly pessimistic when we predicted trouble. After all, at least we had been supplied with a brand new machine and it looked shiny and reliable. Indeed, for a couple of weeks Hal's optimism seemed justified. "Well dears, at least it hasn't sliced the bloody film up the middle." he sighed, whenever we bemoaned the dim picture and the lousy sound. It must be owned that, as it was brand new, the Acmade behaved reasonably well for the first couple of weeks. They must have had a wizard at the factory who could adjust them to work acceptably on delivery but, in regular use, they soon reverted to type. It wasn't long before Hal had to revise his opinion.

After we had restored programme one of the 'Great Acting' series, (the one the Keller had split up the middle) and we had nearly completed programme two, Hal announced that we really should ask his head of department over for a 'work in progress' viewing. Hal and Dick decided that programme two would be the best one to show the great man. This was an interview with Lawrence Olivier which, with Kenneth Tynan asking the questions, had gone particularly well. I was only the assistant editor but I had been ordering up film clips and stills from the great man's career and, thanks to Dick's good nature, I felt very much involved. Hal's boss Stephan Hertz gave us a date when he 'might be able to squeeze us in' and I set about booking a viewing theatre. Unfortunately nothing was available for the time Herr Hertz had granted us. Dick and I begged Hal to put him off until we could view the programme in a theatre but Hal refused, arguing that Stephan Hertz was a busy man and notoriously easy to upset. We would be forced to run the film for him in the cutting room and this, of course, meant running it on the Acmade. Well, we did our best. I got in some coffee and biscuits, also some comfortable chairs. We decided that as the Acmade's picture was so dismal we would black out the room to watch the programme in the dark. Stephan Hertz was due at 3pm on Wednesday afternoon, so by 2.30 we had everything ready for the viewing. I was pretty certain that it wasn't coincidence that Dick was wearing a smart new waistcoat that day and that Hal was wearing a smarter-than-usual suit. As 3 O'clock approached Hal even found an excuse to take off his hat. I hadn't bothered to smarten myself up much because, by this time, I had been working at the studios long enough to know that executives, like Stephan Hertz, would scarcely notice or acknowledge my existence.

He arrived in whirl of spurious activity at 3.15. This was late enough to be 'executive' but not so late as to be insulting to Hal. After all, Hal was some twenty years his senior. But, of course, we could not start the viewing immediately as Stephan had several important calls to make to Television Centre. Once these had been completed and he had had ostentatiously dictated a number of memos to the two secretaries that he had come with him he probably reckoned that he had generated sufficient anxiety to allow the viewing to commence. He sat down right in front of the Acmade, making it impossible for anyone else to see anything much at all.

"Are we ready?" inquired Dick.

"Vee are," snapped Herr Hertz.

"Very Well," said Dick. "Lights!" I turned off the room lights and Dick leant over and pushed the Acmade's green 'go' button. Stephan Hertz looked rather startled but he said nothing as the machine clanked its way into life.

Despite our anxieties, despite the dim picture and the distorted sound, the viewing went remarkably well. There were a few strange noises from the Acmade but we seemed to get from start to finish without a hitch and at the end, and when I turned the lights back on, the usually hypercritical Hertz was almost complementary. "It is much less boring than I thought it would be; the section on Richard III needs more shape, otherwise it is acceptable." and with that the great man and his entourage swept from our presence.

Hal was, naturally, delighted and couldn't immediately understand why Dick looked ashen faced and I looked pole axed. We were both starring at the Acmade. The reason was almost super-natural; there was no film on it. No picture on the feed spool and none on the take up spool the same was true for the sound track. We had just watched and listened to a 50 minute programme but it had now vanished.

"That seemed to go pretty well, "said Hal. "Whatever's wrong with you two?"

"It is probably nothing to worry about," said Dick, in a singularly unconvincing way, "But the film seems to have disappeared."

"But we've only just viewed it."said Hal. "It can't have got far, Dear Boy."

"I suppose not," agreed Dick. "I just don't know where it is or how it got there!" At that moment the Acmade gave a sort of dyspeptic, mechanical, burp.

"Oh my God," I said, "I think I know where the film might be." I approached the Acmade with a large screwdriver, which we kept for opening rusty film cans, and I took off the front cover. On the last turn of the screw the cover almost leapt off and this, we quickly realised, was because of pressure that had built up inside the machine. This pressure was caused by enormous quantities of powder. There was a pile of black dust that had once been the picture and a pile of brown dust that had once been the sound. Four weeks work turned to dust in the course of one 50 minute viewing. By watching the film in the dark we couldn't see that the Acmade's take up motor had jammed with the result that both picture and sound had been sprocket fed into the machines inner workings. Once inside, the greediest, greasiest, gearing known to British engineering had ground our programme to bits.

Chapter Three.

<u>Pranks, Porn and Privilege.</u>

Hal seemed remarkably unconcerned about the destruction of yet another programme. Once we assured him that we had a safety copy of the sound track and that the picture could be re-printed from the negative, he was, if anything, pleased. It meant that he had the perfect excuse to extend the editing schedule by yet another four weeks. Dick did, however, insist that we asked for the return of the, newly repaired, Keller machine before we stated editing anything else.

"Better the devil you know, dear boy," he explained to me.

Our film devouring Acmade was overhauled and delivered to a cutting room further up the corridor. It became the property of the editor Paddy Heath. Paddy was a jolly soul and a very good editor. He was somewhat portly, about forty four, and his cutting room always seemed to be a centre of great hilarity. The BBC's motto was, and still is 'Nation Shall Speak Peace Unto Nation'. Over the door to Paddy's cutting room he had hung a sign which read 'Nation Shall Transmit Crap Unto Nation.' This sort of self-deprecating humour was rife throughout the film department. Film technicians are notoriously unimpressed by bullshit.

The unfortunate consequence of this was that, all too often, time serving toadies were promoted to manage their more sceptical colleagues. Paddy was happy enough, though; confident in the fact that he was a very competent film editor and many directors actually relished the undercurrent of anarchic humour which would always liven up the atmosphere when you edited with 'Uncle Pad'.

Shortly after Paddy inherited our Acmade an incident occurred which exactly demonstrated his humour. Eddie, one of the assistant editors on our corridor, was a bit of a lad. One day he started boasting about his expensive new watch which he had bought for very little money from a mate in the East End. "Fell off the back of a lorry, if you know what I mean Pad? Me brother's well pissed off 'cos he wanted one too, but I got the last of the bunch. Good innit?" Eddie never tired of showing off that damn watch or of gloating about how little he paid for it.

Then one day, about the time that Dick, Hal and I were starting on episode three of 'Great Acting', Paddy was sitting on the toilet. The studio toilets all had old fashioned high flush cisterns. Suddenly a hand reached over the top of Paddy's cubicle and pulled the flush on him giving him an extremely wet bum. Paddy was pretty sure that it was Eddie who had pulled the flush; it was just the sort of prank that would have appealed to him. Paddy, however, was quick witted enough not to react with a loud curse but instead he let out the sort of elderly bleat that Hal might have made. Paddy had the satisfaction of hearing Eddie mutter "Oh Gawd," as he scurried away. When he met Eddie in the corridor, some twenty minutes later, Paddy said nothing. That was his master stroke. It was only after some hours had past that Paddy joined Eddie in the canteen and said "My God Eddie have you heard about what happened to Hal Burton in the toilet?"

"Er no," gulped Eddie, What was then?"

"Well apparently Hal was sitting on the bog, reading Noel Coward's memoirs, when some idiot reached over the top of the cubicle and pulled the flush on him. Hal was soaked: the water came up all round his trousers. He is furious. He went straight up to the front office to complain; they took it very seriously too. I mean, he may be a bit of an old fairy, but he is a very senior producer.'

"Er yes" said Eddie uncomfortably, "what a thing to happen eh? Don't suppose they have any idea who it was?"

"No," said Paddy, "but Hal is pretty sure he will be able to identify the person easily enough."

Eddie flushed. "How's that then Pad?" he said as casually as he could muster.

"Oh Hal said he caught a glimpse of the hand as it let go of the flush and there was a very expensive watch around the wrist. Anyway management are planning to hold a surprise wrist watch inspection tomorrow and nail the bugger." Paddy took a sip of his tea and he noticed that Eddie seemed to have lost all interest in his doughnut. Eddie didn't come into work for a couple of days and when he finally returned he was wearing his old watch. "What happened to your watch?" asked Paddy. "Oh nothing really," said Eddie. "I just got fed up with me brother pestering all the time, so I gave it to 'im."

A few weeks later Paddy and his assistant Bob made a discovery which was to make quite an impact on life in the cutting rooms. The two of them were in the film vaults clearing some storage space for the negative of their next film when they found a collection of ancient porn mags stuffed behind one of the shelving racks. They were all editions of a publication which rejoiced in the name of 'Rubber News'. The pictures inside all showed sexual activity between men and women of all ages, shapes and sizes; the one thing that they had in common was that, if they were wearing anything at all, they were all wearing rubber. One issue seemed to have been more heavily thumbed than the others. This was a 'Latex Special' issue. Lying nearby to the secret hoard of magazines they found several rusty film cans so, fascinated with the thought of what they might contain, they decided to take them back to the cutting room and investigate.

Back in Paddy's room, the cans took some opening as the lids were heavily rusted on. They had to be cautious because it was quite likely that the film inside would be on nitrate stock. Cellulose nitrate was the base of all film

stock before 1953 after which safety film, on cellulose acetate, was used. Nitrate stock was anything but safe. It was
highly inflammable and became unstable, even explosive,
as it deteriorated with age. Despite all danger, and with a
total disregard of the fire regulations,, Paddy and Bob
eventually prised open one of the cans. The film inside was
in surprisingly good condition but Paddy could tell, from
the distinctive smell and the glossy image quality, that it
was Nitrate stock. They knew that they should call the Studio fire officers straight away.... No, of course they didn't;
they loaded the film onto the Acmade and locked the
door. A title came onto the screen; the film was called 'A
Free Ride.' A young lady was driving a car down a country
road and she picked up swarthy young hitch-hiker. By the
look of the car and the hat that the young lady was wearing the film seemed to have been made in the 1920's.
Mind you, the lady's hat didn't remain on her head for very
long, in fact none of her clothing remained on for very
long, for the film was vintage pornography. Like all films
made before the advent of sound 'A Free Ride' had been
shot at 16 frames per second so, running on Paddy's machine at the modern speed of 24 frames per second, all the
action, no matter how lurid or graphic, simply looked
comic; A sort of Keystone Cops with no knickers. This gave
Paddy an idea and he looked on his shelves for some
comic music. Eventually he found a music track that had
been used on a film about performing penguins and he fitted it to the vintage porn. It was shortly after that, in the
run up to the Christmas break of 1967 that the 'Penguin
Club' came into being. On Wednesday and Friday

lunchtimes, members would gather in Paddy's cutting room to view one of the porn films that he had rescued from the vault. He spent ridiculous amounts of time creating sound tracks for each of them, using circus music and comic sound effects. We thought that they were hilarious, but then people who are feeling a mixture of guilt and embarrassment often escape into laughter. Dick Coutts could never be persuaded to watch one - he was far too much of a gentleman but Hal, to our surprise, did attend a viewing. He said he was almost sure that girl involved was an actress he had known in Eastbourne rep in the 20's. "Edith Gribble," I think he said, "She was always grumbling because she never got big parts."

"Well she hadn't got anything to complain about in these films."said Paddy.

Of course we were a bit worried in case the management got to hear about our lunch time viewings; so it was decided that, during the show, Paddy's cutting room door would be locked. Anyone who wanted to gain entry would have to knock and give the password. It was Bob who decreed that the password was 'Latex'. The Penguin club only lasted a few weeks but for many years afterwards certain BBC film editors would approach each other, mutter 'Latex' in a gruff whisper, and then fall about in inexplicable laughter.

Dick Coutts, as I said, never became a member of the club. Some people thought that he was too posh by far and even sarcastically started to refer him as 'Lord Coutts'. This always struck me as extremely mean as Dick was simply an old fashioned gentleman and there were not very many of them working in television. He was smart and polite; he was also unfailing kind and helpful to those who worked for him. Still, his upper class manner and the fact that he was sometimes a bit vague got on the nerves of the front office. Unfortunately for Dick, about this time a slimily piece of work, called Keith Taitem, was appointed to the newly created post of film editing manager. Taitem had never liked Dick and one of the first things he did was to move him from the arts documentaries, which he really loved, to a BBC backwater where tele-recorded pro-grammes were packaged for sale abroad. Dick seemed to take this in his stride but those who knew him saw him gradually loose his sparkle .If Taitem's plan had been to take the wind out of 'Lord Coutts' sails, then he was cer-tainly succeeding. Dick became increasingly demoralised.

Keith Taitem was a typical example of BBC middle manage-ment of the period. He had never been much use as a film editor and held a grudge against any one with more apti-tude than he had himself. Needless to say that was almost every editor under his new command. Dick Coutts' move from the programmes which he enjoyed to an area he dis-liked became an almost standard management strategy. Editors who loved the arts were allocated to sports pro-grammes and football enthusiasts found themselves cut-ting films about Bartók. It was perverse and members of the editing staff soon realised that the best way to be allo-cated a film that they particularly fancied was to talk loudly in the canteen about how much they would hate to work on it. For a while morale started to sink very badly and no one was more depressed by it all than poor old Dick Coutts.

Then, one day, supreme good luck and wonderful irony combined to bring revenge upon the loathsome Keith Taitem. Richard Coutts asked for a private interview. Taitem reluctantly agreed but, of course, he kept Dick hanging about in the outer office for ages; finally he was called in. "Alright Coutts, what have you come to moan about now?"

"Oh I haven't come to moan about anything, dear boy," said Dick as he placed a du Maurier into his ebony cigarette holder. "It is simply that I thought you should know that there has been a change in my circumstances and amend my personal file accordingly."

"What change?"Taitem snapped back, "Getting divorced?"

"Oh not at all dear boy. Emily and I are very happy, especially now. You see, as a result of the sudden death of two distant relatives and, quite unexpectedly, I have inherited a title. I shall not wish to use it on my screen credits but, in future, I should properly be addressed as Lord Coutts."

"My God!"

"No... Just Lord Coutts, or 'milord', either will do."

Chapter Four.

Paddy Heath's Christmas.

The BBC always gives its staff an extra day off for Christmas. It is known as the Corporation Holiday and is the day after Boxing Day. In 1967, Christmas day fell on a Monday so you only had to take off two days annual leave to gain nine days off, including the weekends. Needless to say everyone in the cutting rooms took full advantage of the situation. Paddy suggested that the editors and assistant editors on our corridor should go out for a Christmas lunch on the Friday before the holiday. A new Indian Restaurant had recently opened, opposite the studio on Ealing Green and Paddy suggested that a meal there would make a pleasant change from the endless round of roast turkey and mince pies. I have never liked turkey so the idea suited me fine but I was delighted to learn that the others were also in favour of a festive curry. We might have guessed, indeed I suspect that Paddy had already guessed, that the one person who wouldn't fancy an Indian meal would be Teddy Ballstrobe. "I'm not giving meself the shits, just before Christmas, with a load of foreign muck." was his gracious excuse and that was just fine with the rest of us.

We were aware that Paddy knew a thing or two about curries. He had managed a tea plantation in Ceylon in his early life and had developed a real taste for spicy food. If he thought the new curry house was good then in had to be worth a visit. The meal turned out to be a great success. It seems odd, now, to think that some of the party had never had a curry before; but in 1967, whilst curry houses were becoming popular, they had not yet achieved the universal acclaim that they enjoy today. Still everyone agreed that their food was delicious and those who were unfamiliar with the menu were grateful for Paddy's advice. He enjoyed sharing his expert knowledge and making sure that nobody ordered a meal that was too fiery for them to relish. At the end of the meal we all wished each other Merry Christmas and then Dick, Paddy, Bob and I walked together to Ealing Broadway Station. We chatted about our plans for the holiday. Dick was going to stay with his grand relatives in Norfolk, Bob and I were off for a family Christmas with our respective parents while Paddy was staying at home with his wife and daughter. "There's one thing I'm not looking forward to," he said. "A very 'upper' family have moved in opposite and they have invited us over for a drink on Christmas Eve. My wife is desperate to go. She thinks it would do us good to have some better class friends than the mates from my Merton Park studio days. Frankly I'd rather stay at home and get quietly sloshed, besides, what I've seen of the Courtney-Smythes has not exactly endeared me to the prospect of having them as neighbours. He is something big in the city. She is a magistrate and a leading light in the local Conservative association. They have a daughter at Cambridge and a son at Harrow."

"Well that sounds like a barrel of laughs." said Bob.

"The recipe for a bloody awful evening," agreed Paddy, but at that time he had no idea of just how awful. We only learned the full horror of the evening when we came back to work after the holiday.

According to Paddy, he, his wife Jill, and their daughter could see, from their front room that people had started to arrive at the Courtney- Smythes. Paddy fortified himself with a large scotch and said that he was ready to cross the road and bite the bullet. The door was opened by Mrs Courtney-Smythe. She welcomed Paddy's wife and daughter but seemed somewhat cooler towards Paddy himself. "So Mr. Heath, you work for the BBC, I hope you're nothing to do with those frightful satire programmes?"

"Yes I work for the BBC, and please call me Paddy and if you mean The Frost Report, I don't work on it, but I do enjoy it."

"Oh Dear, I hope you're not a socialist."

"No, no not at all; just an old fashioned anarchist."

Mr. Courtney-Smythe came over and offered Paddy a glass of punch.

"Hello I'm Douglas, I see you've met Isabelle. She is rather tense tonight, I'm afraid. We should have had all our building work completed by Christmas, but of course it has over-run. Damn builders. So as a result we only have one bathroom at the moment. That means that everybody will have to traipse upstairs when they need the loo I'm afraid."

"Oh I expect we'll survive," said Paddy.

So the evening got underway and as more and more people arrived Paddy realised that he had nothing in common with any of them; but as more and more punch flowed it didn't seem to matter much. He found a comfortable chair next to the punch bowl and, while Jill politely circulated, he topped himself up at frequent intervals. Isabelle Courtney-Smythe seemed to have invited more people than her husband had, so the conversation naturally centred on how badly the Wilson Government was doing and the fervent hope that, as soon as the Conservatives were back in power, they would bring back the death penalty.

"Especially for farm boys caught stealing sheep," Paddy shouted across the room as the punch took hold.

"Take no notice" Isabelle whispered very audibly. "That is just one of our frightful neighbours. He works for the BBC. I really didn't want to move to this area at all, you know but, with the station just up the road, it is much easier for Douglas to get into the city. It's always the wives who make the sacrifices isn't it?"

Paddy wanted to shout, "No it bloody well isn't! My wife forced me to come to this awful party!" but he decided against it. He decided this for two reasons. One was that he was beginning to lose the power of speech the other was that he suddenly realised that he was desperate for a pee. He managed to get up from the chair. "Upstairs you said?" he inquired of Douglas.

"That's it old boy. I hope that next time you visit us we will have the downstairs bathroom fully functioning."

Paddy crossed the room and made it up the stairs. By the time he got to the bathroom door he was desperate. He had started to unzip his fly in order to save as much time as possible but then he discovered that the door was locked. He prayed that the occupant would not be long and wished that he had gone outside in the garden. After what seemed an age he heard the flush but this only made matters worse because his body took this as cue that relief was at hand and it became even more difficult for him to contain himself. The flush went for a second time and then followed the sounds of hand washing. This, too, seemed to go on for an agonising eternity. When the door finally opened Paddy was propped up against the wall with his legs crossed. An elderly lady emerged, who Paddy dimly recognised as Isabelle's mother. He pushed past her with considerable force and slammed the door. This was to prove to be his last co-ordinated movement for some while because he entered the bath room with such reck-less speed that he failed to notice the bath mat. He tripped and lost his balance. This in turn produced an adrenaline rush which, when combined with the alcohol in Douglas' lethal punch had a truly devastating effect. Fearing that a loss of balance would further delay his attempts to reach the lavatory Paddy flailed about like a wounded bear.

Downstairs at the party all conversation was suddenly stilled by a chilling cry of pain which was followed by a thunderous crash reminiscent of the last hours of Krakatoa.

It was Douglas Courtney-Smythe who was the first to open the bathroom door and witness the dire consequences of his festive cup. Paddy lay on the floor unconscious, with his trousers undone. He had cut his head. There was blood on the bathroom cabinet, so Paddy must have collided with it. Further evidence for this deduction was the fact that the bathroom cabinet was no longer on the wall, it was lying on the floor. It was face down close to Paddy near the spot where the toilet had stood, until recently, for the falling cabinet had landed on the W.C. and reduced it to a pile of porcelain splinters. Where once the toilet had been there was now simply an ugly, gaping, hole in the floor, the entrance of the soil pipe. It took a moment or two for the full horror of the situation to sink in but, as he turned to go downstairs and tell the guests that the party was over it dawned on Douglas Courtney-Smythe that tomorrow was Christmas Day and that after that came Boxing Day and that he and his family were likely to be without a lavatory for at least a week.

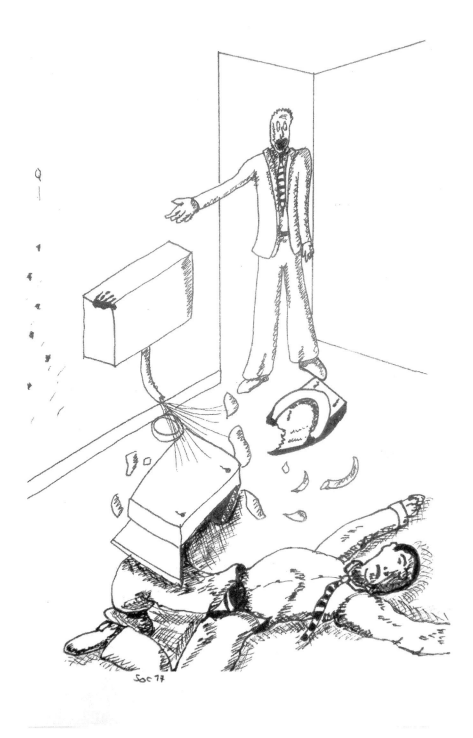

Jill did her best to bring some harmony back into the season of good will by giving her front door key to Isabelle. The Downstairs lavatory in Paddy's house was fully operational so the Courtney-Smythes could come and go as nature dictated. It was perhaps no surprise that such intimacy did little to kindle any flicker of friendship between the two families and tidings of comfort and joy had a very hollow resonance as, for the Courtney-Smythes, achieving comfort involved opening the front door and walking across the road; in all bitter weathers and at all times of the day and night. Paddy decided that the only way he could cope with the situation was to remain permanently drunk for the whole week. He spent the holiday asleep on the sofa. Jill feared that their daughter, Emily, might be traumatised by such scenes of drunken excess but later Emily said that she just thought that Daddy was doing his funny Christmas act.

It was several months before Jill forgave him .The Courtney-Smythes never did.

Chapter Five.

<u>Negative Influences.</u>

As we returned to work in the New Year of 1968 I doubt if many of us gave much thought to the changes that we were about to experience in our working methods. We should've done because, after all, 1967 had seen the first tentative steps into colour transmission on BBC2 and the plan was for BBC1 to go into colour by the end of 1968. As far as film editors were concerned one big difference would be that each individual cutting room was no longer saddled with the burden of having to provide safe storage for the negative of the film on which it was working. It is worth remembering that professional movie film is sent by the camera crew to the laboratory at the end of each day's shoot. It is there developed to a negative. A print is immediately taken from the negative and it is this 'rush' print with which the editor will work until he and the director are satisfied with the final cut. By the time the editing process is complete the cutting copy looks in a pretty sorry state. It is often scratched and will be covered with cue marks for the sound mix or to indicate picture effects in the final version. There will probably also be a few rips and tears to the picture that have been inflicted by the likes of the Acmade editing machine. None of this matters, however, because once the editor has agreed the fine cut with the director he sends this cutting copy, together with the negative to the 'neg' cutter. Neg cutters work in clinically clean conditions to match the virgin negative to the editor's fine cut. It is then possible to strike a pristine copy of the film from the cut negative and everyone breathes a sigh of relief. In feature films for example, the insurance premium drops dramatically once the first print has been struck from the cut neg. All this may seem to be tedious detail but it will, I hope, give some idea of the anxiety caused when a can of negative goes missing. In the days of 'black and white', when all the negative was returned to the cutting rooms, it was not uncommon for a can of negative to go astray and it always caused major stress. There was a famous incident at Ealing involving a documentary about waste disposal. It was given the jaunty working title of 'Junk'. It seems odd to think that nobody thought it risky to send dozens of film cans marked 'Junk' through the BBC's film transport system. Needless to say neither negative nor print ever arrived at the designated cutting room, neither did any of the master sound tapes. A land fill site somewhere in West London may well conceal the germ of a lost cinematic masterpiece.

The advent of colour provided the laboratories with the chance to alter custom and practice and hold all the negative in their own vaults, sending only the rush prints to the editor. They argued, correctly, that colour negative is much more fragile than black and white and therefore the handling of colour neg should only take place at the lab. The BBC management probably baulked at the additional cost of storage but everyone in the cutting rooms breathed a sigh of relief. At last there was to be an end of the cutting rooms been crammed full of cans of negative. The studio's own vaults were already full to overflowing. However, as I said, this new regime only applied to colour productions; for a while black and white films continued in the same bad old way. In early 1968 this resulted in one of the most awful cock-ups in film editing legend.

Nobby Pratt was coming to the end of editing a 90 minute drama. It was in black and white, so all the negative had been sent to him. As the time for neg cutting approached he asked his assistant to bundle up all the cans of negative and leave them in the corridor outside the cutting room. They would then both go for a coffee and, on the way to the canteen, drop into Film Despatch and ask one of the lads there to come, with a sack truck, and collect the pile. The heavy cans would thus be taken to the despatch office and, from there, by van, to the neg cutting firm in Soho. However, Nobby and his assistant had not taken into account the hectoring megalomania of the studio's fire officers. At that time all BBC studios had firemen on the staff and the ones at Ealing were a particularly miserable mob of misanthropic jobs-worths. It was fate that they should have chosen to make an inspection of the telerecording corridor on the day that Nobby had left the pile of negatives outside his door. The trouble was that other editors had dumped cans of out-takes and other junk film outside their doors too. As soon as they saw all this the firemen headed straight for dear old Dick Coutt's cutting room.

Dick was the chief editor on that corridor and, what's more, he too was having a clear out, so that there was a particularly large pile of cans outside his door.

"Get those bloody cans out of the corridor right now."

"They will be gone by lunch time, we're having a clear out."

"I said now and I mean now."

"I don't see that a couple of hours will make any difference."

"In case you didn't know, film is highly inflammable, even explosive."

"Well you obviously don't know that it hasn't been since 1953.You are talking about nitrate film, all that stuff out there is safety film."

"Well the fire regulations haven't changed, so get it shifted NOW."

It must be admitted that in this detail the fire officer was correct. Like so much British legislation the law lagged behind the existing state of the world and fire prevention laws, which were so sensible when cellulose nitrate stock was in use, had never been rescinded even though safety film (cellulose acetate) was about as flammable as wet cardboard. But there was no way that Dick Coutts was going to win this particular argument; he hated confrontation, the fire officer loved it. No amount of reasoned nego-tiation was going to change that. Nor were matters helped by Eddie, of wrist watch flushing fame. He had been pass-ing when the fireman first confronted Dick Coutts and had decided to stand on top of the largest pile of film cans and to sing "I don't want to set the world on fire" at the top of his unattractive voice. Sensing that the situation might quickly degenerate into farce, the firemen marched off, barking a parting, "Get them cans shifted," as they did so.

Meanwhile, in the canteen, Nobby and his assistant were blissfully unaware of the drama that was taking place in their corridor and the imminent danger in which their pre-cious negative was now placed. They decided to have a second cup of coffee before returning to face the slow and painstaking task of 'track laying' the film.

Tracking laying is the process whereby the editor prepares the sound for final mixing in the dubbing theatre. The 'synch' sound recorded at the time of filming is mixed with music and additional sound effects to produce a smooth and seemingly unedited sound track from the original, much cut about, location recording. Each 1000ft reel of picture may have as many as eight reels of sound tracks, assembled in the cutting room, to run in synchronisation with the picture and be combined on to one master sound track in the dubbing theatre. For the picture and sound to run in synch a lot of blank spacing is required. For exam-ple, if the picture reel contains four scenes and there is music in scene one and four, then there will be blank spacing on the music track during scenes two and three. In that way picture and music run in synch with each other. The same is true for all the other tracks, containing spot effects (such as doors slamming) and atmosphere tracks (such as bird song or traffic). Track laying took a lot of time and required a lot of spacing. As 35mm spacing was expensive, editors were always under pressure to be as economical as possible whilst track laying their films.

When Nobby returned to his cutting room he was pleased to see that the negative was gone. The news lads in film dispatch were obviously keen and had made the collection in double quick time. He put the film on to the 'horse' on the synch bench so he could begin the track laying process. They already had enough spacing with which to make a start but certainly not enough to complete the whole job. Nobby therefore sent his assistant, Bill, to see what he could scrounge from other editors along the corridor. Bill didn't have to look very far because, two doors along, Dick Coutts was just completing the clean-up ordered by the firemen.

"You're in luck, dear boy, there's a whole lot of junk negative in that bin. Take the lot you'll be doing me a favour, it weighs a ton and I wasn't looking forward to carting it over to the waste point."

And so for several hours all was peace and tranquillity along the telerecording corridor. Dick, at last, managed to get on with editing he had intended to do, before the invasion of the fire officers. Eddie couldn't find any more situations to inflame, so he settled down to fiddling his overtime sheets and Nobby and Bill cracked into the track laying. Thanks to Dick, they now had loads of junk negative to use as spacing, so they worked as fast as they could. The sound mix was booked for the day after tomorrow, there was no time to lose.

It was just before 5pm when the lad from film dispatch knocked on the door of Nobby's cutting room to say that had come to collect the negative. Nobby thanked him and said that it had already been collected. The lad seemed surprised. It was at 2 minutes past 5 that an unearthly wail of anguish echoed down the length of the corridor. It was a cry that chilled the hearts of all who heard it. It was Nobby and it was the sound made by a man who has just realised that he has spent the last five hours track laying his film using its own negative as spacing.

Dick Coutts went home that night bitterly regretting that he had been so compliant to the demands of the brutish firemen. Nobby went home wondering how he was going to explain to the director that he had cut up their film's negative into lengths of spacing. The Firemen went home satisfied that they had done a good days work saving the studios from the risk of a possible conflagration of un-in-flammable safety film. So, what happened? Well Nobby and Bill had only one choice, they worked like demons to clean up the cutting copy as best they could and use that for transmission. Of course, when the play was broadcast, the picture quality was bloody awful.... but the sound was great.

Chapter Six.

A Hat Trick.

Harold Binns was a sound recordist who was coming to the end of his career. He was too old to be out on location in all weathers and he didn't fancy an office job. The Transfer Suite was the ideal place for him. It was here that location sound, which was recorded on quarter inch tape, was transferred to magnetic film so that it could be easily edited with the picture. Sound from other sources was transferred to magnetic film here too; sound effects from discs and music of course. It was a busy place and Harold had quite a large staff of young assistant recordists working under him. The one big difference between Harold and his staff, apart from their ages, was that Harold was happy to be working there whilst the youngsters were not. They all wanted to be out 'on the road', working with the top location recordists, learning their trade and earning a great deal of extra money in overtime and expenses. The management were very aware of this so assistants were only usually allocated to the Transfer Suite for three months at a time and then only when they were very new to the job. But, of course, sometimes things went wrong and if an assistant recordist had the reputation of being a rebel they might well find themselves stuck in the Transfer Suite for a very long stretch. It was a bit like Borstal.

Harold had one such rebel in his team He was known to his mates as 'the Prof' and he used to give impromptu concerts during the lunch hour, when Harold was not about. Prof would accompany himself on guitar in a series of variously obscene songs which were mainly about masturbation in all its many sophistications. Needless to say the Prof and Harold did not get on. It was not that Harold was a particularly bad boss it was just he was obsessive about time keeping and he totally lacked any sense of humour. Worst of all, he was inflexible. If a film editor came in with a genuinely urgent request the sound assistants would be happy to help them out but if Harold found out that anyone had jumped the queue he would make a terrible fuss. His was a perfectly regulated life; so too should everyone else's be. He was one of those people who had always been 62. The Prof, on the other hand, was an eternal teenager.

There was always plenty of work to do in the Transfer Suite, but it was boring, repetitive work. An averagely bright sound technician could learn the operation in a matter of days and, so far as job satisfaction was concerned, it was all downhill after that. With a group of intelligent young guys working at much less than their full mental capacity conditions were perfect for the cultivation of elaborate practical jokes and it was the Prof who had the reputation of thinking up the best ones.

Harold was certainly not a snappy dresser. Like most middle aged BBC technicians at that time he was very much a sports jacket and flannels type of man. The clothes he wore for work had certainly seen better days and he looked like a maths teacher at a broken-down grammar school. It therefore came as a bit of a surprise when, one blustery March morning, Harold arrived to work wearing a brand new Trilby hat. He was, perhaps, both disappointed and surprised that none of his team made any comment as he carefully took off the hat, brushed it down with his hand and then hung it on the hat-stand, near the door. Maybe they hadn't noticed?... Of course they had but no one was going to do anything so sycophantic as to compliment him on his new purchase. The person who took the most notice of the new hat was 'Prof' but he said absolutely nothing.

It was during the lunch hour, when the Prof was looking for some new strings for his guitar that he wandered into Bentall's music department. On his way out he passed through the men's wear department. Usually this would have been of no interest to him whatsoever as all the clothes were much too old fashioned and traditional for the likes of the Prof.. However one display caught his attention. It was billed as 'The Great Spring Hat Event.' All sorts of awful hats were on display at bargain prices. In amongst them were several like Harold's. So that was where he got it…. A really devious scheme came into the Prof's mind. He looked at his watch. If he was quick he had just got enough time to put his plan into action. He ran back to the studio, entering through the back gate, which was nearest the Transfer Suite. He was in luck, nobody was yet back from lunch. He took Harold's new hat off the stand and noted its' size; it was an 8. He then rushed back to Bentall's men's wear and was able to buy a hat exactly the same as Harold's; except that it was half a size larger. Then he ran back to the studio as fast as he could. It was, by now, five past two, so everyone was back from lunch .Harold glanced up at the clock as the Prof came in and he gave a meaningful sigh.

"Sorry I'm a bit late back, I'll make it up, and I'll work through the tea break, OK Harold?"

"Well, see that you do," Harold snapped back

"Oh I will, I will," thought the Prof and he congratulated himself that he had thought to hide the new hat under his bulky pullover.

When tea break came everybody, except the Prof, set off to the canteen. This gave him the perfect opportunity to switch the hats. He replaced Harold's original size 8 on the hat stand with the other, larger, one and he hid the original hat at the back of his locker.

At knocking off time no one took much notice as Harold put on his coat and his new hat but the more observant may have noticed that his new prized possession seemed to be slipping down over his ears. When he arrived the next morning, Harold was surprised to find that Prof was already hard at work. Perhaps the lad was not as lazy as he had thought him to be? Harold rather regretted that, only yesterday, he had been complaining about the 'Prof' to the suits in the front office. Prof looked up at Harold and he too was surprised by what he saw, because Harold's new hat was fitting perfectly once more. At coffee time Prof lagged behind a little and as soon as Harold was out of the room he examined the hat. It had been padded out with newspaper. Prof carefully removed the padding and equally carefully fitted it into the smaller hat. He hung the small hat on the hat stand and hid the larger one. He then set off to the canteen for a well-earned coffee, whistling as he went. That evening, when Harold set off for home his new hat perched uncomfortably on the top of his head, he looked faintly ridiculous.

Harold was a full fifteen minutes late for work the next day. This was most unusual. He had missed his train, which was unusual in itself but the reason that he had missed it was stranger still. The truth was that he had spent twenty minutes in front of the hall mirror trying on his hat. With the paper padding and without the paper padding. Today it seemed that it was a much better fit without the padding, but only yesterday it fell down over his ears. Harold was getting quite worried. He eventually decided to take out the padding and when he arrived at work his hat fitted perfectly. Prof noticed it immediately and guessed the reason. There is no doubt that Prof was cunning. He would have been brilliant at psychological warfare because that day he didn't swap the hats. In fact he waited until the middle of the following week before he swapped the size eight for the eight and a half once more. Harold went home with the hat around his ears yet again. Then for two or three days the cycle of fitting and removing the newspaper padding started all over again. Harold became a noticeably less confident person and started to take a lot of time off work. His doctor diagnosed stress and privately considered the onset of dementia. This was because Harold had confided to the doctor that that he was sure that sometimes his head changed size overnight... The studio bosses decided that for the remaining nine months, before his retirement, Harold should be allocated light duties in the sound equipment purchasing office. He accepted this suggestion but said he was sure that the transfer suite would grind to a halt without his vigilant supervision. In this, his opinion proved to be about as accurate as his belief that his head was in the habit of changing size. The Transfer Suite functioned perfectly well without him; some said a great deal better. It certainly soon became a much more cheerful place.

When the day came for Harold to retire there was a small ceremony in the canteen and he was presented with several 'leaving gifts'. The management always put in about £20 and the rest of the money was obtained by collection. Considering his rather dour charisma the collection for Harold had been quite generously supported. He was given a gold fountain pen and £25 worth of record tokens. There was one surprise present that puzzled him, however. It was the last package that he opened. In it was a hat. It was exactly the same as one he had at home; one he didn't wear much anymore; one he had decided didn't really suit him.

Chapter Seven.

<u>The Night of Napoleon.</u>

In the mid 1960's, if you were working as for the BBC as a film editor or an assistant editor, there were a number of studios to which you might find yourself allocated. The Ealing Film studios (re-named Television Film Studios by the BBC), The Television Centre at White City or the Lime Grove Studios in Shepherd's Bush. There were a few other cutting rooms elsewhere in West London, but the most of them were housed in one of those three locations.

The Lime Grove Studios had been built by Leon Gaumont, as a film studio; he later sold them to the Rank Organisation. When the BBC needed to expand television from its original base at Alexandra Palace the corporation bought the studios and thus established their television base in West London. The old Shepherd's Bush Empire was just around the block, on Shepherd's Bush Green and the BBC bought this too and converted it into 'The Television Theatre'. Lime Grove had three sound stages but the BBC decided to convert only two of them into television studios. The largest studio, in which 'The Wicked Lady' and 'The Man in Grey' had enacted their nefarious deeds suffered the ignominy of becoming a 'prop' store.

With Alexandra Palace still 'on stream' it was thought that two extra studios, at Lime Grove, would be sufficient until the completion of the sparkling new Television Centre. But remember, at that time, the early 1950's, all television was still 'live'. This sometimes had the most unexpected results. In 1955 David Attenborough was presenting one of his 'Zoo Quest' programmes in Studio 2 Lime Grove when a fruit bat seized the chance for liberty by biting him on the hand and flying up into the lighting gantry. Nothing could persuade it to surrender itself. It lived in the studio for about a month and suitable food was left out for it. Unfortunately Studio 2 was also the home of the BBC's very first soap opera, 'The Grove Family'. For three weeks life in the Grove household was considerably enlivened by impromptu appearances of the fruit bat. It would swoop across the sitting room in a most disquieting fashion and, on one occasion Granny Grove came into the sitting room to find a fruit bat hanging from the standard lamp. The fact that the characters made no mention of the exotic new family pet must have perplexed the viewers but the plots of the show were usually so mundane that this hint of British eccentricity was probably considered a master stroke of creative production. Eventually the bat was recaptured and the life in 'The Grove Family' returned to its regular litany of post-war tedium. Mind you, bizarre events in live TV drama of the 50's could occur at any time and did not require the appearance of stray animals. Jimmy Perry, the creator and co-author of 'Dad's Army' tells a good tale about his first TV appearance. Jimmy had the small role of a police constable in a crime thriller. Naturally. as this was to be his first part on television, his Mum was watching at home. At the end of the drama the detective hero has a huge fight with the chief gangster in the villain's pent-house flat. The climax comes as the detective knocks the gangster out of the window and he falls to a grisly death. At that moment constable Perry bursts into the room, looks out of the window then turns to the Detective and says the last line of the play: "Well, sir, perhaps it's for the best?" That is what was supposed to happen .On live transmission, however, things went badly a-wry. Flooded, as they were, with the adrenaline of performance the actors playing the detective and the gangster got so excited that the fight became much more energetic that it had ever been in rehearsal. The unfortunate consequence was that as Jimmy burst onto the scene both actors fell out of the window. This put Jimmy Perry into something of a quandary as he could see the camera light come on for his final close-up. Quick as a flash he adjusted his dialogue, he looked out of the window and said. "Well...perhaps it's for the best?" His Mum, watching at home confessed that she found the ending rather extraordinary but said that she thought that Jimmy had been very good!

In 1964 the eight new studios at Television Centre were finally up and running. The original plan was that Lime Grove would be quickly phased out once the new centre was completed, but this didn't happen. No more drama ever came from Lime Grove but the studio soon became the home of current affairs and sports department. In the

late sixties BBC2 ran a late night current affairs programme from Monday to Friday. It was the forerunner of
'News-Night' and had the somewhat uncharismatic title of
'24 Hours.' It consisted of studio interviews and location
film reports. There were five film editors and seven assistant editors attached to the show and they each worked,
on average, four 13 hours days a week. Almost without exception they hated the show, but many of the editors
were, in fact, senior assistants awaiting full promotion and
working as 'acting editors'. They could be busted back to
ranks at a moment's notice. It was the management's solution to staffing a programme which very few established
editors would touch with a barge pole. In fairness most of
the acting editors did eventually gain their promotion and
move on to more satisfying projects and it must be admitted that the pressure of working on a daily news programme certainly taught you how to cut film in a hurry. I
hated working on the programme but it surely sharpened
my technique as an editor.

There were a number of things that made working on '24
hours' a pain in the arse. The first was that as an 'acting
editor' you couldn't risk there being any complaints about
your work or your attitude. You quickly got used to an editor's pay and status so, however awful the show was to
work on, being thrown off it was unthinkable; it would
mean going back to being an assistant for a very long time.
If there was one thing to be gained it was experience.'24
Hours' used a lot of film; an editor might well have three
fifteen or twenty minute stories on air in one week. It

could have been exciting, it could have creatively stimulating, the reason it wasn't can be summed up in one word....' Journalists!' All films were directed and presented by reporters and they had about as much visual imagination as a deaf bat. Wall, to wall commentary was the name of the game, the images were merely used as a way of keeping the picture in synch as it linked the various 'talking heads' and interminable pieces to camera from the reporter. On the rare occasions when a new director tried to make something more cinematic it was invariably hacked to pieces by the programme editor. The programme editor is not to be confused with a film editor, by the way: Certainly not. The programme editor is first, last and at all stages in between, a journalist, with all the social disadvantages and personality disorders that calling demands. When I joined the programme, this job was being performed by the extraordinarily named 'Peter Portermento.' He was a pituitary giant with all the intellectual challenges of the species. His inability to make bold decisions was a legend throughout the studio and I first encountered it very soon after I had joined the programme. At this period, the late 60s, every current affairs programme was stuffed to capacity with stories about Northern Ireland and the IRA. In my eighteen months on '24 Hours' I, alone, must have edited about 60 films on the subject. You might think that such constant exposure to detailed reportage would have made me some kind of expert on the history of the period, but it simply didn't happen like that. Once you had edited about ten films concerning the troubles in Northern Ireland each story seemed to dissolve into a toxic miasma of boredom as various people, all of whom had largely unintelligible accents and most of whom were extraordinarily ugly, paraded their mindless agendas. It all seemed hopeless and it all seemed bollocks. However it was whilst editing one such story that I witnessed Portermento's supreme talent for dithering ineptitude. The story that I was editing had a bit more substance than our regular Irish items. It was about accusations that British troops had been illtreating IRA suspects. There was some pretty startling and convincing evidence in the film and both the reporter and the director were justly proud that they had managed to obtain it. The most powerful sequence had been filmed in a village hall in Southern Ireland. In front of a packed house a heavily built man of about forty stood on a stage and then he stripped off to reveal bruises and cigarette burns all over his body. His buttocks were covered with savage blisters. These had been filmed in close up. The commentary for the sequence was responsible and factual, it ran....'This man claims to have received these injuries at the hands of British troops. Scenes like this have shocked the Southern Irish.' Of course it was exactly the sort sequence to send Peter Portermento into a loop. He squirmed, the director and I argued but his word was law so when the film was transmitted his censored version was all that the viewing public was allowed to see. It was this. An extreme long shot of a man standing on the stage of a crowded village hall. As he drops his pants the truncated commentary exclaimed, 'Scenes like this have shocked the Southern Irish.' This was my first encounter with the withering power of fearless television journalism.

Editorial indecision was not the only cause of disaster on the programme; when it combined with technical breakdowns the scene was set for some wonderful cock-ups, some of which took on an almost surreal nature. Such an edition was 'The Night of Napoleon'.

Now, remember '24 Hours' was a, live, studio based, programme. The presenter varied from week to week. Sometimes it was Ludovic Kennedy, sometimes Austen Mitchell, in his pre MP days. It was often David Dimbleby or Kenneth Alsop. The presenters introduced the show, conducted the interviews with studio guests and provided the links into the film items. Each show had three or four items on film and there was always a standby film in case some item had to be dropped unexpectedly, (if a studio guest failed to turn up, for example.) I seem to remember that Kenneth Alsop was the host on the night in question and I certainly remember that the stand-by item was a rather dull film about Napoleon's treasure.

The programme always used two telecine machines. These are the TV equivalent of film projectors; they transmit film. It takes a good few minutes to lace up a telecine machine and at Lime Grove they were nowhere near the studio control gallery nor, for that matter, the cutting rooms. That was one of the reasons for the programme using two machines. The films that were ready ahead of transmission would be made up on a reel for telecine A and then any late stories could be loaded onto telecine B. It was quite common for films to be in the process of editing when the programme actually started transmission. The completed film would then be rushed down to telecine in time to be screened before the end of the programme. Another piece of equipment that played a vital role was the 'Telejector'. This was a device that televised slides. Photographs of politicians, maps of war zones, things like that. They were loaded into the Telejector in programme order. By pushing a button in the control gallery the slide was transmitted. When the vision mixer cutaway from the slide, back to the studio presenter, for example, the Telejector automatically went on to the next slide so that new one was then ready to be 'punched up' on cue. That is what was supposed to happen, but on the 'Night of Napoleon' it sure didn't work like that.

The ironic thing was that it had been a slow news day. Come the supper break, at six o'clock, all the film stories for that night had been completed and the reels of film for both telecine machines had been made up and delivered. They were the standard mix; An interview with the Shah of Iran, in which he insisted that his regime had never been more secure or more concerned with human rights (a pack of lies which sure came back to haunt him). There were two depressing items from Northern Ireland featuring the predictable parade of incomprehensible bigots. Then one of those 'social problem' pieces which always seem to start with a commentary like, 'Arthur Remnant is 84, he has a limited income and an even more limited intellect.' Finally, there was the standby film about Napoleon's treasure. As per usual the films were split between telecines A and B. The telejector machine had been loaded in advance too and contained slides which showed a photograph of the Shah of Iran, for use during the studio introduction of the film, some maps of Northern Ireland, in case anybody watching had forgotten where it was, some graphs which attempted to explain why there was little hope for Arthur Remnant and finally a portrait of Napoleon, the classic one with the hat, for use if the standby item was required.

There was an unusually jolly atmosphere amongst the 24 hours film editors, in the bar, during the supper break that night. It was very rare for all three film editors, on shift, to have their films completed so early so what better way to celebrate than to go to the bar and have a few drinks? We might have guessed that it was too good to be true and, indeed, it was. At about 6.45 that we were told that a really important story was coming in from Northern Ireland. The film labs had been told to pull out all the stops and we were to expect the rushes in at about eight o'clock. The production office hoped that we would be able to get a fifteen minute story cut and dubbed in time for transmission at ten thirty. It was a vital news story, so we were told. We were also encouraged to prove how fast and professional we could be. That sort of talk was guaranteed to rub us up the wrong way. We were always bloody fast and we had been cutting current affairs stories long enough to know that today's hot story is tomorrow's fish and chip wrapping. That is how it seemed to us but then we weren't journalists, and we thanked God for that.

So we downed our pints, finished our sandwiches and headed back to the seventh floor cutting rooms to await the arrival of the vital news footage. In a situation like that the main problem is not so much the time it takes to cut the story together but the time absorbed in breaking down the rolls of film into individual shots and matching the sound rolls to the picture. Still, there were three of us so we hoped to that we could divide the film into three sections, cut a section each and then join it all together. And that is what we did. I remember that it was a sweaty close shave but we made it. By transmission time the film was ready and we were told that it was to be the lead story of the night. Indeed one studio item had be dropped to make room for it and poor old Napoleon's treasure was certainly shelved. One of the assistant editors took the film down to Telecine and joined it on to the front of Telecine A, ready to be run as the 'lead story'. We had made it in very creditable time, so there should have been no cause for panic or confusion in the control gallery. However current affairs people don't seem to operate like that. They get high on panic and confusion; indeed they are adrenaline junkies. That was probably the reason that no one took any proper notice of the message from the cutting rooms. The other reason was that the telejector machine had suddenly decided to play up and it kept jamming and not moving on from slide to slide. Because of that distraction the production were so glad to learn that the vital story was in telecine, ready to run, that they failed to listen to the rest of the message. It was this. The old running order had the films on telecines A and B in alternate order so that the vision mixer would run telecine A and get the Shah of Iran, then telecine B for the boring IRA bastard, then A for the protestant Belfast bigot and then B for Arthur Remnant. But now telecine A had the new film on the front so the new running order had to be A then A AGAIN before reverting to B, A as per normal. It didn't seem much of a complication to us in the cutting rooms but then we didn't know about the telejector crisis. So, as the programme went on air, all the elements were in place for a cock up of monumental proportions.

The show started smoothly enough, the pretentious title music swelled and the lights faded up so that the silhouette of Kenneth Alsop became fully lit. He looked uncomfortable, but then he always did. Perhaps, on this occasion he was anxious because the late arrival of the lead story and the messing around with the telejector had meant that there had only been enough time for the sketchiest rehearsal. However he introduced the first item with aplomb, the director said 'Run telecine A', and our vital late story hit the air waves. When the film came to its' vital conclusion, and shock waves of apathy and indifference had echoed around the nation, the director cut back to Kenneth in the studio. He started the introduction to the Shah of Iran interview. During this intro various slides were supposed to come on screen via the telejector: A map of Iran, a photo of Tehran and a formal portrait of the Shah himself. They were supposed to, but they didn't. Instead what came up at each cue was the portrait of Napoleon with the hat. The Telejector had jammed again and nothing could shift it. Kenneth was obviously getting a bit rattled but he used all his professional suavity to make light of the problem."Well we are evidently having a few technical problems so let's go straight to our interview with His Royal Highness, the Shah of Iran." But we didn't. We didn't run telecine A for a second time, as instructed, we ran telecine B, so we didn't get the Shah of Iran we got the boring IRA bastard ranting on about the 'Farken Brahtish Trouarps'. If this was not enough to perplex the viewer at home another strange visual distraction punctuated the interview. The vision mixer had decided to make a determined effort to clear the jammed slide in the telejector by jabbing the button in an increasingly frantic fashion. He thought this might finally clear the problem and he also thought that the machine was 'off line' .He was wrong in both assumptions. The result was that during the interview with the Irish 'Shah of Iran' the viewer was treated to an apparition of Napoleon flashing on and off the screen in an increasing frenzy, redolent of the early stages of epileptic seizure. Such was the distraction caused by the telejector problem that it was about two minutes before anyone in the gallery noticed that the 'Shah of Iran' was wearing a black berry and talking a lot about the Falls Road in Belfast. The film was abruptly abandoned and we returned to a very rattled and confused Kenneth Alsop in the studio. "I'm sure you don't need me to tell you that that was not an interview with the Shah of Iran. However, I am told that we are now able to run the exclusive interview, which his Royal Highness gave to our reporter Tim Mangle." At this point a still of the intrepid reporter was scripted to appear but, dear reader, you will have probably have guessed that the image that leaped on to the screen was the, now familiar, face of Napoleon. It may have been this that caused the vision mixer to scream, 'Run Telecine' without actually mentioning which one. As a result the telecine operators decided that the previous machine must be the one required, so they started it up again. We were back to Belfast and our IRA activist.

From that point onwards the programme degenerated into s surreal farce. A furious presenter made ever more apologetic appearances. Nothing he introduced had anything to do with the film which followed. Napoleon continued to flash on to the screen, now and then in a frenzy of imagery which would normally only result from the ingestion of hallucinogenic mushrooms and when the Shah of Iran did, at last, appear it was after an introduction which had described him as 'a pensioner of restricted means'. When at merciful last it was time to run the end credits the background image did not dissolve into the programme logo, but rather,.... to the picture of Napoleon.

As I drove home from the studios that night I didn't relish the thought of the inevitable post mortem and acrimony that we would all face the next morning. Then I started to shake with laughter. It suddenly occurred to me that, had any viewer been daft enough to stick with the programme from start to finish the most bizarre feature would have been the countless appearances of Napoleon. After all, we knew that his treasure had been the standby story, which is why the fated slide had been loaded, but no mention of the Emperor himself was ever made during the programme. His unexplained multiple appearances must have been completely baffling to the home audience. It was exactly the sort of incident that might prompt the likes of the Daily Mail to fabricate stories about the BBC having been infiltrated by dangerous republican revolutionaries.

The result of that calamitous broadcast was a further decline in the already unpleasant relations between the programme's cutting room staff and production personnel. The film editors were really pissed off that any blame should be placed at their door especially as they had worked like demons to get the vital story ready in time, only to see the inclusion of this decidedly unremarkable item cause total chaos. Some of the *soi-dissant* directors on the show now felt the desire to become even more aggressive towards the film editors and the atmosphere in the cutting rooms went from bad to worse.

One man in particular was really unpleasant bastard. His name was Toby Winters. "For God's sake get it right!" he would bellow down the phone and when he actually bothered to visit the cutting room, to see work in progress, he would put his feet up on the editing machine and generally behave like the school bully. We could always tell when he was in the area for he would crash through the double doors at the top of our corridor and shout something self-important like, "I've only got ten minutes, so this better not be a waste of bloody time." His bullying days however, were about to come to an end and it was to be brought about, quite literally, by his own hand.

What happened was this. When directors were abroad for location filming they would send their editing scripts back to the cutting rooms by post. Now, nobody would have ever guessed that Toby Winters had a humiliating secret of a sexual nature; he seemed much too blusteringly confident for that. Then one day he made a classic fatal mistake. After he had written up the editing notes for the day's filming, complete with his usual insults and threats, he wrote a letter to his wife detailing, his erectile dysfunctions, his misery on learning that his wife had found herself a virile lover and stating that he felt 'like a man with no legs.' He then posted the letters off to England, without realising that he had put the two letters in the wrong envelopes. The editing notes were of little use to his wife but the letter intended for her was of considerable interest to the film editors. About a week later Toby was back from location, he came to the studios directly from the airport and blustered his way to the cutting room where the last of his reports was being edited for transmission that night. "My film is the lead story tonight and I'm not having you lot cock it up!" The great man's voice reverberated down the corridor as he crashed his way through the swing doors up by the lift. Then another voice shouted back, "Look out boys, here comes the man with no legs." The effect of that disembodied voice was both instant and miraculous. Toby Winters stopped dead in his tracks, he went very pale, and then he turned and ran back to the lift shouting, "Oh God, Oh God, Oh God." That is all we could hear until the doors shut and the lift sped him away.

Toby went on to make many more films for the programme; no other mention of the incident was ever made, but from that day forward his manners in the cutting room were always impeccable.

Chapter Eight.

Genius at the Helm.

Under the indecisive and ineffectual stewardship of Peter Portermento the viewing figures of '24 Hours' went from bad to worse. It must be said that the transmission times didn't help. The programme went out on BBC2 every night from Monday to Friday but never at the same time. Sometimes it was 10.30, sometimes 10.45, sometimes even as late as 11.20. Hardly ever was on the same time twice in one week. There was, therefore, hardly any chance of the programme becoming habitual viewing. Mind you the fact that it was often bloody boring and that ITV invariably ran an action feature film against it didn't help. The production team became more and more sensitive about the plummeting viewing figures, especially as it made their insistence that this or that story was 'Vital' have a distinctly hollow ring. The knowledge that the production mob was becoming increasingly touchy about audience numbers planted an extremely wicked idea in the heads of the lads in the cutting rooms. Legend had it that when the BBC's hugely successful dramatisation of 'The Forsythe Saga' had been transmitted the national grid had requested to know the precise running times of each episode. This was because as soon as the programme finished there was always a huge surge in the demand for electricity; 20 million people switched on kettles to make a cup of tea, or went to the lavatory, (the pumps at the water works are powered by electricity.) It was this fact that gave us the idea for our unsettling joke. As I had an ability to do 'funny voices'; I was chosen as the man to carry it out.

For a period of about three weeks I would phone the production office, using an outside line, and pretend to be a supervisor at the National Grid. This was in the days before 'ring back' or number identification, of course.

"Hello is that the chief executive for the 24 hours programme?" I would ask. "This is control command at the National Grid. I wonder if you could give me the exact start time of your programmes for every day this week?"

"I think that might be possible," came the excited reply. "Why would you like to know?" It seemed likely that whoever I was speaking to had heard of the 'Forsythe Saga' power demands and was fool enough or vain enough, to think it possible that '24 Hours' had entered the same elite class.

"Well it is simply that every time your programme starts transmission there is huge surge of spare power capacity throughout the UK. We imagine that it is because millions of people are switching off their televisions, all at the same time. If we knew exactly when it was going to happen we could be ready to shut down our end and save a fortune in surge fuses." There was no reply from the production office, just a gasp of horror. We thought the joke was a good one and couldn't believe that the production seemed to be taking the calls seriously; but then journalists are never very sharp about separating fact from fiction. It may have been that the joke calls tipped the balance for change, or it may just have been co-incidence, but it wasn't long before the programme had a major overhaul and our jokes very much back fired on us. Two changes of staff were to affect our lives and make life in the cutting rooms even more miserable than they already were. Peter Portermento was to be replaced as the programme editor and a new post of 'Chief Film Editor' was to be created in the hope of bringing some discipline into the perceived anarchy of the cutting rooms. These new faces were not really new at all as they had both worked on the hugely successful fore-runner of '24 Hours', a show which had been called, imaginatively, 'Tonight'. The fond hope was that these two fresh talents would bring with them some of the sparkle of old. But television doesn't work like that, mainly because the world moves on, times change, tastes change and, in the case of the two new faces, people change most of all.

The new chief film editor was a humourless Welshman called Manfred Jones; the new programme editor was an ageing 'bright young thing' and his name was Dennis Bodmin. The problem with Jones was that his knowledge of technical developments in film hadn't advanced in fifteen years and the problem with Bodmin is that he had developed from being a heavy drinker into being a dangerous dipsomaniac.

Jones' first attempt to assert himself was to order that the film editors went back to the old method of joining film, using film cement. For at least five years joiners which used specialised sellotape had been in general use. Tape joins were much faster to make and could easily be undone if alterations were required, but 'No!' Jones insisted cement joins had had been how things were done on the 'Tonight' programme so, from now on, they were to be used again. This was patently daft. The films on the 'Tonight' programme were much less complex than those on '24 Hours' so the extra time involved in cement joining made it much harder to meet the deadlines to which the production team had become accustomed. It is true that cement joins were less noticeable on screen than tape joins but this was only because the BBC was too mean to buy the proper optical tape and supplied us with the sort of adhesive that you would probably decline to use if you had been wrapping a parcel. Jones was intransigent and for about a month we struggled on. After I had nearly missed a transmission, because of the extra time taken to cement-join my film, I decided to take drastic action. I visited the studio one Sunday, when I knew that the film block would be as dead as a door nail. I went to the store cupboard where Manfred Jones had deposited his fresh supplies of film cement and I adulterated the whole bloody lot with film cleaning fluid. This was undoubtedly a rat's trick. It was particularly so as I had the next week booked off as holiday. When I came back I had to feign amazement when I was told that tape joins had be reinstated at the demand of the production team. Hardly surprising after a week in which every single film had fallen to bits on transmission.

The fiasco of the failing cement joins had greatly reduce the esteem in which the ghastly Manfred Jones was held and he never really recovered his influence or authority. After a short while we learnt that he was to be replaced and we were delighted to discover that the new Chief Film Editor was to be none other than my old friend Paddy Heath; he of the porn films and penguin music. At least Paddy's arrival might provide with some buffer against the awful regime of Dennis Bodmin. That was our hope at any rate.

Dennis Bodmin had joined the BBC straight from University as a general trainee. As such he was part of the corporation's 'crème de la crème'. To become a general trainee you had to have left Oxbridge with at least a double first. The interviews for the, very few, places were legendary. A candidate could expect to enter the room and have a question fired at him (occasionally her) in ancient Greek. If they flashed back a witty riposte in fluent Neanderthal, they had a chance of being accepted. It was by the use of such innovative practices that the BBC expected to keep closely attuned to grass roots of popular taste.

After a year or two spent observing all aspects of the Corporation's work, the general trainee was guaranteed a job in the department of his/her choice. Many chose admin. because the career path was more certain and there they could make best use of their Neanderthal. Dennis Bodmin, however, chose current affairs. In all fairness, his first job, on the 'Tonight' programme had shown him to be a programme maker of considerable talent but gradually he succumbed to the malaise that all too often afflicts those of inter-galactic intelligence; he was so clever that he was daft and what is more, he was daft enough to allow himself to drink to excess. He had reached that stage by the time we were lumbered with him on '24 Hours'.

The first glimpse we had of Bodmin's odd behaviour was at the eleven o'clock viewings, which he instigated. The idea was for all production staff and film editors to gather in the large viewing theatre at Lime Grove Studios and view the films which were likely to be included in that night's programme. This was a throwback to the production practices of the 'Tonight' programme, but that show had been a general interest magazine programme. Morning viewings were not much use on '24 Hours' because it was chiefly a news programme. We seldom had any films ready in advance because most stories were edited on the day of transmission and hanging around in the viewing theatre simply reduced the amount of time we had available for cutting the films. Still Bodmin was the boss so, for a few weeks the viewings took place and we watched the films that were on' stand-by' (and, by definition, not exactly' hot news'.) Naturally Bodmin himself was always late for the viewings. At about ten minutes past eleven we would hear the familiar sound of the studio's ancient lift grinding its' way towards the fourth floor, then we would hear the clang as the doors opened; (they were manual, by the way, as the lift was the 1930's original.) Then, in a flurry of shouting and self-importance, Bodmin and his team would sweep in. For such a little man he made an awful lot of noise, but that, perhaps was the reason. He was about 5ft 6ins and rather sickly looking, despite his dark complexion. He always wore tight fitting Italian -style suits which, combined with his tinted glasses, gave him a distinct air of 'Mafiosi'. But whilst he might have looked like a minor character in 'The Godfather', his behaviour more closely resembled the major role in 'The Lost Weekend.'

Bodmin would lurch in, shouting over his shoulder at the projectionists to "Get on with it. Run the film for Fuck's sake." He would then slump down in the middle of the second row and put his feet over the back of the seat in front. "So what's this one about then?" He would demand of no one in particular. "It looks boring, it is boring, boring, boring, BORING!" That was his favourite word, 'boring'. He would shout it over and over again sometimes before the film had even started and the leader was still running through the projector. He was drunk. We knew that. But he was roaring drunk and this was still only eleven fifteen in the morning. By transmission time, at ten thirty in the evening he would be uncontrollably rat-arsed!

The programme had a hospitality for guests and key production staff. There were sandwiches, a very generous supply of drink and a big colour TV on which to watch the programme. As this was a time when the BBC still had confidence in itself programmes, like '24 Hours,' all had a generous hospitality budget and they sure knew how to spend it. Film editors and reporters were lucky in as much as, come transmission time, their work was usually finished for the evening. They could, therefore, go to hospitality as soon as it opened at the start of the programme. Guests from the studio would be shown in, as soon as their item was over and at the end of transmission the studio crew, director, vision mixer, programme editor etc would make an entrance. In the days before Dennis Bodmin joined the programme hospitality was something to which we looked forward, but he changed all that. It quickly became evident that he was a total liability if he was in the control gallery during transmissions. He would shout and throw things at the monitor screens and often roll around on the floor, banging his fists on the carpet. As that sort of behaviour was hardly conducive to the smooth direction of live television, and it was not long before Bodmin found himself banned from the production gallery of the programme of which is was the titular head. Unfortunately that meant that he came, instead, to the hospitality room as soon as the show started. His actions had to be seen to be believed. His favourite pastime would be to take a plate of sandwiches, separate the slices of bread and then stick them on to the television screen shouting "Boring, Boring, Boring!" His judgement of the on screen item was usually correct but, coming from the man who was directly responsible for the programme's content it was an unsettling, even frightening, action to witness. Then, as is so often the case with deranged behaviour, Dennis Bodmin's went from bad to worse.

It was probably in a desperate attempt to improve the audience ratings that a woman who had recently been the girlfriend of Micky, (The Mad Axe Man,) Mitchell was invited to appear on the show. Viewers were treated to an in depth interview exploring every fascinating detail of what it was like to sleep with a mad axe-man. The answer, presumably, was 'bloody uncomfortable' depending on whether he insisted on bringing the axe to bed with him. The item was shameless sensationalism but it was argued that it was what was needed to give the programme a welcome boost. What was less welcome was Bodmin's attempt to grope the mad axe-man's girlfriend in the hospitality room after her interview. Had he been sober enough to comprehend her interview, he would have realised that the young lady was no fool and was certainly not the type of girl to be attracted to a shrunken, drunken, television executive with an inflated opinion of himself. However all Bodmin could see was a sexy young woman who was provocatively dressed and therefore bound (in his way of thinking) to be easily seduced by a T.V. sophisto. A slap round the chops and a threatened kick in the bollocks soon put him right on that score but the resultant cries of "I'll see you never appear on television again you bitch." did

little to impress the other studio guests who had been expecting to spend an enjoyable time in hospitality while
they awaited their cabs home. And it got worse. He threw
a whole plateful of canopies at the TV screen and then
rolled around, on the floor, in a temper tantrum. Paddy
Heath, who was duty chief film editor that night, had had
enough. He came over to me and my assistant, Dick Allen,
and said quietly, "Come on lads, help me throw the bastard out." I am happy to say that we needed no second
bidding. The three of us picked up Dennis Bodmin, which
wasn't very difficult, as he was not heavy and was beyond
resistance. We carried him to reception to await his cab.
There he made a bit of a rally and started kicking and
screaming again so Paddy, Dick and I picked him up, once
more and threw him out of the double doors of the Lime
Grove Studios and into the street. He landed in the gutter
and that is where we left him.

"Well lads," said Paddy, "I Doubt if we will have jobs tomorrow."

"Don't worry Pad, it needed doing," said Dick. "And he is
so pissed that I doubt if he'll remember what happened
anyway."

Dick was right. Next day everything was back to normal
but a few weeks later Dennis Bodmin was away on special
leave. Rumour had it that he was in the drying out ward at
Hammersmith Hospital. Rumour also had it that the BBC
had six beds in that ward permanently reserved for its executives. Fortunately for us, Dennis Bodmin was never to

return to '24 Hours'. When he was discharged from the dypso ward senior management obviously needed to consider his future very carefully. They needed to, but they didn't. Instead they decided to appoint him to head of BBC Television News; proof, if ever any was needed, that it is often easier to live a charmed life than a charming one. However his next excursion down skid row was not long in coming and was precipitated by the IRA.

In December 1975 four IRA gunmen broke into a flat in Marylebone and held a middle aged couple hostage. The incident became known as the Balcombe Street Siege. BBC news was determined to bring its viewers every nerve tingling moment of inactivity and they persuaded a young woman whose flat overlooked the 'siege apartment' to let them use her front window as a camera position. She was doubtless paid well for her trouble but, in the event, nothing like enough for the distress she actually was to experience. The siege lasted six days and it must be stated that the police behaved in an exemplary fashion, eventually securing the release of the hostages and the surrender of the terrorists without a shot being fired. This must have been a huge disappointment for the Head of News, Dennis 'Boring' Bodmin. On day three he decided to visit the location to see what was going on. He felt sure that it must be possible to get some more exciting pictures than those which had, so far, emerged from the young woman's flat. He threw his weight about and upset everybody especially a number of newspaper journalists who had conned their way into the 'BBC flat'. This infuriated Bodmin because it was his budget that was paying for the prime viewing position. It soon transpired that there was more drama taking place in the camera flat than in that of the hostages because, on day four of the siege, Bodmin arrived, pissed as fart. He ejected all the Fleet Street reporters from the flat and then tried to sexually assault the girl who lived there. This time it was the BBC camera crew who threw him out. A staff photographer from the Daily Mirror took a picture of Bodmin lying in the gutter and the Mirror's picture editor sent it to the BBC with the ultimatum, "Either you replace this shit or we will put this picture on tomorrow's front page!" The next day Dennis Bodmin was back in Hammersmith hospital.

The Balcombe Street incident still didn't finish him. About nine months later he was back at Television Centre with a large office on the fifth floor. He had been given charge of a special project. He was to be allowed to make a documentary on any subject of his choice and he chose the architecture of ancient Greece. He went out to Athens with one of the film department's finest cameramen but little came of the adventure. This was largely due to the fact that, in contravention of all filming agreements Bodmin overflew the Parthenon in a helicopter. Determined, as he was, to photograph details that had never been seen before he ordered the pilot to fly much closer to the monument than was either safe or sane. As a result of the chopper down draft great chunks of masonry were dislodged from the monument and they crashed to the ground. Not since the visit by Lord Elgin had the Parthenon suffered such disfigurement at the hands of an Englishman. After several heated exchanges between the Greek Government, the Foreign Office and the BBC it was at last decided that Dennis Bodmin's employment at BBC television would have to be terminated ... and so it was...and he was moved to a highly paid position in BBC local Radio.

No reminiscence of the Lime Grove Studios would be complete without a reference to the infamous lift. Not until the re-privatisation of the railways was there ever such an unreliable method of transport. It was on the left as you entered the reception area through the main studio doors. It was one of those lifts that you see in 1930's crime movies... the sort that travels in the central stair well and has sliding lattice gate doors which you can see through. You had to open the outer gate yourself but the inner gate closed automatically. Obviously, as a safety feature, the lift would not move if the outer gate was not properly closed and this meant that if someone had got out of the lift, and not bothered to close the outer gate behind them, the lift would not answer calls from other floors. After lunch there were frequent arguments in reception about who should run up the stairs, find where the lift was stuck and close the open door. Only then would the lift respond to the frantic button pushing that was taking place on the ground floor. It was a very small lift and could only hold four people. There was, therefore, always the temptation to over load it. However if a fifth person did manage to squeeze in the lift could wreak a terrible revenge. It would go up about half a floor and then stick. Mind you, it often stuck anyway, even when it wasn't overloaded. One lunch hour when four of us were hoping to travel from the ground to the seventh floor the lift stuck, when it had only ascended about four feet. We thought that it might be possible to force the gates and squeeze ourselves out because we could still see the reception area, if we knelt on the floor. However the lift was having none of it, the gates were shut fast. We shouted to the lady in reception and she called the studio firemen. They took an age to arrive and then took even longer to discover that the lift would only un-jam if it was winched up a few feet before being lowered back down again. The four of us in the lift were in no danger whatsoever but we were getting pretty fed up as we were losing editing time. An hour passed and the fire men were still mucking about, with little sense of urgency and we were increasingly agitated. I suggested that if we pretended that we were panicking it might speed things up. We decided that 'full on' hysterics might be going too far so we hit on the idea of singing 'Nearer My God to Thee,' in mournful, weak voices. The Film 'A Night to Remember', about the sinking of the Titanic, had been on television the previous week and that is what gave us the idea. The effect on the firemen was almost miraculous. They started winching with much greater fervour and we heard them phoning for reinforcements and a nurse. When the lift at last descended the four feet necessary for us to be able to make our escape there was a group of anxious first-aiders waiting for us, with cups of hot strong tea; they even had a wheel chair with them. I seem to recall that Paddy Heath, who was one of the trapped heroes, even managed to con a large brandy out of them.

It was about ten o'clock one night, about half an hour before transmission that the lift pulled its dirtiest trick. One of the assistant editors was taking reels of films for that night's programme down to telecine when the lift stuck between floors. This time there was some danger as the lift was stuck high up in the shaft, between floors six and seven. It was late at night, so there was only one fireman on duty and he had to phone Television Centre to get extra help. This was not good news for the poor trapped assistant who now had to prepare himself for several hours of waiting. The other problem was that he had the reels of film with stuck in there with him and, as sod's law would have it, 60% of that night's programme was planned to be on film. It was a major production crisis. If it was simply a problem of manpower, then all the men in cutting room were ready to help but the fireman insisted it was not that simple He was not sure how to winch down the ancient lift and insisted that it would be much safer to wait until someone arrived who was more familiar with the mysterious machinations of Lime Grove's antique Otis. So there it was, an assistant editor stuck in the lift with twenty five minutes of film that was due on the air in thirty minutes time. The fact that the lift was so old fashioned was the reason why it was always breaking down but, on this occasion, its' out-moded design provided the solution to our problem. As I have said the lift doors, on each floor were sliding, open lattice, metal frames, so you could see the lift shaft through the diamond-shaped gaps in the doors' metal struts. Someone realised that if Louis, the lad trapped in the lift, unspooled some of the film and fed it out of the lift door we might be able to catch when it reached the level of the floor below. Once we had got hold of the end of it we could wind it onto another spool easily enough. We shouted our idea to Louis and he unwound some of the film. Actually getting hold of the dangling end was not that simple, as the gaps in the gates were small, but, by taping a wire coat hanger onto a broom handle, we eventually succeed. The re-spooling procedure took while because we were anxious not to damage the film. If it flapped around too much in the lift shaft it was in danger of picking up some of the decades-worth of muck and grime that had gathered in the workings. Careful, as we were, the film suffered a bit but at least we were able to get it down to telecine in time for that night's transmission. It was not long after the start of the programme that Louis surprised us all by walking into the hospitality lounge. Apparently the lift had un-jammed itself about five minutes after we had completed winding the film down the shaft. This merely confirmed our belief that the lift was possessed by a mischievous spirit. As soon as we had out-witted it, it gave up But it had had its' fun.

Chapter Nine.

<u>Light Fingers.</u>

It was not long after my great escape from 'The Great Lime Grove Lift Drama', that I actually managed to escape from the wretched studio altogether. The management at last decided that I had served my time on current affairs and that I could move back to the Ealing Studios and work on some real programmes. At long last I was to be appointed a full film editor, my days of 'acting editor 'were over. I would have my own cutting room and my own assistant. The first person to fill that illustrious position was Kikki Torville, to whom I introduced you in chapter one. However Kikki was on a short term contract and once that had expired she was keen to continue her Globe Trotting. We said a very fond farewell and Kikki headed off to the U.S.A. She kept in touch with her friends at Ealing and she had many adventures to recount. She visited Harlem with a friend. Two white woman alone in that part of New York was asking for trouble, if all the advice was to be believed but there was only one unfortunate incident and Kikki proved more than capable of dealing with it. She and her friend had just got out of a cab when three large youths emerged from the shadows and demanded money, threatening them with a knife. Kikki, in her most imperious tones, simply told them that she had never before experienced such appalling bad manners and that the three young men ought to be thoroughly ashamed of themselves. The assailants were so surprised by this turn of events that they vanished back into the night. A lot of the people at Ealing thought that story was simply a bit of comic invention on Kikki's part but knowing the intrepid lady, as I did, I didn't doubt it.

It wasn't long before I was told that I was to be joined by a newly appointed full time assistant called John Thornicroft. He was tall, thin and had a rather eccentric hippie look about him. He was hugely energetic and a really positive person to be around. We quickly became both good friends and a strong editing team. I had developed some bad habits while I worked on nightly current affair's films. I had become a very fast film editor but I was disorganised and terrible at filing trims (those parts of each shot which, though not included in the first cut, may well be needed later). John soon sorted me out. "Right," he would say, "that's enough. If you don't let me do some filing we will never be able to find anything. You go for a coffee, or go into town for half an hour. When you come back I'll have everything sorted." And he did, it was marvellous. We never lost a trim.

John was also a great sound editor. I always found the preparation of sound tracks, for the final mix a tedious process even though I knew that it was essential for a good end result. John was great at it and he also enjoyed the overtime, which came with the task. It was the combination of my speed and editing skill with John's methodical, organised, approach that made us such a good editing team; plus the fact that we each appreciated each other's contribution both technically and creatively.

John owned a narrow boat on the Grand Union Canal at Harefield, about thirty minutes' drive from the studio. He had bought it with the overtime that he earned on the TV film *'Cider with Rosie'*, so he called the boat 'Rosie'. My editing speed had one hidden advantage in that it allowed us to take very long lunch hours. Come twelve thirty on most days I had cut as much film as most editors would achieve in a full day so two or three times a week we would simply down tools and head off for a canal trip on Rosie. After a pleasant lunch, in a canal side pub we would return to the Studio, sneaking in by the back gate at about 4.pm. (in time for tea.). If we were working with a civilised director we would include him, or her, in the excursions. The point is that we never went over schedule. Had we not taken time out we would have frequently come in well under schedule and this would have made us extremely unpopular with the other editors. There was always a lot of bullshit pedalled by some of the editing staff about how long the various processes took and how difficult they were but the skilled editors could cut very fast indeed. No one wanted to have to work any harder than absolutely necessary and if, at the end of a long schedule the editor and assistant put in some overtime it all helped with the pay packet at the end of the month. Not many editors seriously fiddled their overtime claims but a few hours added on here and there seemed fair game. This was mainly because the film editors felt hard done by in comparison with the pay given to cameramen.

Cameramen were on a higher basic salary than editors and because they spent a lot of time on location, living on their generous expenses, they were able to bank more of their take home pay. Film editing was always a somewhat 'Cinderella' sort of occupation There was an old, bitter, joke amongst editors that if a film was good, then it has been 'beautifully photographed' but if it was a dud then it had been 'badly edited'. The strength of this prejudice was tangible and as many editors had rescued many a badly directed and badly shot piece of junk by their skill with the scissors, they resented the lack of esteem in which their talents were often held. From the management point of view it was a simple matter; if a cameraman cocked up completely the only solution was an expensive re-shoot, whereas if a film editor loused up it was always possible to re-print the rushes and start again, with a different editor, if necessary. This, too, would be costly but nothing like as expensive as a re shoot. *Ergo,* cameramen deserved more pay.

It was in the late 1960s and early 70s that some of the more cavalier film cameramen hit on a scam that was to increase their income in a spectacular fashion. It was spectacular, not only in the amount of money it made for them, but also in the scale and cheek of its dishonesty. The amazing thing is that it went undetected for so long and that, when the management finally realised what was happening, the magnitude of the fraud was almost too much for them to comprehend.

The scam was simply this. Until the mid-sixties all film lighting equipment was bulky and difficult to use; it had been designed for studio rigs. Even a small documentary unit would require a couple of lighting electricians on the crew if they were to film any interior locations. Any Ealing crew, working in the UK would take a BBC lighting crew with them but if they were going to film abroad then it was cheaper to hire the lights and the lighting men locally. That, at any rate, was the theory. Then suddenly the lighting world was revolutionised by the introduction of the first lightweight lighting kits. They were called Colour-Trans, primitive by modern standards and still fairly heavy they, nevertheless, packed down into a couple of large cases. Suddenly lighting documentaries became much quicker and easier. The BBC still believed it to be an extravagance to send their own lighting crews abroad so the practice of hiring lights and men from foreign lighting companies continued. But, in fact, it didn't. It didn't because a large number of cameramen bought themselves a new set of Colour Trans and used them to light foreign locations. On returning to BBC Ealing they would submit a false receipt for the hire of local electricians and equipment and would trouser a handsome sum when they came to claim their expenses. There was one small drawback. Because the new lights were still a substantial piece of baggage, everyone in the crew had to lend a hand with lugging the cases about. For the swindle to work the cameraman, assistant cameraman, sound recordist and the director were all required to be in on it and literally all lend a hand. So the booty had to be split four ways, but it was well worth it. It quickly became obvious that the receipts for cash payments to bogus European lighting companies needed to look more convincing than a had written scrawl torn from the pages of a foreign receipt book; but the embezzlers were soon across that. They had note paper specially printed with the names of their various fictitious suppliers emblazoned at the top. The BBC film department happily passed the expense claims made to such concerns as ' Bougies Truques Bordeaux', 'Lucas Falsas' Madrid or 'Scintillias Impostores', Milan. The camera crews concerned were on to real winner and the fraud succeeded for several years.

It was never very clear as to how the truth finally came out. It is possible that the lighting electricians got wind of what was going on and dropped a word in management's ear. It is even possible that the honest cameramen, (and they were in the majority) were sickened by the dishonesty of their unscrupulous colleagues, but, from whatever source, in about 1974 the management was, at last, tipped off. It would be inadequate to say that the shit hit the fan. It would be more accurate to imagine the flow from the main London sewer being fed into the turbines of a jumbo jet.

Over the next few days the reaction of the managers in the front office of the BBC's Ealing Film Studios ran a bizarre course. At first there was total disbelief, then vengeful fury, and finally frustration and fear. They feared that if the facts got into the press they would be made to look completely foolish and felt frustrated that, if they pursued criminal charges against the crews involved, the press would certainly get hold of the story. They therefore decided to find a strategy that would put the fear of God into the miscreants and force them to pay back every last dishonest penny. It turned out to be a fond hope.

One uncomfortable decision that the film managers felt forced to make was to refer the problem upwards to senior executives at Television Centre. Their report soon landed on the desk of the newly created 'Head of Television'. This was Hugh Welshborn. Part Druid, part intellectual, Welshborn liked to think of himself as a polymath and indeed other people might have thought him to be one too, if only his range of knowledge had been less limited. He had only been in his newly created, post a few weeks when the great lighting scandal broke and in it he saw the chance to assert himself as a man to be reckoned with. He would apply his finely attuned mind to the problem and all would be amazed by his wisdom and strength of purpose. At that time few senior executives in British television were held in higher regard than Hugh Welshborn; certainly none were by Welshborn himself. The more he thought about it, the more Welshborn was convinced that the great lighting debacle would give him a chance to shine.

He would summon a meeting of all the Ealing camera crews and address them in his most authoritarian tone. He would make sure that a good number of other senior managers were present to witness his triumph. It would be a meeting to remember, he would speak for at least an hour. The errant film crews might find it extremely uncomfortable but personally he could think of nothing more enjoyable than sixty minutes spent listening to the sound of his own voice. All he had to do now was to decide exactly what he was going to say. The shiny suits at Ealing had suggested a method of retrieving the looted cash. They planned to open a discreet office where those crew members who had been involved in the fraud could pop in and pay back what they owed. This seemed a rather gutless approach to Welshborn, but he could see the need for discretion. He would like to have sacked every techie who had had even the slightest involvement but then, it was pointed out, and this would have reduced the number of film crews by about 20%. The consequent cancellation of important forth-coming productions would be devastating. All in all the 'pay back' scheme was probably the best but Welshborn was convinced that this 'softly softly' approach would only succeed after a powerful piece of oratory had shamed the wrong doers to the very core. Yes that, he decided, must be the effect of his harangue. As he thought about it he realised that he had a lot of experience on which to base his speech. He had worked with film crews in his days as a very wooden presenter on Arts documentaries. Some of the crew members were rough diamonds, no doubt about that but, basically, they were decent chaps. He would therefore frame his address in the tones of an irate commander with a touch of 'incensed head master' and a good deal of hell-fire Methodist minister. In fact he had had very little military experience but his Welsh up bringing had provided him with plenty of exposure to the wrath of headmasters and ministers of religion. So that was it. He wrote a memo to the film managers instructing them to call a meeting at the Ealing Film studios at 18.30 on the following Wednesday. Everybody, repeat, *everybody* in the camera and location sound departments must be ordered to attend.

Over the next few days there was a distinct frisson pervading the Ealing Studios; a definite feeling that 'something was up.' The film crews had all been summoned to a meeting. *'Why, what was it all about?'* The film editors, paranoid to a man and woman, convinced themselves that the cameramen and sound recordists were about to be awarded even higher salaries; then later they began to fear that the meeting heralded the start a crackdown on excessive overtime claims. The editors thought that it wouldn't be long before the management called another meeting, just for the cutting room staff. The day before the great show down something like the truth behind it all began to emerge. It was something to do with a lighting fiddle and vast sums of money were involved. Thousands, perhaps tens of thousands of pounds, certainly a lot more than the odd few quid that the editors were used to fiddling from their overtime. Paddy Heath, who had a lot of mates in all departments at the studio, got closest to the truth.

"It's all about false claims for lighting gear when some of the camera crews were working abroad. That devious old bugger Reg Bishop is a ring leader and Aidan Feathers is up to his neck in it too. Some big wig from Tele Centre is going to be at the meeting to read the riot act and it isn't impossible that some of them will end up in the slammer." In this last bit Paddy was wrong, of course, but it all seemed quite plausible to us and the two cameramen he mentioned were unpleasant, arrogant and pretty damn useless as cinematographers. That afternoon the Tuesday before the Wednesday evening's great reckoning a lot of the film crews were looking extremely worried and Reg Bishop and Aidan Feathers were looking more worried than the rest. Most of the studio electricians however, seemed bright and cheerful and the phrase, "Serve the buggers right," echoed on the wind.

The local managers had done their best to play their cards close to their chests. They had deliberately leaked some details about the purpose of the meeting, in order to unnerve the guilty parties, but they had kept the fact that the event was to be chaired by no less a luminary than Hugh Welshborn a deadly secret. On the Wednesday morning, however, the strategy was to advertise Welshborn's attendance, convinced that this late information would further unsettle the fraudsters. They could not possibly have guessed that in fact it would provide a glimmer of hope to the likes of Reg Bishop and Aidan Feathers.

Earlier that same morning Hugh Welshborn had looked in his wardrobe to decide exactly what suit to wear for the evening meeting at the Ealing Studios. A meeting which he felt confident would establish him as a powerful management figure, perhaps even Director General material. He selected the suit which he had intended to wear for Princess Anne's wedding, an intention which had been unfulfilled as he had not received an invitation. He had attended the event but only as part of the BBC's team, crammed in to the sweaty confines of an outside broadcast van. Even achieving that had cost him a bottle of Scotch, (a bribe to the engineering manager) but it had enabled him to impress his neighbours with tales of the event.

Never mind, the suit would, at last, be put to good use and on this occasion it would be centre stage.

Welshborn just knew that the Wednesday morning in the office would drag, and indeed it did. He spent an hour shuffling papers around and then decided it was no good; the only way to kill time before he set off to Ealing was to do a tour of Television Centre. He enjoyed putting in surprise appearances around the building and would often make a helpful suggestion to a nervous young director or suggest a change in the running order of a light entertainment show. He felt sure that these 'walkabouts' did his reputation a power of good and proved that he was still in touch with the 'coal face' of production. Unfortunately one of his recent interventions had cost the variety show concerned a fortune in musicians' overtime, but this was well compensated for by a grateful comment that he had overheard as he was leaving the studio, it came from the guest French singing star, Jonnie Rallabol who muttered *'Quel Branleur'*. Welshborn was not exactly sure what it meant but thought that it must mean that Monsieur Rallabol had recognised an executive who had 'hands on' experience. However today he thought it best to play safe and pop into a studio where his august presence would be most strongly felt. He noticed that *'Blue Peter'* was in studio 6 and he was sure that the, somewhat naive, presenters of the programme would be suitably overawed by a visit. He wouldn't barge in, that was not his style at all. No, he would slip in, very quietly, and stand at the back of the studio until some junior technician recognised him and a muttered buzz of excitement ran round the studio and betrayed his presence. Then at a suitable moment he would emerge from the shadows and charm everybody with a word of encouragement, here, a joke with a prop man, there, and, perhaps a gem of advice based on his years of experience.

When he got to the studio he was rather annoyed to see the red 'No Entry' light flashing. This was odd; surely *'Blue Peter'* was transmitted live at about 5pm? After some thought he realised that they must be prerecording an item for some reason or other. He knew that he should wait for the red light to go out before he entered but then

111

a wicked thought came into his head. After all, he was the Managing Director of television so he could do what he liked. He would ignore the red light and go straight in. Of course he would be as discreet and quiet as possible but if some member of the crew berated him for not observing 'the red', it would be simply delicious. He would appear to be suitably chastened and then, when he was recognised as the important person he truly was, he would be penitent and insist that the lowly minion had been absolutely right to admonish him. It would provide him with a chance to be humble, noble and patronising all at the same time. He trembled with excitement at the prospect. The studio door opened quietly and easily enough and Welshborn found himself in a dimly illuminated part of the studio. The brightly lit set stood a good distance away at the far end of the studio floor. He was rather disappointed that no one had noticed his entrance so he walked forward a little. Suddenly he felt something strangely soft under his foot and immediately afterwards the efficient calm of the studio was disturbed by a horrendous yelp. Hugh Welshborn had trodden on the tail of one of Blue Peter's menagerie of pets... A large sheep dog type, taking a rest away from the heat of the lights, had fallen asleep near the door right in Welshborn's path. At the far end of the studio the presenter, who up to that moment, had been demonstrating how to make a model of the Kremlin from three cornflake packets and a couple of onions, stopped what he was doing and exclaimed,

"WHAT THE FUCK IS GOING ON? IT'S LIKE A FUCKING CIR-
CUS IN HERE TODAY." Welshborn was shocked to hear
such language from a, much loved, children's presenter
but, before he could emerge from the shadows and berate
the offender in his most schoolmasterly tone, he felt the
most violent pain in his buttocks.

The dog he had so rudely awakened had decided on a
campaign of revenge and was sinking its teeth into Welshborn's arse. Now it was his turn to curse but, ever mindful
of the dignity of his position and also the fact that he was
within the sanctity of a *'Blue Peter'* studio, the swear-word
he shouted was in Welsh. It was, nevertheless, a disgusting

oath containing, as it did, an inordinate number of consecutive consonants and a plethora of double y's. He could see an angry floor manager heading towards him followed by an infuriated dog handler. This was no time for pleasantries or erudite quotations, he made a run for it. He dashed out of the door and hid himself in the Gents which adjoined assembly area outside the studio. Here he was able to examine the severity of the bite and extent of the damage to his trousers. Both looked pretty bad. He sat down on the seat with his head in his hands and muttered the YY word under his breath. One thing was clear, there would be no problem filling in the time between now and the meeting at six thirty. He would have to see the BBC Nurse and get an anti-tetanus shot then he would need to get his driver to take him home so that he could pick up the suit's spare pair of trousers. Thank God he had taken the tailor's advice and had an extra pair made. No all was not lost, he could rise above it; indeed he must! What was it Kipling said? *'If you can meet with triumph or disaster and treat those two imposters just the same.'* But as the line came into his head he felt immediately ashamed. He remembered that all modern critics held Kipling in very low regard.

Four hours later he was sitting in the back of his chauffeur-driven limo and was, at last, on the way to the meeting at the Ealing Studios. He adjusted the pillow under his bottom and was very glad that he had thought to take it from the bedroom when he had gone home to change his trousers. He was also thinking about suggesting that 'Blue Peter' do an educative special to help children cope with the grief that they might experience when a pet had to be destroyed. To make the point both powerful and realistic the programme's own dog would be put to sleep as part of the project. Something also needed to be done to put that damned BBC nurse in her place. It had been embarrassing enough to have his buttocks examined by a talkative Irish S.R.N. without having to put up with her insensitive comments about his physiognomy. *('Sure I'd have to be asking me self why in the world a doggie would want to bite a bum like yours, when there is not enough flesh on it to feed a Chihuahua?')* Cheeky bitch! She hadn't just kissed the Blarney stone - she had bitten a bloody great chunk out of it. Well he'd sort her out, he'd get personnel to invent a shed load of forms that she would be required to full in at the start and end of every shift. One way and another it had been a pretty awful day, but this made him even more determined to be dazzlingly effective at the great lighting scandal showdown. He decided to take another look at the notes which the Ealing people had sent him; at least 20 crews involved, sums of money around £600 per trip falsely claimed, been going on for about seven years, probably started by the cameraman Reg Bishop. He knew that name but couldn't think why, must have seen it on a screen credit sometime. Ah well, his speech would soon have them jumping over themselves to pay the money back. He glanced at his watch, they were running a bit late but, never mind, he would have less time to spend before the meeting with the ghastly little runt who styled himself

'Head of Film'. His name was Jim Blewett. He had been put in charge of the film department years ago when all in consisted of was three men, an apprentice and three old newsreel cameras left over from D day. As the department grew so Blewett grew with it until now he had become insufferably self-important. He was red faced and affectionately known a 'Jug Ears' by the film technicians.' Worst of all, he had less interest in cinematography than a rabbit has in family planning; as a result his staff both despised and loathed him. 'Yes,' thought Welshborn, 'the less time spent with 'Jug Ears' the better'. He glanced at his watch, it was already ten to six. the car would arrive about fifteen minutes before the meeting was due to start; perfect timing if you wanted to spend as little time as possible before the main event with a lot of managerial non-entities.

In fact, the traffic cleared and it was only five minutes later that Welshborn's car swept into the Ealing Studios. Well, it would have swept in but they had a brush with security. The man on the gate turned out to be a prince amongst that breed of paranoid misanthropes which the BBC traditionally chose to employ as commissionaires. Welshborn had left his identity card in the back pocket of his other trousers so this enabled the commissionaire to start on his practiced course of bloody-minded obstruction. Things were getting pretty heated when a cheery voice called out, "It's OK Bert, he is the bloke who is going to give the speech in the canteen."

"Very well, Mr. Bishop," replied the job's-worth, "As long as you think it's alright." The car was waved through and, as they headed for the cramped car park, Welshborn realised that he had just recognised, not only the name, but also the voice of Reg Bishop. He had no time to give the matter much thought because the car door was hastily opened by the sweaty hand of 'Jim Jug Ears Blewett'. "Welcome to Ealing Sir", he spluttered, even more red faced than usual. "Sorry about that trouble at the gate. Henderson is a good man but a trifle overzealous; still can't be too careful, eh?"

"Perhaps you should put him in charge of checking the expenses claims?" retorted Welshborn, enjoying the chance to deflate the blustering Blewett.

"Quite so, bad business this. Still, come and have a drink before we get stuck in". Welshborn glanced at his watch again, "Have we time?" "Oh yes twenty minutes at least, besides no bad thing to keep the buggers waiting."

Drinks in Blewett's office were every bit as tedious as Welshborn had feared. He had to endure endless anecdotes from the red faced little bore about his time as a Major in the Catering Corps and how this had uniquely prepared him for the management of men and woman who had determined to devote their lives to world of film. And there was no chance to escape either, because all the other people in the room, who Blewett referred to as 'My senior staff,' were even more uninteresting than Blewett himself. However another glance at his watch persuaded

Welshborn that, at last, they should head for the canteen, where all the crews would be anxiously waiting to learn of their fate.

As they walked down the studio roadway, from the front office towards the canteen, it certainly didn't sound as if the crews were exactly gathered together in fear and dread. Welshborn was expecting a hushed awe to have descended over the assembled miscreants and was somewhat unnerved, as he grew nearer, to hear sounds more usually associated with a bear garden. Thank God he had prepared a powerful speech; he'd soon bring them all to heel.

It had been agreed that Jim Blewett would make a brief speech of introduction before Welshborn 'let them have it.' so Blewett entered the canteen first, followed by Welshborn and after him the assorted minions who had proved to be so dull at the drinks 'do'.

The chatter died down a little as they approached the small stage which been put up at the end of the hall. The sound department had provided amplification but, inevitably, Blewett failed to realise that he needed to switch on the microphone. A deal of time and charisma were lost as he pratted about. There was a lot of, 'Is this thing working?' and 'Can you hear me at the back?' until finally the system leapt into life with the inevitable high pitched shriek of feed-back howl- round. Welshborn sat in chair which was just behind, and to the right of Jim Blewett; the lesser management apparatchiks sat in a grim faced row along the back of the stage. Blewett had already spoken for longer than had been agreed and was in danger of stealing some of Welshborn's thunder. 'Breach of the sacred trust between the corporation and the licence payer. The most appalling case of expenses fraud in the history of...' These were all surely phrases which would have sounded better coming from Welshborn himself. He glanced again at his watch and shifted uneasily in his chair; the dog bite was beginning to throb like the very devil. He decided to give Jug Ears another minute and then take over. Suddenly his eye was caught by a squat little man in the front row who seemed strangely familiar. Could it be? Was this Reg Bishop? Their eyes met but then, instead of looking embarrassed and contrite, Bishop simply grinned at Welshborn and gave him a most disrespectful wink. This was too much. Hugh Welshborn was on the point of grabbing the microphone when Bishop winked again and made gestures towards his watch. A deathly chill flooded through Welshborn's veins. He dimly remembered why the name Reg Bishop had seemed familiar. Bishop had been the cameraman on a film which he had directed, years ago in Paris. Welshborn had interviewed Lawrence Durrel on the steps of the Sacre Coeur. Durrel had talked about the influence that the French poet Henri Mensonge had made on his philosophy of life and Welshborn had agreed that Mensonge, though largely forgotten nowadays, was certainly one of the most important of all the late nineteenth century French writers. Durrel and Welshborn entered into an erudite discussion about the neglected author. Then, after shooting about two hours' worth of film, Durrel suddenly fell about laughing and revealed that Henri Mensonge was his own invention; the man had never existed! Hugh Welshborn had been revealed as a pretentious, gullible, ignoramus. But that was years ago, and if Reg Bishop thought that knowledge of the warped prank of a dubious author would get him off the hook he was in for a shock, and no mistake. Welshborn glared back at Bishop, as fiercely as he could, but it had no effect. Bishop winked in an even more grotesque fashion and made yet more frantic gestures towards his watch. Then, suddenly, the penny dropped and the pain which gripped Hugh Welshborn's heart made the savage dog bite on his arse seem but as a gnat's nip. He remembered it all, He remembered that he had told Reg Bishop how much he wished that he could afford the Rolex watch in the hotel shop. He remembered getting drunk with Reg Bishop after the humiliating interview and rambling on about being nothing more than a sham and a failure. Worst of all, he now remembered how Reg Bishop had cheered him up by saying that there was a way he could afford to buy the Rolex, all he had to do was to help the crew carry a few lighting boxes around!

Only a few seconds before Welshborn had been longing for Blewett to shut up and hand over the proceedings to him, but now he just felt sick. Jug Ears could ramble on as long as he liked, Welshborn just wanted out of there, besides he was beginning to feel very strange indeed.

"An office will be opened for the discreet repayment of the money and to explain how this will work and to emphasise the dire consequences of any failure to comply I now hand over to no less a person than the Managing Director of Television, Hugh Welshborn." At last Blewett was finished and, with his last remark, he turned and made a dramatic gesture towards Welshborn. At that same moment the stage was shaken by a heavy thump as Welshborn fell off his chair and rolled around on the floor in a state of nervous collapse. He was apparently delirious and was mumbling meaningless words; meaningless, that is, unless you happened to know the Welsh for, "The bastards have got me by the balls."

The meeting came to a sudden and inconclusive end. Welshborn, wrapped in a blanket, was helped back to his car and hurried home. His collapse was conveniently explained as an allergic reaction to the anti-tetanus shot. Reg Bishop and his cronies knew better. They diagnosed an allergic reaction to the bitter truth and they headed straight across Ealing Green to celebrate in the Red Lion....

The 'discreet payment office' was duly opened but closed three months later having only recouped one payment of £380, the price, at that time, for a Rolex Watch.

Chapter Ten.

It Makes You Deaf.

Some months after the great lighting scandal I was able to discover, at first hand, the lengths to which some cameramen were prepared to go to squeeze the very most out of their expenses. Though the case I witnessed was completely 'legit', it was none the less deliciously third rate. I had got myself a production attachment to the Light Entertainment Department in a bid to progress out of the cutting rooms and into direction. This was not a permanent position, just a six month trial to see if I fitted in. In some ways I did and in many ways I didn't; that was always how my life in Light Entertainment would prove to be. It was decided that I should be attached to the production office which was about to embark on a new series featuring the comedians Wally Baker and Wally Cubit. The imaginative title of the show was *'The Two Wallys'*. We didn't know at the time, of course, but it was destined to run and run.

The producer was a guy, in his mid-thirties, called Gerry Pews. He was tall, slim, artificially tanned with peculiar, dimpled, good looks and luxuriant, prematurely silver hair. He was highly regarded as the brightest of bright young talents and, as is so often the case, this was the result of ego, vanity and talent combined in him in unequal proportions, with talent coming a poor third. Still he was a nice enough man for whom to work and, as long as nothing went wrong and he wasn't required to do anything, he was perfectly charming towards his staff. Gerry's second in command was production manager, Barry Fender. He was shorter than Gerry and a deal more portly. I think he was a bit older than Gerry, he had rather unhealthy looking, parchment-like, skin. He was one of those out-going show-biz types who appears to be everybody's friend and who you'd be a fool to trust further than you could throw a grand piano. He seemed to be involved in three divorces at once, and, whilst I know this seems unlikely, that was the impression that I got from the frequent heated phone calls which he always made the instant Gerry went out of the office.

I joined the office as the second production manager with special responsibility for the film element in the new show. Wally Baker had written a spoof classic serial which was to be shot on film and provide a ten minute episode in each of the six shows. Baker himself was a keen cineaste and the scripts were quite demanding in their requirements for locations, props and film technique. Neither Gerry Pews nor Barry Fender had any knowledge of film making and I quickly realised that I had been attached to the pro-gramme to fill the cinematic knowledge gap. I set to work preparing a shooting script. It was an enjoyable task as the script was inventive and funny, in fact very much better than a lot of the stuff Baker was to write for later series. Baker would often pop in to the office to see how I was getting on and approve, or criticise, my efforts. This unset-tled the paranoid Fender and I gradually became aware that he was beginning to look on me as a threat to his ex-ulted position. He never lost an opportunity to regale the office with endless tales of his time as stage manager to hit

West End musicals. The point of these anecdotes was always to prove that 'what he didn't know about West End theatre wasn't worth knowing.' The trouble was that it became increasingly evident that what he *did* know about film-making wasn't worth a tuppenny toss. About a month before shooting was due to start, Fender and I set off for the West Country to look for suitable locations. The most important of these was a large stately home, where our heroine would start her adventures as a Jane-Eyre-style governess. We were lucky. With the help of some guide books and a local taxi firm we found a large country hall called Dorrington Abbey, not far from Bath. It's most attractive feature was a collection of horse drawn vehicles, including a stage coach, together with a team of horses and driver for them all. The script required a number of horse drawn carriages, so the fact that we were able to negotiate an 'all in deal' was a great saving on the show's overall budget We returned to London feeling quite pleased with ourselves.

Fender had been good company on our location hunting trip, but as soon as we returned to the office, and he had people around who he felt he needed to impress, he quickly reverted to type and never missed a chance to make me look a fool. I have to admit that I gave him plenty of opportunity. I was new to the politics of television and naively believed that, for success, all you needed to do was your professional best. Grovelling to stars and producers was not part of a film editor's everyday life, and it did not

come easily to me. Shortly after our return I was to encounter another Prima Donna who had been allocated to
our production. This was, film cameraman, Rupert B. Parnell.

Parnell was a white South African who had come to England to further his career in cinematography. He was
about forty three, with thinning blonde hair, he was ambi-
tious, assertive and potentially very boring indeed. Production accommodation at the BBC was never very generous
and our first planning meeting for the forth-coming location shoot saw us all rather uncomfortably crammed into
Gerry Pew's office. There was Gerry himself, looking cool
and unconcerned, his secretary, Anne, Barry Fender, his
assistant, Mark, Wally Baker, Rupert B Parnell and me.
Anne was about the only person present who hadn't got a
hidden agenda for self-advancement; there was a lot of
laughter as people tried to evaluate each other, who was
to be trusted, who was safe and reliable and who was
likely to prove a treacherous wanker. Wally Baker was almost certainly working hardest to reach some judgements.
He seemed jolly and relaxed, even unconcerned, but then
he was always a consummate actor. However the person
who seemed most determined to make an impression was
Rupert B. Parnell and he chose to do this by rubbishing
most of the shooting script that I had prepared. I was not
sure exactly why he did this because it honestly was a
competent piece of work. I think he resented the fact that
there was going to be someone else around who had some
knowledge of film making. He was hoping to be the show's

cinematic guru, to whose expertise everyone would bow in open mouthed wonder. As he damned my ideas, with condescending faint praise, I hoped that I wasn't the only person present to notice that he didn't actually offer any alternative suggestions.

"Oh you want to shoot it like that do you? Oh well now, let me think of a way we can do it properly." After half an hour of put downs like that I was feeling humiliated and extremely pissed off, especially as Barry Fender was eager to stir it.

"Actually, Mike, I was never really sure about that bit of your shooting script myself. Good job we've got the expert in, eh Gerry?"

Frankly, I could have stuffed his kipper tie into his fat mouth and watched him choke on it. Bloody Barry Fender had suddenly become an authority on film technique, when, in fact, what he knew about movie making could be written on a postage stamp and still leave room for Lord's Prayer.

I suppose that I was most disappointed by the fact that neither Gerry Pews nor Wally Baker had said anything to support me. Up to that point they had both said how pleased they were with the shooting script and how glad they were to have a film editor in the team; but now they were apparently quite happy to see me slapped down. Had I been less insecure I would have understood that each of them knew that they were embarking on a new series which could make, or break, their respective careers. There was no way that they intended to let petty production politics frustrate their ambitions. I was discovering that in the wonderful world of show business the only standard you can depend on is the law of the jungle.

So the meeting dragged on to the subject of artist and crew accommodation whilst on location. Here Fender came into his own. There were two hotels nearby. The White Hart was four star and snooty. Its restaurant was impressively furnished but served indifferent food. The Brown Jug had three stars, was friendly and had an excellent restaurant. Fender naturally proposed to book Gerry and the Two Wallys into the White Hart, together with the makeup and costume people. This made good sense as it meant that the two stars could be made up and dressed at the Hotel before setting off to location. As many of the other actors as possible would be booked into the White Hart, and everybody else would stay at the Brown Jug, including Fender and me. The camera crews and electricians always found their own lodgings, as they liked to stay in cheap B&Bs in order to make as much on expenses as possible. Even so, Fender was a bit surprised by the reply he got when he offered to book a room for Rupert B. Parnell. "Oh I'll stay at the White Hart, of course, so I can be on hand in case Gerry or Wally wish to discuss anything; just fix up for me to park my camper van in their car park, there's a good fellow, and make sure that I can get hooked up to some power."

What a cheap skate! I thought. I'm sure Fender thought so too but he wasn't going to admit it.

For all their determination to always play a perfect hand of production politics, Gerry Pews and Wally Baker had made a bad mistake when they called the production meeting. It was this: they failed to invite the other Wally, Baker's co-star, the diminutive Wally Cubit. There was no reason for him to be there; Baker was present, not as a performer but as the writer. What Pews failed to realise was that this in itself was enough to sow seeds of resentment in Wally Cubit. Baker was the more talented of the two; he was not just a comedian but an actor of versatile skill, as well as being a gifted writer. Cubit was simply a vaudevillian. He was only about 5ft tall and it is possible, that had he grown to a normal height, he might never have achieved success as a comic at all. Like all comedians he was insecure and this, combined with his lack of inches, made him a volatile, difficult performer to direct. Wally Baker almost certainly knew all this but he chose to ignore it and, indeed, to exploit his superior position. So, there it was, right from the start: the double act of Baker and Cubit was an unpalatable cocktail; varied talents mixed with jealousy and insecurity which was to be occasionally infused with malevolence. My first proper taste of location filming had every chance of being a baptism of fire.

A couple of Sundays later I was checking into the Brown Jug, ready for the filming, which was scheduled to start on the Monday. Fender and I had agreed to visit Dorrington

Abbey mid-afternoon to check that everything would be ready for us first thing the next day. We had decided that it would be a good idea to start the filming with some general shots of the stage coach travelling through the country-side. As this would not involve any actors it would give the costume and makeup departments a day to unpack and get settled in. It would give us a chance to establish a working relationship with the crew and it also allowed the cast to enjoy a full weekend before travelling down on the Monday. In theory, it was a good plan. The trouble was that Wally Baker wanted to be present for all the filming, in fact he planned to take over the direction if at all possible. The shots on Monday may only have been of the stage coach, but they were shots for his script. It was vital for him to be there, or so he thought. He therefore decided to travel to location a day earlier than expected. This had two unfortunate consequences. The first was that it made Wally Cubit feel even more side-lined and unimportant. The second was a pure mischance, but it was to upset Mr. Cubit even more.

When Wally Baker arrived at the White Hart, a day early, the room he had been allocated was not available as it was occupied until noon on Monday. By chance the room intended for Wally Cubit was available for the Sunday night, so the Hotel solved the problem by swapping the Two Wallys' rooms. Unfortunately Fender had printed a list of who was in which room as part of the schedule. This information would be useful to costume and makeup and hardly likely to be the cause of bitter conspiracy theories.

However in the world of diminutive comedians they are matters of sinister import. When Cubit was shown to a different room on the Monday he was convinced that Baker must have arrived a day early purely to secure better accommodation for himself.

Fender and I were surprised to see Wally Baker strolling around the grounds of Dorrington Abbey on the Sunday afternoon. He was in a jolly mood and was already talking to the stage coach driver about suitable locations for the travelling shots. I wondered how Gerry would receive such shameless trespassing on his directorial territory, but Barry Fender, who knew Gerry a lot better than I did, reckoned that there would not be a problem. If Baker wanted to direct, then he could .The fewer decisions Gerry had to make the happier Gerry would be. Fender was more concerned that Baker might have trouble getting a room for the Sunday night as he was not expected until the next day. When Baker told him that there had been a slight problem but that he had sorted it out, Fender was much relieved. As all seemed in order at the Abbey we decided that we could go back to our hotels for supper and an early night. Gerry was expected at the White Hart that evening and Wally Baker said that he would dine with him and talk over ideas for the first day's filming. It was all looking good. The last thing that Fender and I did, before leaving the location was to fix two important signs to the two entrances which lead to Dorrington Abbey. There was a good reason for this. Any vehicle bigger than a transit van could not reach the car park if it took the first entrance. This was because half a mile up the drive there was a low stone archway and no possibility of turning around. All large vehicles (and we were expecting plenty) had to use the second entrance about a mile further down the main road. We had printed warnings about this, in block capitals, in the film schedule but, as Fender remarked, 'Most of the buggers never read schedules.' That is why we took a belt and braces approach and put up our signs. With that task completed we drove back to the Brown Jug feeling ready for our evening meal.

We were about half way through the main course when the landlord came to our table to say that a young lady wanted us on the phone.

"Her name is Tina and she is having trouble with her car," our host informed us. "It's the makeup girl," said Fender, and he was off like a shot. He never missed an opportunity to play the hero to damsels in distress, which is ironic because, I knew from all those office phone calls, that he had been directly responsible for the distress of a good many damsels. I finished off the rest of my steak knowing that this was sure to mean the end of a pleasant meal and realising the awful truth that a production manager is never off duty. Fender returned to the table and took a large slug from his wine glass. "Yes, it's Tina and her assistant Sue. They are only about three miles up the road; something wrong with the steering apparently. I said we'd set off straight away."

As Fender didn't drive the rescue mission was going to be entirely down to me but that wasn't going to stop him from trying to take full credit for it. We found the car easily enough and the young ladies were pleased to see us but not at all distressed. They were made of sterner stuff and were treating it all as a kind of 'Girl's Own' adventure.

"Ok Tina, why don't you drive our car back to the hotel with me and Sue and Mike can wait here for the breakdown people?" I was gobsmacked, Fender must have been working that strategy out from the moment we set out. 'What a prize shit you are,' I thought, but then I noticed something that cheered me up no end. "I've a better idea", I said. "Why don't you help me change the front tyre, its flat; that is why the car hasn't been steering properly."

"You can't be sure of that,'" said Fender, sorry to lose his chance to put one over on me.

"Well I'm pretty damn sure that's the reason and anyway we need to change the tyre before we can tell if anything else is wrong. Come on, help me get the spare out." Very reluctantly Fender followed me to the boot of the girl's car.

"I must say its jolly clever of you to know it's the flat tyre." said Sue. "'I noticed the tyre was a bit flat when the hire firm delivered the car but I didn't think it would matter.'"

"We are a couple of dizzy tarts, aren't we?" asked Tina, confident of our immediate, insincere, denial.

"Well you were very wise to phone us, it would have been really dangerous to drive any further on that tyre.'" I said, as I helped Fender carry the spare round to the front of the car. I took the hub cap off and then I realised that if I was not careful, I would end up doing all the dirty work myself. I handed the wheel brace to Fender. "Ok mate," I said, sounding as casual as I could, "You loosen the nuts and I'll fit up the jack." As Fender didn't drive I was pretty sure that he had never changed a tyre before. I intended to make to make him regret his plan to leave me stranded. I found the jacking point and fitted the jack quite easily, but I pretended it was difficult as this left Fender to sweat and strain in his attempt to loosen the nuts.

"It's no good, they won't budge, you'll just have to wait here, like I suggested." said a now vengeful, Fender.

"Here let me have a go." I said. Fender had been trying to shift the nuts by turning the wheel brace with his hands. As the owner of many a clapped out old car and the changer of many a wheel I knew that the easy way to loosen the nuts was to stand on the wheel brace, even jump on it if necessary. In this way I soon had all four nuts loose. I went to jack up the car having first asked Fender to take the wheel off as soon as it became possible. I was de-vious enough to make it sound as though jacking up the car was enormously hard work and that I was giving him the easier job. Again, my previous experience had taught me that the exact opposite was true and, what is more,

133

taking off a wheel and replacing it with the spare is not only hard work, it is extremely mucky.

After about ten minutes and a lot of 'jolly hockey sticks' encouragement from the girls we had changed the tyre and this proved that there was nothing wrong with the steering. It was only a couple of miles to the White Hart so we set off in convoy, just to make sure that the girls had no more trouble. It occurred to me that it was significant that Fender choose to ride in their car, leaving me to travel alone. Perhaps in my determination not to be side-lined I had made a potentially dangerous enemy.

It didn't take us long to reach the car park of the White Hart and, as we parked, I was quite relieved to see Gerry Pew's Morgan was there, next to Wally Baker's new Ford Granada. The real quality that Gerry had, as a producer, was that his presence was always reassuring and inspired confidence. The truth was that he was much better as a producer than as a director.

The vehicle which commanded the most attention in the car park was the motor caravan belonging to Rupert B. Parnell. This was parked close to a rear door of the hotel and already had a power cable hooked up to a supply in the building.

"Whatever is that?" asked Tina, reprovingly.

"I think it belongs to our esteemed cameraman," I said. "He plans to pocket his expenses by sleeping in the van."

"How charming," said Tina. "I expect it reminds him of life on the Veldt."

Once Fender and I had helped the girls unload and we had cleaned up a bit we looked into the bar where Wally and Rupert were deep in conversation about 'the look' of the film. A slightly bored Gerry was with them and doing his best to seem involved. Parnell looked up as we walked towards them. "My God, I thought this was an exclusive establishment," he quipped acidly, "But apparently they let anybody in."

"Oh this place can't be all that grand," Sue replied. "They allow gypsies to park in the yard."

"Gypsies?" Parnell inquired.

"Yes, haven't you seen that frightful van out there? It looks like one of the props from 'The Grapes of Wrath.'"

Wally and Gerry grinned, Parnell glowered and Fender rescued the moment by offering to buy the girls a drink. I assumed that Sue hadn't heard my conversation with Tina in the car park; or then again, perhaps she had heard all of it and was just much more adept at good 'put downs' than I would ever be.

We didn't stay long as we had to get back to our hotel; the planned early night had departed long since. However Rupert B. Parnell lost no time in persuading his mate Fender to include his bill for parking and electricity charges on the production account. Rupert B. Parnell would therefore be able to pocket every last penny of his overnight allowance. I was amazed that that he had such a nerve and couldn't believe that the others didn't seem to have registered what was going on. I was wrong of course; nothing escaped the notice of ladies like Tina and Sue.

The following morning Fender and I arrived at the Abbey and hour before the crew call time of 8am. This was unfortunately not early enough to prevent an incident which got things off to a very bad start. The driver of the wardrobe caravan had gone ill and been replaced by a freelancer. Of course, the new driver had not read the warning notice in the schedule or taken any regard of the signs we had put up, about which entrance to use. 'Ah so when he reached the low arch he had enormous difficulty turning round,' you might be thinking; but you'd be wrong. Oh no, he could see the other vehicles, which had taken the correct entrance, properly parked up on the other side of the bowling green; so he simply drove his 15 ton load straight across the green and joined them. In less than two minutes he destroyed a bowling green which had been nurtured at Dorrington Abbey for three hundred years.

As Fender and I got out of our car we were collared by the estate manager, a man called Major Pointer. For some reason he styled himself as the 'comptroller' of the Abbey; whether from some arcane nod to feudalism, or simple dyslexia, one could only guess but as he rushed towards us he was not showing much sign of self 'comptrol'. "Look at the bowling green, you bloody vandals," he shouted, "It's been destroyed! When I tell Lord Dorrington do you know what will happen? Do you know what he'll do? He'll have a heart attack that's what he'll do!" With a skill normally only associated with stage illusionists, I noticed that Fender had disappeared. As I looked over the major's shoulder I could see him legging it over to the catering wagon, where the crew were having their breakfast. I knew that amongst that lot there must be the infernal idiot who had just managed to erase three hundred years of herbaceous history, but for the moment, such knowledge was of little avail. The major was warming to his theme.

"Mary Queen of Scots played bowls on that green two years before she lost her head. James II played bowls on it two months before he lost his throne. George III played leapfrog on it two weeks after he lost his marbles, and look at it now; it's like the battle of the bloody Somme."

"You two boys look like you'd be better for a cup of coffee and a bacon roll; I've brought you some over." Tina, bless her had come to my rescue.

"Young lady, we are discussing the appalling events of this morning and I don't think that a cup of coffee is likely to provide me with any comfort."

"You must be Major Pointer?"

"Yes I am."

"Hello I'm Tina the makeup supervisor, so you are the Comptroller? I must say that does sound frightfully important. Do you comptrol everything that happens around here?"

"That is the general idea and that is why....." the Major's voice was rising again to a frenzy.

"Yes I know it's absolutely dreadful what's happened to the bowling green, what with King Alfred playing on it before Trafalgar or whatever. But really there is no point yelling at poor Mike. It's not his fault that some brainless relief driver couldn't be bothered to follow the very clear instructions. Anyway, now it's happened the thing to do is to get it all fixed and you want Mike on side for that as he's the one person who can speed up the insurance claim." Tina had that upper class female way of making all men feel like obtuse school boys. It was the magic gift of being able to flirt and patronise at one and the same time. It was certainly beginning to work on the Major.

"You see Major, darling, the BBC may not always employ the brightest pixies in the dell but it is insured up to the hilt."

"Well thank God for that," said the Major and I could see that he was calming down."I just hope that we can get it repaired before his Lordship returns, that's all."

"When is he due back?" asked Tina.

"The week after next." replied the Major.

"Oh, good heavens darling, that's heaps of time, isn't it Mike?" with that remark Tina cast me a very knowing look "Oh yes," I said. 'Heaps'. Fortunately I had read Tina's mind. We would be long gone the week after next. I had every intention of seeing that the bowling green was repaired as quickly and expertly as possible but, thanks to Tina's diplomacy, the awful event was not going to disrupt our filming. Indeed it didn't take long for the Major to be persuaded to come over to the catering wagon for a second coffee. Almost as soon as we arrived Rupert B. Parnell glided up to the Major. "Good morning sir, may I say on behalf of the camera crew, how deeply we regret the tragedy that has befallen the bowling green. Of course you must appreciate that it was most certainly not caused by any of the camera vehicles." You smarmy sod, I thought as I gritted my teeth to make the introduction. "Ah Major, this is our cameraman Mr. Rupert B. Parnell."

"Morning Parnell,"snapped the Major and I got the impression that the Major could tell a creep when he met one. At that moment Fender emerged from the costume wagon, he was holding a clip board and doing his best to look important. "Ah Mike, there you are, is everything sorted?"

"Yes I think the Major and I have reached an agreement." I said as I thought 'and no bloody thanks to you.'

"I have to say, Mike, I did wonder, yesterday, if those signs of yours were clear enough." Barry Fender must have taken a double first in shit stirring.

"Well after all this is his first time on location." Parnell added, with a smile that could have curdled a quart of milk. "Just let's hope that there aren't any more production cock-ups." I was trying to think of a suitably withering reply when all attention was drawn to the sound of the approaching stage coach. It clattered across the cobbles in front of Dorrington Abbey and pulled up close to the catering wagon. Wally Baker and Gerry jumped down from the top of the coach talking excitedly. Wally shouted across to us, "We've found the perfect place to shoot the title shot, it's not far up the track." He pointed back in the direction from which they had just driven. It was amusing to see how differently they had each dressed for the day. Wally was wearing twill trousers, green water boots and an old anorak, whereas Gerry looked as if he had just stepped out of an Austin Reed catalogue. The thing that I remember most about Gerry's outfit is that he was wearing an extremely expensive soft leather coat. It was cream in colour and therefore totally unsuitable for the wear and tear of location filming, but I had not yet deduced that Gerry had no intention of exposing either his coat or himself to wear and tear.

"What I suggest," said Wally, "is that Gerry takes Rupert, Barry and the crew up to the place we've found, then Mike and I can come up on the coach. We need it to look like it has a few passengers on it and, in long shot, nobody will recognise me. We won't even need full costume, just a couple of frock coats. Agreed Gerry?"

"Absolutely," said Gerry, who was discreetly admiring himself in the polished paintwork of the stage coach, "Good idea."

It was certainly very obvious who was going to be in charge of this film. Just before the crew drove off to set up the camera on the hillside, the assistant sound recordist, Terry, gave me a walkie talkie radio set. In the days before mobile phones this was the method used to communicate over short distances and was essential when filming the sort of thing we were about to attempt. I had one on the stage coach, Fender had the other beside the camera. He was not very careful about switching it off when it was not in use. We were thus able to eaves drop on conversations and comments that would have been best left unheard. Parnell's irritable tones featured a lot. "Christ, why is it taking them so long to turn the coach round? I suppose that bumpkin driving it is even more stupid than he looks."

Brian the driver flushed with anger and grabbed the hand set from me. "I suppose you think that a stage coach has power steering and a reverse gear," he shouted down the microphone, "And I may be a bumpkin but I am the only bumpkin within a hundred miles of here who knows how to drive a stage coach. Perhaps you'd better remember that?" It was a good threat and for the rest of the morning all the instructions we received were transmitted with studied politeness. The rest of the morning past pleasantly enough. It was fun riding about on the stage coach and being away from both Fender and Rupert B. made it lot easier to relax. Just before one o'clock the message came that Gerry was breaking for lunch so Brian cracked his whip and the team of four brought us quickly back to the stable yard and the catering wagon. As I jumped down from the coach I saw Rupert B. walking towards us. Driver, Brian, cut him dead and carried on getting the nose bags ready to feed the horses.

"Pity that the driver had to hear that joke of mine, don't you know anything about using walkie talkies? You don't keep then switched on all the time you know."

"Thanks for the advice Rupert. Are you going to tell Barry then, or shall I? Of course he might think that there is not much point having radio communication if it is not switched on, let's ask him." I was becoming sick of being made the fall guy for every cock-up and the exhilaration of the morning's coaching had done my self-confidence a power of good.

"Ah there's Gerry," said the great cinematographer and he rushed off towards the coffee, leaving me to ponder why I had ever deserted the cutting rooms. The rest of the lunch hour passed without incident. Major Pointer was certainly in a better mood. I think that when he realised that for the next ten days Breakfast, Lunch, and Tea would all be free and excellent, his concern for the ruts in the bowling green took on a different perspective. He was also looking suddenly more fashionable. It took me a minute or two to decide what the difference was but then the penny dropped.

His hair had been cut and styled by courtesy of the makeup department.

"Never had me hair cut by a gal before," he boasted to Wally Baker.' "Great fun and the young ladies did a damn fine job too, don't you think?"

"They certainly did,"said Wally and I felt a bit happier. At least some members of the team were doing their best to smooth out ruffled feathers and help the production along.

Inevitably Parnell complained that his sautéed potatoes were over cooked but, all in all, lunch went off quite well and most of the crew rated the caterer better than average. One of the laws of film making is that, however good the caterer proves to be, someone in the unit will know of a better one and will have just come from a production that used it. I thought that the lunch was amazingly good, but this was my first experience of location food. As for Major Pointer, he declared it to be 'Just the ticket' and simply couldn't get over the fact that it was 'all free.'

After lunch we spent a couple of hours with the camera mounted to the stage coach to get shots looking over the driver's shoulder towards the galloping horses and other useful material for the journey sequence. For a while I rode inside the coach, just to see what it was like. Take it from me, travelling in the inside of a stage coach was sheer misery. I never become travel sick so quickly, before or since. The suspension of the coach used springs but shock absorbers had yet to be invented so the unfortunate traveller was thrown from side to side and bounced up and down like a slug of gin in a cocktail shaker. Even though the passengers who rode on the top of the coach were exposed to the elements they still had a much more comfortable ride and, therefore, paid more for their tickets.

By four o'clock Wally Baker and Gerry thought that we had probably got enough general stage coach footage so it was decided to break for tea and then spend the rest of the day filming shots of the carriage and pair, which were needed in episode three.

We returned to the stable yard, where we grabbed a cuppa, and Brian, the coachman hitched up a fresh pair of horses to the Barouche. We were just about to go back to work when the third and most unpleasant incident of the day burst upon us. The horses were hitched and about to leave the yard when a Bentley Sports Saloon swept impressively, in fact recklessly, into the yard. The driver was the other Wally, co-star Wally Cubit. The huge door of the limo swung open and the diminutive Wally Cubit stepped down and out. If he had purchased the over-sized automobile to sublimate his own lack of inches then it had been a bad decision. The contrast between the size of the car and size of it's driver only served to make him seem even smaller, especially when one noticed that the foot pedals all had wooden blocks attached to them in order for his feet to be able to operate them. He was immaculately dressed; cavalry twill trousers, lamb's wool car coat and kid leather driving gloves but, again, his size compromised the effect so that, instead of looking dashingly successful, he looked *jejune*, like a small boy dressed 'grown up' for his part in the school play. None of this helped his entrance to be the dramatic event that he had intended. He was angry and he wanted the world to know it.

"Well Wally, this is a lovely surprise." said Gerry as he stepped forward with a disarming smile. He had sensed trouble and was anxious to nip it in the bud.

"I've no doubt it's a surprise," came the rejoinder. "What I want to know is what the bloody hell is going on? Why was I not called until tomorrow?"

"Well we are only filming carriage shots today, we thought you'd welcome the extra day off."

"So I'm not needed today?"

"Well no, not really, but it is lovely to have you here." Gerry's lie was a brave, if unsuccessful, attempt at diplomacy.

"No I'm not needed but Wally Baker is, just like he was at the planning meeting that I wasn't even told about! I star in this show too you know. It's called *'The Two Wallys'* not the one and a half Wallys." The joke was better than he intended but no one dared laugh at it.

"I'm treated no better than a bit player and, to cap it all, when I try to check in at the hotel I'm told that I have to change rooms because Wally Baker has taken mine over. It is unbelievable, that's what it is, one bloody insult after another."

It has often been remarked that when someone gets angry they appear to grow in size, unfortunately, for Wally Cubit the converse was true. As he continued to list the slurs and festering resentment that he had been harbouring for weeks he went red in the face but actually appeared to become smaller. The sorry display brought to mind Rumpelstiltskin when the Queen succeeded in guessing his name and he ran round in ever decreasing circles and vanished up his own trouser legs.

"Look, there has obviously been the most awful misunderstanding and I take full responsibility," said Gerry. "think that the Wallys and I need a quiet chat so we'll have a cup of tea in the makeup caravan, Mike, you know what we need for the rest of the carriage shots, so you'd better direct for the rest of the day."

"Don't worry Gerry," came Parnell's instant response, "I'll see that the boy doesn't screw up too badly."

"You patronising shit..." no, I didn't say it but, my God, I thought it.

So, for the last two hours of the filming day, Gerry was embroiled with the Two Wallys in a session of heavy ego massage and feather un-ruffling, whilst I was involved in a battle of wills with Rupert B. Parnell. I am not sure which of us had the worst time. By six o'clock Parnell claimed that the light was fading so I decided to call, "That's a wrap." thus ending the day's work. When we got back to the stable yard Gerry and the Wally's were friends again, largely thanks to Tina, as I later learned, who had given each of them a head massage. Gerry called over to me. "Hi Mike, how did you get on?"

"Well we got nearly everything," I replied. "I would have liked a couple more passing shots, but the light was going."

"In point of fact we could have filmed them but our esteemed director called 'wrap' before I could stop him." came the mendacious comment from Rupert B. I was becoming truly puzzled about how it was possible that, in his ten years as a cameraman, Parnell had managed to escape without someone sticking a tripod up his arse. However, before I could defend myself, he rushed across to Wally Cubit and was busy brown nosing his way into the star's good books. Gerry had an announcement to make. "Well everybody, it's been a bit of a problem day for all of us, but the Wallys and I think we have the answer and this is it. Tomorrow evening cast and crew are all invited to have dinner with us at the White Hart. That will help us all get to know one another and you can all relax because the production will be paying." "Much more of this sort of thing and the budget will be buggered, that's for sure." It was Fender whispering in my ear.

"Wouldn't it be better to feed everyone at the Brown Jug?'" I whispered back. "The food's better and a whole lot cheaper too?"

"Christ no." said Fender. "If the Wallys were to find out that our hotel is better than theirs the shit really would hit the fan."

The next day's filming certainly went much better than on that awful first day. One reason for this was the arrival on set of the curvaceous young actress Millie James, who had been cast as the heroine in Wally Baker's spoof classic serial. All the straight men in the crew fell immediately in love with her, as did some of the gays. Her presence certainly helped to keep everyone on their best behaviour. Gerry became suddenly much keener to appear to be in charge and was therefore apparently able to direct Millie with suave expertise. Wally Baker made use of every opportunity to take Millie aside and hint at the chance of a role in his forth-coming sit-com. Every time a close up of her was required Rupert B. took inordinate trouble with his exposure meter which, for some reason would seem to give a more accurate reading when held in close proximity to Millie's tits. As this was a comedy both tradition, and Wally Baker, insisted that her costume should display her ample bosom to the very limit of decency. Yet, despite all this attention from senior members of the team Millie seemed more interested in Terry, the assistant sound recordist. He was a nice enough lad, though what she saw in him was a puzzle. But it didn't matter, a little sexual rivalry on set worked wonders for the cause of good manners. This did not, however, completely save us from Wally Cubit's temper tantrums. He had another 'Rumpelstiltskin' rant when we were trying to film the sequence in which his character gets splattered with mud from the wheels of the departing stage coach. Thanks to much buggering about by Rupert B. the shot needed four takes before it was successfully 'in the can'. By take four the much discomforted and humiliated little man was spitting blood. He started to shout, in his irritating Edinburgh brogue, that everyone in the unit was an incompetent fool; that he wished that he'd never signed the contract (we were all with him on that one) and that the special effects man in charge of the squirt device was obviously some sort of myopic moron. Now, the one thing that no actor, however illustrious, should ever do is to make an enemy of the special effects man. They, after all, are the people who decided on the strength of the explosion, the solidity of the chair which is to broken over the actor's head or, as in this case, the quantity, temperature and ingredients of the substance which Wally Cubit was to get full in the face. It was therefore probably as a result of the insults that the successful take was such a spectacular affair. Bert, on effects, loaded the squirt pump with three times as much gunge as previously and delivered it at twice the pressure. The result was hilarious for everyone, except Cubit who was knocked almost breathless by the force of the jet. He stood there covered from head to foot in nameless filth and was beside himself with rage. It took Gerry at least ten minutes of flattery and commiseration to calm him down again. Meanwhile I went over to Bert and thanked him for his efforts. "By the way,'"I asked, "what was the stuff made of exactly?"

"Oh just thin porridge, vegetable dye and a bit of soot, It'll wash out easily enough. Mind you, once I realised what an objectionable little sod he actually is, I pissed in it too."

It was now tea break time and, partly because of scene created by Wally Cubit, Gerry decided to release the actors for the rest of the day. "After tea you can pick up those carriage shots you couldn't get yesterday, OK Mike?"

"Fine Gerry,'" I said, "I'll get Brian to hitch up the carriage and pair." I was talking to Brian when I saw the dreaded Rupert B. sidling up to me. "Look, old boy," he smarmed, "I've had a bit of a trying day. What with Mr. Cubit's little tantrum an' all; I'll let my assistant be your cameraman for the rest of the day, if that's OK?"

"Oh yes fine," I said, much relieved.

"Well have fun," with that he hurried off and, to my surprise, I saw him knock on the door of the makeup caravan.

It didn't take long to pick up the remaining carriage shots, mainly because Rupert B's assistant, Ian, was a lot more cooperative than his boss. We were back in the stable yard an hour later and, though most of the actors had already headed back to the White Horse, Tina and Sue were still in the makeup caravan dressing wigs and cleaning false whiskers ready for the next day. I popped my head round the door.

"Don't forget the production dinner tonight." I said.

"No chance of that,"said Tina. "Especially after the special favour that our esteemed cameraman has requested."

"Favour?"

"Cheeky old sod," explained Sue." He has asked if he could use our bathroom to shower and get ready for this evening. Old skinflint; he should have damn well booked a room, like everyone else. Fancy staying in that ghastly camper van."

"So did you tell him to get lost?"

"Of course not darling; no point having a row is there?" came Tina's diplomatic, reply. "I think the problem is that he has the hots for Millie and plans a charm offensive over dinner. There won't be much of a chance if he emerges from the van in a miasma of B.O. Hence the sudden requirement for our bathroom. Anyway we are all meeting in the bar at 7.30. So see you there darling."

"OK Tina. I owe you several drinks anyway, for calming Major Pointer down."

"Oh he's a sweetie really, darling, just a bit of an old tight-arse. You know I think it would be a good idea if you invited him along tonight. I'm sure he'd love it; he seems quite star struck."

"Yes, Good idea, I'll do it now. Thanks Tina; I'll be there about eight." With that I headed to the car and returned to the Brown Jug to have a bath and change.

I met Barry Fender in the bar of the Brown Jug at 7.15. As ever, he needed a lift from me to get to the dinner at the White Hart. He was wearing a brown pin striped suit and a particularly virulent after shave. He told me that it was extremely expensive and called 'Ebullience'. Frankly, 'Effluent' would have been a more appropriate name as that would have intimated both the aroma and the fact that, at any price, it was money down the drain. Certainly, by the time we arrived at the car park of the White Hart, I was only too glad to get out of the car and away from the heavy scent of that oppressive lotion. If Fender thought that it was sophisticated then I pitied him. I have smelt more seductive air fresheners. As we crossed the car park I resolved that I would certainly not be sitting near Mr. Fender during the meal. I wanted to be well away from his musky pong and also be distanced from his insidious personal comments.

As soon as we entered the reception area of the hotel we heard gales of laughter coming from the bar. It was that peculiar type of forced merriment that television production people always feel obliged to feign when in the company of star comedians. There were two groups, of approximately equal size, each gathered around one of the Two Wallys. As far as I could discern Wally Baker was recounting hilarious tales of his early career during the death throes of weekly rep whilst Wally Cubit held his listeners spell bound with rib tickling yarns of his experiences during the arse end of vaudeville. I decided to hang around at the back of Wally Baker's coterie and I was pleased to find Tina and Sue hovering there too. "What can I get you ladies to drink?"I spoke quietly so in no way to upset the flow of Wally Baker's exquisite timing. He had reached the climax of a particularly amusing gem involving Laurence Harvey, a bell boy and a French loaf. Tina threw her head back and roared with laughter.

"What did he say?" I whispered.

"God knows, darling," came her reply. "I gave up listening half an hour ago; just laugh when the others do and everything will be fine."

"I hope it's not long before we eat," said Sue, "I'm bloody starving."

The head waiter came in and had a word with Gerry and then, as soon as there was a brief lull in Baker and Cubit's seemingly endless canon of unremarkable anecdotes, he jumped in with the announcement that it was time to go into the dining room.

It was only when we were seated that I realised that Rupert B. had not yet joined us. "Anyone know where Rupert is?" asked Gerry. "It would be best to order in one go."

"He must still be in our room." said Tina, amid the all too predictable cries of, "Oh I see." and "It's like that is it?" from most of the lads.

"'I'll go and find out what's keeping him," Sue volunteered.

"God knows he's been in there long enough," Tina said to me under her breath, "I gave him my key when we came down to the bar and that seems like hours ago."

"Well I've got my key on me, "said Sue. "I'll soon flush him out."

As we waited for Rupert's arrival and Sue's return there was much self-conscious perusal of the menu by those around the table. More interesting than the menu, perhaps, was a perusal of the assembled bunch of television archetypes. We sat at a very large round table, which had the advantage of blurring the divisions of rank. I have found it amusing that few societies are more conscious of status than the, supposedly egalitarian, community of Broadcasters. It was noticeable, for example, that no electricians, or drivers, were present at the dinner. I wasn't sure if they had been invited or not. Most probably they had been but they knew, from past experience, how deadly dull such meals always turn out to be. At any rate I was glad that the fool of the driver who had destroyed the bowling green wasn't present. Major Pointer was seated next to Gerry and therefore close to the Two Wallys. He was loving every minute of it.

Megan, the costume designer, sat not far from me. She was rather a strange young woman, who dressed in a sort of 'new age' fashion. With her long blonde hair, long hempen skirts and ethnic jewellery she looked like a cross between a Saxon princess and a Camden Town infant school teacher. When I glanced across at her she was vainly searching the pretentious menu of the White Hart for a Vegan option. Nearby sat the sound recordist Bob and his assistant Terry. Their conversation revolved entirely around decibels and impedances; they were in a happy world of their own and the rest of us were happy to leave them there. Everyone, that is, except Millie. Somewhat to the chagrin of Gerry and the Two Wallys she had not joined the star end of the table but was sitting beside her new friend, the slightly geeky Terry. What on earth did she see in him? I felt sure that Tina or Sue would soon find out.

Barry Fender, of course, had established himself at the 'star end' of the table and was determined to impress. Unfortunately he was convinced that the way to do this was to be discourteous to the waiters. I have often marvelled at how grand and difficult some restaurant customers can be and that those who probably think that a *sommelier* is someone who walks in their sleep are usually the most awkward of all. Such a diner was Mr. Barry Fender. Brimming with insincere good will towards Gerry and our two stars and grasping for an illusion of urbanity he thought that Mickey - taking jokes at the expense of the elderly wine waiter and unwelcome flirtatiousness with the pretty young waitress would be good for his 'cheeky chappie' image. I found myself hoping that, before it left the kitchen, some disgustingly insanitary revenge would be wrought on the food that he was shortly to be served; but as he sat there in his brown suit, with the pink silk shirt, blue polka dot tie and matching hanky in the top pocket, I had the unsettling feeling that he was going to be much more successful in the world of television light entertainment than I ever would be. Perhaps that's why I disliked him so much; I was jealous and hated the fact?

Meanwhile the elderly wine waiter was being much better treated by the Wallys themselves. I had noticed, in the bar, that neither of them were exactly big spenders so they were now wrestling with a difficult decision. To order an expensive wine would be good for their image but such extravagance would be hard for either of them to stomach. Such are the trials of stardom. The wine waiter was doing his tactful best to assist. As Wally Baker was the cleverer of the two it didn't take him long to realise that if he pretended to spot a mid-priced bargain on the wine list he could both save money and look extremely knowledgeable.

"So you have a Chateau Degolas 1972 at only £3.25p?"

"Yes indeed sir."

"Oh Wally, we should have that, it's delicious; I don't think the management here can realise how sought after it has become."

"Oh well then Wally," replied the other, diminutive Wally, "I happily bow to your superior knowledge." But he wasn't happy at all and he immediately notched up ten more points on his tally of bitter resentments.

While all these petty dramas were taking place in the restaurant a far more interesting one was about to unfold in Tina and Sue's bedroom. As she reached the top of the stairs and started down the corridor which led to their room, Sue was wondering what on earth could be keeping Rupert B? She hadn't thought about it while we were all socialising in the bar, but now, as she glanced at her watch, she knew that it was more than an hour since Parnell had tapped on their door to ask Tina if it was a convenient time for him to use the shower.

"Absolutely we're all done, help yourself," Tina said. "We're off to the bar now so see you later."

"Thank you, dear ladies, the van is very comfortable but I have to admit that the sanitary arrangements are somewhat primitive."

"Quite so," said Tina meaningfully; and with that the girls were off to join the party.

Sue recalled some of this conversation as she approached the door but she was snapped back to the present by a noise. It was not very loud but it was, nonetheless, alarming. It seemed to be a series of low moans. "Oh my God," she thought, "he's having a stroke! "she hastily unlocked the door and entered the room.

Sue's worst fears were accurate to some extent but the stroke that that Rupert B. Parnell was experiencing was not apoplectic, it was venereal and, what's more, he was bringing it on himself. If you haven't already guessed, the unfortunate scene that Sue witnessed as she stood transfixed in the doorway, was this: Rupert B. Parnell, cinematographer, world traveller and *soi-disant* polymath had left the bathroom door open so that Sue could see his reflection in the bathroom mirror. The fact that he was naked did not concern her overmuch, although it was not a vision that was likely to improve her appetite. No, what temporarily made Sue doubt the evidence of her own eyes was the fact that the naked man in her bathroom had abandoned all thoughts of washing but was, instead, masturbating into the wash basin. He had his willy in one hand and something else in the other. It was some sort of handkerchief and he was forcing it into his face. This was the reason that he hadn't noticed Sue's arrival. Then, as incredulity melted into mind-numbing comprehension, Sue recognised what it actually was that the great man was shoving into his chops. It was a pair of her knickers.

"Oh good, Rupert's coming now." said Gerry, as a rather flushed, but immaculately dressed, Parnell joined the restaurant table.

"Sorry I've been so long, I fell asleep in the bath. When I woke up it had gone quite cold."

158

"I expect it had shrivelled up as well." quipped Wally Baker, with the incisive wit and timing that only comes from years of comedy experience.

Sue returned to her seat between Tina and me.

"So did you find him in the bath then?" asked Tina.

"Tell you later." said Sue.

The rest of the week's filming went comparatively smoothly. Mille and Terry continued their innocent romance and Rupert B. Parnell seemed to have transformed into a perfect gentleman. "What actually happened when you went to find him in your room?" I asked Sue several times a day. "I can't tell you yet," she would reply. "We struck a deal, OK?"

Apart from the odd sarcastic comment directed towards Terry, from, the now jealous, Fender, the only friction that spoiled the atmosphere was that between the 'Two Wallys' and I must admit I that I was beginning to feel a bit sorry for Wally Cubit. Admittedly he hadn't endeared himself to me very much but the point was this. The script involved the two of them in a lot of physical slapstick but the accidents that befell Wally Baker's character were always large scale; Falling off ladders, falling down stairs or over cliffs. These stunts were too dangerous to be performed by the star himself so, naturally a stunt double was employed for them. However the accidents that befell Wally Cubit's character were on a smaller scale; mud in the face, a bucket of white wash over the head, tumbling into the pig sty; all jokes which could safely be performed by the actor himself and much funnier if shown in close-up. So, while Baker had a relaxed and comfortable week Wally Cubit spent a lot of time being sprayed with gunge, soaked to the skin or wallowing in festering filth. It was not very long before Cubit realised that the distinction between these types of accident was not an accident in itself. After all it was Wally Baker who had written the script.

It was on the Friday, the last day of the first week of filming, that Wally Cubit at last managed to achieve some sort of revenge. We were shooting the sequence that was to close episode two. Wally Baker's character, doubled of course by the stunt man, was to fall off the barn roof and upset a manure cart. The contents of the cart were to land on Wally Cubit as he dozed in the sun. The final shot would be of Wally Cubit as he emerged from the shit heap. "It is sure to get a huge laugh," Wally Baker reassured the unenthusiastic Mr. Cubit. There was a pause and then a slight gleam came into Cubit's eyes.

"Surely it will get an even bigger laugh if we both emerge," he said. "After all Wally, you tipped the cart over so it is quite likely that you would have landed in muck too; and, if you appear a beat after me, the laugh will be even bigger; just what we need for the end of the episode." There was no doubt he was right and it was probably this fact that made the experience doubly unpleasant for Wally Baker. And that is how it was filmed. The sensible decision was made to make the shot of our two stars emerging from the muck the last shot of the day; they could then clean up and change at their leisure. Gerry called "Well everybody thank, you and that's a wrap for this week."

Wally Cubit's dresser approached him with a towel in order to wipe the worst of the muck from his face but, the ever creeping Barry Fender beat him to it.

"Well done sir," he enthused, "At least there are no more grunge gags in the schedule for next week."

"There'd better bloody not be, I've suffered enough this week to last a bloody life time."

"I'm sure you have, poor darling," said Millie.

About an hour later I set out for home and the weekend. Fender had persuaded Millie to give him a lift back to London so I was spared the company of both him and his after-shave. I was blissfully alone for the first time in over week and I thought over how much we had all learned about each other in those first, eventful, days.

We were to learn even more at the start of the second week. Fender was getting a lift back to location from Millie and must have been hoping that his plans for seduction could be advanced by regaling her with his fascinating tales of back stage dramas during the runs of, long-forgotten, West End Musicals. However his plans were frustrated by the fact that, when Millie arrived at Fender's flat Terry, the assistant sound recordist, was already in the car with her. They had spent the week end together so that Terry could install her new Hi Fi system. Millie rather enjoyed telling Fender about how diligently Terry had fiddled with her tweeters and that he had taken the sub-woofer out twice before they were both satisfied with the response. Fender sat glowering in the back of the car for the whole return journey.

There were two surprises awaiting us when we arrived back on location. One was that our cameraman had been replaced and the other was that Sue said she reckoned she knew why and would 'tell all' in the bar that evening.

It turned out that on the night when she had discovered Rupert B. Parnell looking less than elegant in her bathroom she had promised to guard his tatty secret; but there was a condition. Sue would say nothing about the incident but Rupert B. must promise to buy a meal for the whole unit before the end of the shoot. "I had worked out that it would cost him about as much as he had fiddled out of his expenses by staying in that ghastly van of his," Sue told us. "Besides I caught him holding my favourite pair of knickers. I have had to throw them out. I would never feel comfortable in them again."

"So you think the reason that he has taken himself off the job is because he is too embarrassed to face you for another week?" I asked "No, I think it is because he is just too bloody mean to buy us all a meal."

"Of course," said Gerry, "it might be that he couldn't face the Two Wallys. You see, all last week's filming looks great apart from the last shot. For some reason Rupert screwed up the focus; so now someone has to tell Wally B and Wally C. that they are going to have to emerge from the dung heap all over again."

"Well who's going to tell them, then?" asked an anxious Barry Fender.

"Surely you should Barry darling? After all, it was you who was rash enough to promise Wally Cubit that this week would be free from all those frightful slop bucket gags." The voice was sweet but with just a hint of venom, and it belonged to Millie.

Chapter Eleven.

The Poor Cat i' the Adage.

Everyone who has been involved in location filming will have a few stories to tell about cock-ups and disasters that have overtaken some unfortunate production or other. By its very nature the whole process of location filming is vulnerable to the fickle finger of fate. It pees with rain on the day that you planned to film the sunbathing sequence, blows a gale when you hope to film the picnic or blazes with sunshine on the day that you have scheduled the storm scene. Film makers get used to these set-backs and do their best to take them in their stride. Problems that are a direct result of idiocy are less easy to forgive. The actors and director waiting at Ashford in Kent for a camera crew that have driven to Ashford in Sussex is a prime example.; less culpable, but equally devastating, was the unit that struggled to find the scheduled location in a run-down street until they realised that the whole area had been demolished in the time that had elapsed between the location hunt and the actual shoot. Then there are directorial decisions that are just plain daft; the director who insisted that the actor should board the departing train at Euston, and that the train should pull out of the station, in one continuous shot. Only after he had called 'Cut.' did it dawn on him that the train's first stop was Rugby and it would be at least four hours before his leading man would be available for another take. But there are times on location when fate seems to play a spiteful hand for no good reason other than to drive the, already stressed, director to the verge of nervous collapse. The case of the cat on location in Liverpool is a prize example of this genre.

The sequence to be filmed was for a sit-com, which concerned the mundane lives of two Scally Lasses. The series was generally about as amusing as a holiday in Slough and the location scene involving the cat was a typical example of the sophisticated humour that pervaded every episode. With an irony worthy of Molière, the writer had conceived an incident in which Lizzie, one of the heroines, is cycling home from the shops when she decides to pay a visit to a friend. She is invited in for coffee and leaves her bike in the front garden. Lizzie has some expensive fish in her bicycle basket which she has bought for a romantic supper; (having learned that her new boyfriend loves fish.) However the boyfriend is not the only hot blooded male in the district with a taste for seafood for when she returns to her bike. Lizzie discovers a neighbour's Tom cat finishing off the last of the fish. I am sure that you can imagine the gales of laughter which this scene was confidently expected to engender in viewers' homes throughout the land.

The man who had been entrusted with the task of bringing this comic gem to the screen was called Robbie Sargent He was a pleasant man and a competent director. Both these

165

qualities were unusual in the BBC Light Entertainment department of the 1970s. However Robbie did have one big weakness. He lost his reason completely when under the slightest degree of stress and, as directing is a continuously stressful occupation, Robbie, on location, became a raving monster at least three times a day. The scene with the cat very nearly resulted in him being 'sectioned'. This is how it happened.

From the moment when Robbie Sargent first read the scene involving the cat he felt a degree of disquiet. He had been in show business long enough to know all those warnings about never working with children and animals and he was determined to do everything possible to avoid problems when directing the 'cat scene' on location. He therefore instructed his production manager to book a performing cat for the job. Many directors would have simply paid a local cat owner £10 for the day, but not Robbie; he wanted to be sure. Unfortunately the only thing that you can be sure about is that there is no such beast as a performing cat; dogs yes, horses yes, seals, elephants, lions, tigers, even goats, but not cats! Several *self-styled* trainers have made money pretending that they owned such a creature but the truth is that the most that anyone can expect from a cat is that it arrives on set with its' owner and stays in one place long enough to be filmed in close up; even that depends on the cat's mood at the time. The cat which the production manager booked for the job was one such moggie.

The weather was not very kind on the day for which the cat scene had been scheduled. Several showers had delayed the start of the filming, so it was not until mid-afternoon that work could start on the shots involving the cat. It was early autumn so they would lose the light about 6.30 but it was a large unit, complete with five electricians and a powerful generator. The fact that the sun was fading fast behind heavy clouds was not going to be too much of a problem now that they were filming in the small area of the front garden. As long as the rain held off, they had enough artificial light to cope.

The shot of Lizzie arriving at the house and leaving her bike propped up against the wall was filmed easily enough. The cat was then summoned and the 'trainer' got out of his car carrying a large, long haired, sleepy white cat. He insisted on showing it round to the key members of the unit; camera, sound, design and then finally he introduced the cat to Robbie Sargent. "This is Cuthbert," said the owner, "he is your featured feline."

Robbie, who was not a 'cat person' did his best to look enthusiastic but he found himself wondering if the trainer might be three kittens short of a litter.

Cuthbert's first shot went ahead without much trouble. It was a close up of the cat apparently noticing Lizzie's arrival on her bike. Cuthbert was persuaded to turn his head by having his favourite toy waggled at him from just out of shot and Robbie was confident that when this close up was edited together with the shot of Lizzie pushing her bike towards the house it would all look very convincing. While they were setting up for the next shot, in which Cuthbert was required to jump into the bicycle basket and start to eat the fish, the sun finally disappeared for the day. There was nothing for it but to start up the generator and use artificial light for the rest of the shoot.

Cuthbert was very uncooperative when the time came for his big moment. He totally refused to jump into the basket and after several takes with Robbie mumbling "I thought the bloody cat was supposed to be trained," one of the prop boys suggested that it might be possible to hold Cuthbert just out of shot and throw him into the basket on cue. The trainer immediately threw a fit, insisting that this was no way to treat a valuable performing animal. Then Robbie said that from what they had seen of Cuthbert's talents so far, they would have been better off with a stuffed cat. This did little to reduce the temperature of the debate. At length the trainer was finally persuaded that as there was no real danger that Cuthbert would be hurt when he landed in the basket they might as well give it a try. The cameraman framed the shot as tightly as possible so that Cuthbert only had to be thrown a very short distance into the basket; the prop man grabbed Cuthbert and Robbie said, "OK turn over, end board it and…Action." With the shriek of an angry demon, Cuthbert landed awkwardly in the basket and then immediately jumped out again and ran for cover under the camera car.

"I warned you he wouldn't like it," said the trainer, with a hint of triumph, "Goodness knows how long it will take me to calm him down now, especially now he has smelt the fish."

"What do mean smelt the fish?" Robbie was aghast.

"Oh Cuthbert hates fish, he's allergic to it in fact. It's all the fish you put in that basket that has upset him."

"But the whole bloody point of the sequence is that the cat eats the fish."

"Well he won't."

"But I've seen him cat food ads on the tele, he is guzzling fish." It was the production manager anxious to cover his back.

"Oh that's not a real fish it's a prop one; they make them up specially from icing sugar. Cuthbert likes sugar alright.

"Would this be a good time to break for tea?" suggested the cameraman helpfully and just in time to prevent Robbie from assaulting the trainer.

"Yes," agreed Robbie, "ten minutes for tea and a re-think..."

"Ok Bert," said the gaffer. "Turn off the generator for a bit mate."

The tea break came as a blessed relief for Robbie. He took the opportunity to smoke two cigarettes to calm his nerves and then he took three yeast tablets to stimulate them again. He was just about to ask the production manager to call the unit back to work when Joe, the prop man, came up and had a quiet word.

"The lady next door has a cat guv."

"Well?"

"Well she hasn't fed it today yet and it likes fish. I was thinking, you have only got one shot of the cat so far. If you wanted to swap cats, now would be a good time."

"Yes I see, do the cat eating the fish stuff first, then, when the next door's cat is full and happy do the shot of it lying and watching."

"Exactly guv."

"How much does the lady want for the use of her cat?"

"Give her a tenner and she'll be your friend for life."

"OK. Let's do it." Robbie handed Joe ten quid.

As the unit went back to work the prop man went to fetch next door's cat. He gave the lady a fiver, the sum he had previously agreed with her.

"OK everyone," said Robbie, "same set up as before tea, but this time with a new cat, a cat that actually likes fish."

"Sorry Robbie, we've got a problem." It was a gaffer sparks.

"What problem?"

"It's Cuthbert.'

'Oh bugger Cuthbert." said Robbie. "We're using another cat. Bloody Cuthbert can't stop us now."

"I'm afraid he can, you see he's got inside the generator. I can see him behind the radiator grill. If we start the genny he'll be cut to bits by the fan."

To describe the effect that those words had on Robbie as 'somewhat dramatic' would be like describing the passenger experience on the Titanic as 'somewhat disappointing'. The sudden release of adrenaline into a blood stream already flooded with nicotine and yeast extracts resulted in Robbie undergoing a personality change that would have outclassed Dr Jekyll.

"See if I care," said Robbie as he ran towards the generator. "Give me the keys and I'll start the genny myself. I'll teach that infuriating, furry, feline, fucker a lesson it won't forget in a hurry."

"He's gone mad," said the trainer, as he rushed after Robbie, "You can't do that to an innocent creature. Besides Cuthbert is a valuable trained animal."

"Now you listen to me Sunshine," Robbie was almost foaming as he grabbed the trainer by the lapels of his stained jacket, "I don't know if you are a charlatan or a simpleton, but that cat of yours is no more trained than my daughter's gold fish. In fact, in an intelligence test, I'd back the fish. Your bloody mog has already wasted two hours of our time and I am not going to let it waste another second." Robbie jumped up into the cab of the generator and was delighted to see that the keys were in the ignition.

"You Monster!" a scream rang out that might have awakened the dead, it certainly delayed Robbie in his act of execution. It was Emma, the continuity girl.

"You must be the most heartless, cruel, selfish and depraved man that I have ever worked with. If you harm that poor cat I will not rest until I see you in prison."

It was certainly something to think about.

"Actually, guv," said the gaffer, "it would be best not to start her up 'cos if you do it will probably bugger the whole machine."

'So what the hell do we do now?' asked Robbie as his mood of explosive fury subsided into tremor of the limbs and a facial twitch.

"All we can do is to take the grill off, then reach in and grab the cat."

"Well how long is that going to take?"

"I don't know, I have never had to do it before; we'll be as quick as we can."

"Try not to frighten Cuthbert," said the trainer. Robbie threw him a look which would have turned a more sensitive man to stone.

For the next half hour most of the unit had little to do except lounge about. The sparks were the only people actually doing anything; they were all engaged in trying to take the grill off the generator.

"How much longer?" asked Robbie.

"Hard to say, guv, it would be easier if we had a socket set."

"I'll see if I can get hold of one." said the production manager, "Where's the bloody cat gone anyway?"

"It ran to the back of the engine when we started taking the grill off, but I think we will be able to grab it once we have access."

"Well don't be too gentle." said Robbie.

The production manager came back with a socket set. "The sound recordist had one is his car."

"Thank God for sound," said Robbie, expressing an emotion which, in ten years of directorial experience, he had never felt before.

The work continued, but the nuts were coming off faster now, thanks to the socket set. Most of the crew were making use of the lull to fill in time sheets for their previous shoot. The assistant cameraman conferred with his boss. "What are you claiming for last Thursday, Dan?"

"Early call, four hours overtime and disturbed meal breaks, should be worth about £90."

"Bit steep, don't you think?"

"Perhaps," replied the cameraman, "but that director was such a wanker, he deserves it."

Their deceits were interrupted by a shout of mild triumph from the electricians. The last nut had been removed and the radiator grill was lying in the drive. The gaffer put on a pair of stout gloves and reached behind the engine. "Right now Cuthbert let's be having you, come on now, come to uncle." The trainer came up to the generator.

"If you want Cuthbert, he's in my car."

"What?"

"Yes, he's been there for ages, he came out at the back, when you started to take the grill off."

"Well why the fuck didn't you tell us?"

"You were busy mending the machine, I knew that you wouldn't need him until you had finished the repairs; and there is no need to swear." The gaffer had no response worthy of the situation and he could see Robbie approaching them from the house. He gave the trainer a meaningful look. "If I were you I wouldn't say anything about this to the director."

"Oh don't worry, the less I speak to him the better, I don't think that he is a 'cat person.'"

"Probably not," agreed the electrician. By this time Robbie had reached the generator, "Ready to go?' "he asked hopefully.

"Five more minutes, we don't need to put all the nuts back on but I must replace enough to make it safe."

"OK fine, and thanks, I'll get the shot lined up." said Robbie. The trainer coughed self-consciously. "Where would you like me to put Cuthbert?"

In later years Robbie would often recall this moment and wonder at the self-restraint that he had displayed in not responding to such a perfect feed line with a suggestion that would have been both unpleasant for Cuthbert and very uncomfortable, not to say hazardous, for the trainer. But, of course, there was no need to resort to crudity for Robbie was relishing the imminent moment when he would tell the trainer that Cuthbert's part had been re-cast.

"Guv!" Robbie turned round, it was the prop man.

"Just a moment Joe. I was just about to break the news, to our friend here that, thanks to you, I am able to give Cuthbert the sack."

"No one sacks Cuthbert," said the trainer very grandly. "Cuthbert has no wish to continue with this engagement, he resigns!"

"Pity about that," said Joe. Robbie felt a shudder of disquiet.

"Why?" he asked.

"Well I was just about to tell you, it's the other cat, it's buggered off. " "Never mind, we found one local cat, I'm sure we can easily find another."

"It's not as simple as that," said Joe.

"What do you mean?"

"Well before he buggered off he jumped into the bicycle basket and ate all the fish, we haven't got any more and we can't buy any more because today is early closing."

Chapter Twelve.

<u>Curse of the Custard.</u>

Jack Morgan was a middle aged, short and rather portly Welshman. He was not a snappy dresser. He was hardly ever seen outside without his grey nylon cap and this was invariably accompanied by his grey nylon anorak. He walked with his feet turned out, and this combined with his body shape to give anyone familiar with Noddy books a powerful reminder of Mr. Wobbly man.

Jack was a pleasant enough fellow. He had worked in film since he was a boy and he had a fund of stories to tell, especially about the British branch of Technicolor, where he had spent his early years. When I first met Jack he was a neg cutter at the BBC Ealing Film Studios. A neg cutter's job is a very responsible one, for it is the neg cutter who matches the virgin negative to the film editor's cutting copy. Once this has been done a pristine, gleaming, show print can be made. Negative cutting therefore takes place in a clinically clean environment. Any dust or scratches must be avoided as they will show up as white lines or blotches on the show print. The neg cutter wears white gloves and works with care and precision. Jack Morgan followed all these procedures to the letter, but he had one huge disadvantage. He was accident prone. It wasn't Jack's fault that a heavy shelf fell off the wall and showered its' contents all over the negative he was assembling. It wasn't his fault that it chanced to be the negative of the most expensive scene in the studio's most prestigious drama for some years. It was just Jack's bad luck. Every professional procedure and many a desperate trick were employed in the attempt to restore the damaged negative into some sort of condition before it was finally sent off for show printing but to no avail .That sequence always looked as though a dog had got at it. . Not long after the shelf incident Jack's ill-fortune struck again…. This time he was the first person to use a tin from a faulty batch of film cement that had been delivered to the studios. Again it wasn't Jack's fault but, as a result, two thousand feet of 35mm negative fell to bits on the printer. It took an age to retrieve all the pieces and even longer to stick them back together again. This time the final print looked as if it had been trampled underfoot by migrating wilderbeasts.

At about this time the camera repair shop took on a new technician. This man, Bob, had worked at Technicolor at the same time as Jack Morgan. Like Jack, he had many a tale to tell, but his repertoire contained a few yarns which we had never heard from Jack. The most dramatic of these was the story of the 'green stripe.'

The Technicolor process was extremely complex and quality control was taken to an almost obsessive degree. The equipment itself was necessarily engineered to the most exacting standards and was regularly maintained. It never went wrong; until one night it did, as Bob remembered only too well.

They were printing the show copy for the West End premier of Olivier's 'Henry V'. The plan was to print that copy then run off 30 more for distribution. It all seemed to go smoothly enough except that, next day, when they came to check the 'Premier' print it had a big green stripe right down the middle of the picture. When they checked the other prints they were the same, every reel of every copy was ruined. Thousands of feet of film and thousands of pounds completely wasted. It was a bloody mystery because, when they came to check the printer, that could find nothing wrong. The day shift were ordered to run off one single print...it was perfect Bob said that he couldn't remember the name of the poor bastard who was the duty supervisor on the 'night of the green stripe' but, as the story unfolded, I had an uncanny feeling that I already knew who it was.

Jack Morgan was spared any further disasters as a Studio neg cutter for the simple reason that the studio bosses decided to close the department. For some while outside competitors had been providing a much faster service. These 'outside firms' would cut a 50 minute documentary overnight and deliver it to the laboratory for printing. The editor could therefore finish his fine cut, send it off to the neg cutters, and see an answer print the following afternoon. This was a revelation. The studio neg cutters had required at least a week for the same amount of work. As editing schedules became ever more pressured it was inevitable that the new system would prevail, (and make the owners of the new neg cutting firms, very rich people.)

Jack and his colleagues were not concerned about the changes because the management offered to find them new jobs within the studio system. So it was that Jack became a rather elderly assistant film editor. He was, tactfully, paired with an even more elderly film editor. They got on well enough and their work load was never very great because the editing jobs that they were allocated were usually very simple. A few shots of church towers and bells for *'Songs of Praise'* or some, poorly animated, graphics for a schools programme was their standard fare.

Jack was happy enough in his new job. The editor, to whom he had been assigned, was Bert Fields. Bert had only a couple of years to go before retirement. He was perfectly happy to spend a week editing a sequence that could have been easily achieved between breakfast and the coffee break. But he was no fool; not only could he always supply a believable technical reason for his slow pace but he was frequently sufficiently creative to invent hours of overtime to swell his pay cheque and, in consequence, Jack's as well. For the first time in a long while Jack was happy in his work and you could often hear him singing as he went about his tasks. Hymns learned in the Welsh Chapels of his boyhood were the favourites in his repertoire, especially *'When the roll is called up yonder I'll be there.'* He may even have dared to think that the genii of his bad luck was back in bottle, but it wasn't; it was just taking a holiday to gather strength.

One Wednesday morning Bert and Jack returned to the cutting room, after an extended coffee break, to find the phone ringing. Jack answered it. On the line was an irate telecine operator at Television Centre. He was had been trying to run the film which Jack had sent them to play into the studio for a recording of the schools programme *'Let's have Fun with Fractions.'* Apparently they weren't having much fun in telecine as Jack's film had buggered up one of their best machines. For reasons which no one could fathom the film was interlaced with bits of grass, dead leaves and mud... Jack rushed over to Television centre to clean the film but, even after his most earnest endeavours, the film still looked as if it had been matured in a compost heap. The investigations which followed proved that his was not far from the truth because eventually the driver of the van, which had transported the film form Ealing Studios to the Television Centre, confessed to what had happened. While he was driving on the bumpy road across Ealing Common the doors of the van had burst open and a load of film cans rolled out across the grass. He stopped and was at once relieved to see that none of the film cans had been damaged. Thank God, they all had their lids on, well, all except one; for when the driver looked more closely he noticed one can without a lid and some yards distant there was 600ft of film uncoiled under a hawthorn bush, blowing about in the breeze. Of course, this was Jack's film; his was the only lid to jolt off when the cans hit

the ground. The Genii was back in town and had also decided to have some *'Fun with Fractions'*.

Just as in the past, no possible blame could be laid at Jack's door but again, as in the past, it started Jack on downward spiral of depression. He did his best to appear cheerful but we sensed that this was a front. His renditions of Welsh Hymns were now very few and far between and were then only from the most mournful of the genre.

It was perhaps because he was preoccupied with his thoughts that, one lunch time, he failed to notice a blob of custard that had been spilled onto the canteen floor. The resulting accident was spectacular. Jack didn't just slip on the custard, he shot into the air like a gymnast performing a backward flip. Unfortunately only the early part of the incident had any vestiges of grace. It was a startling metamorphosis. Jack left the ground like a gazelle but once he had lost contact with the ground he transformed into a 15 stone sack of bricks. There was a sickening crash and he lay in a ghastly heap. We later learned that he had damaged the vertebrae at the base of his spine and would be off work for many weeks.

He finally returned to the studios some three months later but he was a very sorry figure. When we asked him how he was, he told us that he was still in a lot of pain but that was not the only trouble in his life. Shortly after the accident his wife had become seriously ill and on top of all that, his local council had road widening plans which meant that his house would most probably be demolished. The price that the council were offering for a compulsory purchase was 'a bloody insult' according to Jack. The news was truly depressing but, worst of all, so now, was Jack's company. Everyone felt very sorry for him but it was so dispiriting to hear his low Welsh voice relate yet another tale of woe that people started to avoid him whenever possible. He had become a truly tragic figure.

Some months after Jack's return to the Ealing Studios I started my 'attachment' with the Light Entertainment Department and, weeks later still, I was working with *'The Two Wallys'*. One day I had to go to a music recording session at the Lime Grove Studios and, after the recording, I had some time to spare so I decided to go for a drink in the Lime Grove bar. Because of my time on the *'24 Hours'* programme I knew the back stairs and corridors of that ramshackle old studio very well and I was descending one of the least used and dimly lit stairways *en route* for the bar. To my surprise I heard someone coming up the stairs towards me. I say 'surprise' because the existence of that old stairway, in the thickness of the wall, was not widely known. It was hidden behind an uninviting, unlikely and unmarked tatty old door. Anyway, someone else obviously knew about it and I was about to meet them. I turned a corner in the stair-well and there he was. It was Jack. We both stopped in our tracks and were genuinely pleased to see each other.

"Hello Jack!" I said, and then, without thinking, "how are things?'" To my relief and surprise he smiled back at me.

'"Well Mike,'" he said, "at long bloody last things are pretty good. My wife has had an operation and they reckon she's cured. I have had therapy on my back and I am almost as good as new and, to top it all, the Council have lost the appeal so they have had to scrap the road-widening scheme. I like working at Lime Grove; it is easier for me to get here than to Ealing. I like the programme I am working on too. I can hardly believe it mate, but life is good."

We chatted for quite a while. I told him what a pain in the arse the Wallys were to work with and we laughed a lot about old times; Teddy Ballstrobe's awful jokes and Bert Field's shameless false overtime claims and Paddy Heath's Porn films. I even dared ask him about *'Henry V'* and the green stripe.

"Oh yes that was on my watch." he confessed. "Bloody thousands of pounds worth of show prints completely buggered up. No one ever knew how or why, still serve Technicolor bloody right; they were a miserable bunch of bastards to work for."

I was quite sad when the time came for us to go our separate ways so before I finally left the stair-well I paused for a moment to hear Jack's footsteps receding away from me, as he headed for the cutting rooms on the seventh floor. Just before he reached the top there came a familiar sound echoing down those dusty stone steps, Jack's favourite Hymn, *'When the roll is called up yonder I'll be there.'*

185

A fortnight later I was in the Lime Grove bar again, after another music recording session, when an old mate from the film department joined me. The conversation went from this to that and then my friend said, "Did you hear about poor old Jack Morgan? Dropped down dead in the garden last Sunday."

I was shocked and very sad.... then I had the chilling realisation that I was not at all surprised.

Chapter Thirteen.

A Parable of the Talents.

The attitude of the BBC towards talent has always been ambivalent. At a very basic level the senior management has always regarded it with suspicion, whilst outwardly insisting on the corporation's high regard for the artists and writers whom they are obliged to employ. The fact that the concept of true talent is completely beyond them is made evident by the frequent justification of obscenely inflated fees being paid to range of unremarkable chat show hosts. When such a person descends into obscenity then the BBC will trot out the bland excuse that the obscene fee and the obscene language can both be justified by the presenter's cutting edge talent; they come, we are asked to believe, with the territory of cutting-edge broadcasting genius. The corporation simply can't risk losing people of such brilliance. The results of this stupidity are only too obvious. The presenter, who was never a shrinking violet in the first place, becomes over confident to the point of megalomania and a host of up and coming television celebrities feel certain that their route to success will be aided if they adopt the same, revolting, mannerisms.

What is so frustrating for the viewer or listener is that a management that is so eager to support some dismal mediocrity, of its own creation, will run a mile when the need arises to stand by a programme which has genuinely provocative or controversial content; especially if that programme is likely to embarrass some arm of the Government. In such cases the word 'talent' will never enter the argument, however talented the journalist or programme make maybe. No, instead there will be much talk of 'balance' and judgement and the unacceptability of putting only 'one side of the argument'. This is therefore to purport that a programme would be far more responsible if its' content was fifty percent the truth and fifty percent lies.

In general the BBC has more respect for the men and women who appear in front of the camera than for the folk who work behind it. This was especially true in the days when the programme makers were nearly always members of the permanent staff. It was probably considered unwise to acknowledge that Bert was a really talented cameraman or that Beryl was an exceptionally gifted film editor. To do so would have been to court two dangers. 1) That Bert and Beryl might have the temerity to ask for more money and 2), that directors would insist that Bert and Beryl were the only two people they wanted to work with on their productions. It was for administrative convenience that any talk of natural talent was discouraged. The official line was that every staff member involved in programme making was as good as everyone else.

People like Teddy 'plate in the head' Ballstrobe were quite obviously bloody useless but there were others at the Ealing Studios who were nearly as bad. As they were less evidently barmy, it is arguable that they were even more dangerous. The difficulty for any director, new to the BBC, was that most of the film technicians were eccentric and, as the management would always insist that all staff were equally competent, the only way to discover who was 'eccentric talented' and who was 'eccentric useless' was by bitter experience.

One of the most identifiable 'Competents' was Shelia Tombelson. She was a large, cheerful lady who specialised in editing the film sequences for various popular police dramas. She was efficient and unflappable and her elegant cigarette holder suggested a woman of confident sophistication. The image was somewhat diluted by Sheila's propensity to wear red Wellington boots, whatever the weather. I often wondered if she lived on a farm, but I never dared ask her. The boots might have had something to do with her love for her two dogs, 'Bimbi and BoBo'. They were two toy poodles who accompanied Sheila to the studio every day. As they were not allowed past the gates they had to remain in her car and Sheila's working day therefore involved frequent breaks to make sure that they were safe and to walk them as often as possible, whatever the weather. I remember one occasion when she bought an electric dog clipper in a bid to save on the high prices being charged by Ealing's poodle parlour. The clippers had arrived in the post that morning and Sheila was so excited that she brought them into work so all her friends could admire them. The next day Sheila's mood was bad and Bimbi and Bobo's was worse. I happened to notice them sulking in the back of Sheila's car, as I walked along Ealing Green to work. They were shivering and huddled together for warmth; this was because they were both bald and covered in assorted pieces of sticking plaster. Sheila later admitted that she hadn't read the instructions properly and that the clippers had probably been set for an Alpaca.

Adam Tyler was one of the film editors at Ealing who had the reputation of being a near genius at his craft. You might therefore suppose that his eccentricities would be excessive, this was not the case, but, none the less, he did have some. Adam was a small man about 50 years old. He wore glasses with thick black frames, very much in fashion in the 1960s. He had thinning light brown hair and looked a bit like Bilbo Baggins in *'The Hobbit'*. His reputation as an editor had been earned during years of work on BBC arts programmes and his skill had saved many arrogant young directors from cinematic catastrophe. The oddest thing about him was vocal. He had a peculiar way of speaking. This was upper class but very sibilant and delivered in a half whisper. He also had a habit of coming up to complete strangers and telling them something, in confidence, about his current film. This puzzled me for a while but I eventually decided that it was because Adam had a bad memory for faces and he often mistook visitors to the studio for trusted colleagues. So it was that some unsuspecting person would be grabbed in the corridor as Adam informed them, "Hello Dear Boy. You know this film I'm cutting about Schubert is getting nowhere at all; there are just endless shots of the sun shining through the trees. I tell you, if I see another shot of the sun shining through the fucking trees, I just won't wanna know."

He once came up to me in the canteen and whispered, with an excess of sss, "I am supposed to be doing the battle of Bunkers Hill and all they have given me is a few shots of some tatty old flags. You know, dear boy, I jusst don't sseeee a sssequence."

Adam was at his best when dealing with difficult *'enfant terrible'* directors. The Music and Arts department had a number of these and the unchallenged leader of the pack was Russ Kennel. He was a large man with a red face. Strangely his voice did not fit his appearance, for he spoke in a high pitched, complaining, whine. His disciples excused his ungracious manners by claiming that he was tortured by his constant striving for artistic perfection. His detractors put it down to his monumental ego. Mr. Kennel specialised in making films about nineteenth century composers. He had first gained critical acclaim with his film about Sir Hubert Parry. This was a modestly budgeted production which had been well photographed and then exceptionally well- edited, by Adam Tyler. The film's success enabled Russ Kennel to command ever larger budgets and as budgetary restraint went out of the window so too did every kind of artistic self-control. Kennel embarked on a series of 'composer films' and he delighted to find that many romantic composers had bizarre sexual appetites, some even as bizarre as his own. His formula was simple; as a movement from this or that symphony burst onto the sound track, nuns were chased around gooseberry bushes, prostitutes were chased around nunneries, animals were ritually slaughtered and village virgins ritually ravished. If the music was too long for the action, then it was cut; if too short, it was repeated. Then, as success lead on to excess, Russ Kennel became positively cavalier with his treatment of great music. A few bars from one symphony would be stuck onto a section from another, only to be wedded to a tone poem or an overture. The music edits were so skilful that an untutored ear might believe that it was listening to the composer's original intention. Any listener who knew the works well was in for a right slap in the face. All that mattered to Russ Kennel was the impact of his images. He considered it perfectly justifiable that his film about Ralph Vaughn Williams featured a piece of music which had been achieved by joining the first few bars of *'The Lark Ascending'* to part of *'The Arctic Symphony'* and ending with *'Seventeen Come Sunday'*, from the folk song suite. The pictures which were married to this melange included a goat eating a French loaf and Morris men, in various stages of undress, doing improper things with a Maypole. The fact that Vaughn Williams is generally thought to have led a life of almost pious propriety was not going to stand in Russ Kennel's quest for sensationalism.

Very early in his series of 'composer films' he hit on the idea of including a dream sequence. This easily allowed him to film whatever sexual fantasy he was personally craving at the time and pass it off as part of the creative process of some poor sod of a composer who, being long dead, was unable to sue. For a while he got away with it. The television critics were anxious not to appear ignorant or puritanical so they were quick to praise the fiercely original imagery with which Kennel purported to explain the mysteries of the creative process. It was generously assumed that this enlightened new director had actually engaged in assiduous research which had revealed hither-to unknown facts about the mental tumult from which the subjects of his films variously suffered. So it came to pass that the arts world was fascinated to learn that *'The Flight of the Bumble Bee'* owed its genesis to Rimsky Korsakov's erectile dysfunction, whilst it was premature ejaculation which drove Chopin to pen *'The Minute Waltz.'*

It was to Adam Tyler's credit that he saw the way things were going at an early stage and, after editing the first three of Kennel's *'oeuvres',* decided to get out from under. The wise editor had perceived what the head of the Music and Arts department had failed to glean. This was that as

Russ Kennel grew older he became less and less the *'enfant terrible'* and was increasingly just plain *'terrible'*. But Adam was a diplomat; he had no wish for his working relationship with Russ Kennel to end in a blazing row. The strategy he used was to be disarmingly unimpressed with the great director's conceits. It was while they were editing the film about Modeste Mussorgsky that Russ Kennel decided that it might be easier to work with another editor in the future. One who had as high a regard for Russ's talent as he had himself. Alan Tyler had been struggling for several days to shape the final sequence of the film and provide a powerful conclusion.

"No, No," whined Kennel, "that's not it, you just don't get it do you? Look, Mussorgsky is lying there in the gutter. He is pissed as a rat. He has been pissed for most of his life, but this is the binge that is going to kill him. As he lies there he thinks of what a total piece of shit his life has been. Thrown out of the army, his mother dying in his arms; then his best friend, Balakirev, reckons that *'Night on the Bare Mountain'* is a load of bollocks, he blows the family fortune on booze and, before he knows that *'Pictures at an Exhibition'* has been hailed as a master piece, another friend dies. So he goes on a bender for the very last time. That is what this bloody sequence has got to convey!"

"Yes, yes of course, I see it now," said Alan in an excited sibilant, whisper. "Come on then Modeste, old chum, let's take a trip down memory lane!"

The Mussorgsky film was a moderate success, the truth was that some viewers were beginning to perceive that what had once been hailed as a shining new talent was fast degenerating into a succession of cheap cinematic tricks. Even some of the critics were beginning to catch on. Adam Tyler considered himself well out of it. Lesser men might have worried about severing connections with Television's most controversial director but Alan was glad to quit while he was winning and to have some respite from Russ Kennel's domineering whines.

Tyler was still held in high regard and he was occasionally called in to rescue an arts documentary that had run into trouble. One of these incidents resulted in a favourite story which he used to tell against himself.

A novice director had persuaded the arts department to let him make a film about Otto Loon, a contemporary artist who the director considered to be a neglected genius. Loon was an action painter. His technique involved stripping naked, jumping into a vat of red paint and then rolling around on top of a large canvass. It might be argued that a gorilla could have achieved similar results except that a gorilla would have had more sense than to try. Anyhow the film got made but after ages in the cutting room it was overlong, confused and very boring. The executive producer asked Adam if would come to a screening and see if he could make any suggestions that might save the show. Adam agreed on the condition that the original film editor had no objections and, indeed, he didn't because he was at his wits end. So the viewing took place. There was a lot of tension in the viewing theatre that afternoon. The executive producer was not keen to have to tell his head of department that he had thrown £75,000 down the pan so he was hoping above hope that Adam Tyler would have some brilliant ideas. The director, fresh from Oxford with a double first in Etruscan burial rites, was not used to eating humble pie and confidently expected that Adam would declare the film a master piece. The long suffering film editor was simply hoping that whatever suggestions Adam might make could be carried out quickly so that he could be rid of the whole ghastly fiasco. The film started and some very impressive titles hit the screen. 'They cost a few bob.' thought Adam as *'Otto Loon - an Artist for Tomorrow.'* wrote itself across the screen in a golden, gothic script.

The first twenty five minutes of the programme consisted of intercut interviews with three artists: a middle aged woman, a willowy young man and another man with a thick black beard and an even thicker Geordie accent. The woman was engaging; she talked, with great insight, about public attitudes towards art. The young man was also interesting; he revealed his constant fear of failure but also his optimism for art in the 'New Britain' of the 1960s. He was, so Adam thought, very much an 'Artist for Tomorrow.' However there seemed to be no good reason why the bearded man was in the film at all. He was almost impossible to understand, except for his frequent use of obscenities, he was apparently very angry about something but it was not clear what that was; he was also the worse for drink and, indeed, became drunker as the film progressed, a fact which did little for his ability to communicate.

At the end of reel one there was a pause for the projectionist to re-lace and all eyes turned to Adam.

"Well a lot of that was absolutely fascinating," he said, reassuringly. "I know we've only seen one reel so far but you've definitely a got a movie in there. I can see why you wanted to make a film about the guy, what he says is riveting."

"You really think so?" said the producer. The director gave a muted snort of triumph.

"Oh for sure,'"Adam continued. "I mean the woman is good value and young Otto is great. All you have to do is ditch that boring bearded bugger, you can't understand a bloody word he says and what's more, he's pissed."

"That's our problem," said the producer, "Otto Loon is not the articulate young artist, Otto is the boring bearded bugger!"

At the opposite end to the talent spectrum from Adam Tyler was a film editor called Norman Marks. He was so bad at the job that no one could understand how he had managed to be appointed in the first place. In fact there was a popular theory that he had been given the job as a result of an almighty cock-up in which the personnel department had confused him for someone else. A proper inquiry might have revealed the original dire mistake so the easiest thing to do was to hush it all up.

At first glance, Norman Marks seemed normal enough. He was always smartly dressed and, from a distance at any rate, looked almost distinguished. However when he was up close three features became all too apparent. The first of these was a powerful stink. The cause became quickly obvious; it was Norman's addiction to ' *Disque Bleu'*, the smelliest of all smelly French cigarettes. Norman had very large teeth and, as there were too many of them, they protruded. The *Disque Bleu*s had done little to aid dental hygiene and the huge teeth were covered with a coat of nicotine. This mouthful of molars had another unpleasant consequence, for when Norman got excited he spoke very quickly and had a tendency to shower spit. Unfortunately Norman got excited rather often. He also had an unusual nose, with enlarged nostrils. Combined with the teeth the overall effect was a powerful reminder of Lon Chaney's makeup for *'The Phantom of the Opera'*, but it is arguable that the Phantom might well have been better at film editing than Norman would ever prove to be.

It was fashionable for television documentaries of the 1960s to contain music sequences; sections in which the commentary shut up for a welcome period and the film advanced with pictures simply accompanied by appropriate music. It became almost a badge of honour amongst the film editing fraternity as to who was the most skilled in the use of music and the most sensitive in cutting pictures to its form and rhythm. Adam Tyler was generally accepted as the master of this skill but Norman was determined to prove that he was an equal. In fact he believed himself to be better.

The important trick about cutting pictures to music is that the picture changes should be in sympathy with the music but that they should not be slavishly predictable. For example: if the chosen piece of music is a fast waltz then the first change of shot might be on the first beat of the fifth bar (or the first beat of the ninth). In either case the cut will fit a four bar, or eight bar, musical phrase and will seem logical to the audience. If, however, the film editor continues with that formula for more than the first few cuts then the sequence will become horribly predictable and, soon after that, extremely irritating. Sensitive editors therefore 'ring the changes' so after a short while a picture cut might occur in the middle of a bar of music; perhaps when a particular instrument makes an entrance. This removes the hex of predictability and the sequence is no longer at risk of being boring. Unfortunately Norman Marks had only learned the first part of the procedure, and, therefore, all his music sequences were mind-numbingly predictable. Worse still, however, was his actual choice of music. He had a very limited knowledge of the repertoire and there were a few pieces of music with which he seemed to be obsessed. He would never tire of using them, whatever the subject matter might be. So a

Women's Institute outing to Cleethorpes might be accompanied by the *1812 Overture*, or an investigation into artificial limbs by *'The William Tell Gallop'*. His choice of music was not entirely confined to the classics, the slightest commentary reference to foot wear would send him scuttling to his copy of *'These boots were made for walking',* but Tchaikovsky was definitely his first choice.

Film editors who had cutting rooms in the same building as Norman were driven mad whenever he was involved in the creation of one of his infamous music sequences. Those whose rooms were nearest to his suffered the most. This was because of Norman's insistence on playing the music at full volume for hours on end. Often a single musical phrase would be heard going forwards, backwards and then forwards again for hour after hour, sometimes day after day! You are probably familiar with Tchaikovsky's *Piano Concerto no1*. It is the one that starts; Pom pom pom POM Scrunch, Pom pom pom POM, Scrunch, Pom pom pom pom Pom Pom Pom Pom SCRUNCH SRUNCH It soon quickly develops into a very memorable tune but, even the most devoted Tchaikovsky fan would quickly tire if they were subjected to hearing the opening bars played incessantly through the distorted amplifier of Norman's clapped out editing machine. Matters made worse by the fact that for each crashing play forward there was an immediate shriek of musical gibberish, as Norman reversed the sound back to the start for another attempt. For the first week he would seldom get further than the fourth Pom before winding back and starting all over again. The editors in adjoining rooms were becoming desperate men. By the middle of the second week Norman had still progressed no further than the fourth Pom after the first Scrunch. He had ignored all requests to turn the volume down as he insisted that he could only really feel the emotion of the music at full blast. The Desperados decided to act. A bottle of whiskey was bought for Don, the guy who serviced the editing equipment, and the next day he came in early and 'fixed' Norman's machine. What he did was to put a limiter on the amplifier so that it could never play louder than half volume. Norman had only been in the cutting room for ten minutes before he was on the phone to Don to say something was wrong with his machine and could Don come and mend it? Don was no fool and had prepared his reply. "So your machine has gone to half volume, let me guess, is it an Acmiola?"

"Yes," said Norman, "why do you ask?"

"It is a common fault with them, I know what the problem is but I won't be able to fix for a month, we are waiting for spares."

Norman slammed down the phone and hot-tailed it to the Front Office. Ten minutes later he was heading back to his cutting room in an even worse mood than when he had left it. "Useless Bugger," he repeated over and over again as he stormed back in a rage. The editing manager had been unimpressed with Norman's demand for a new editing machine and in fact, when Norman had told him about the problem with the volume control, the manager had a shrewd idea of what might have happened. Besides he was not going to have his morning routine of coffee and the Daily Mail puzzle page interrupted by some trivial staff complaint.

Norman's regular route to his cutting room was to take the stairs immediately to the left at the entrance to the editing block and head up to his room on the second floor. This time, however, he was so angry that he stomped past the stairs and along the ground floor corridor towards the second set of stairs at the far end. The change of routine was fateful; it led straight past Adam Tyler's cutting room. The door was open and as he bustled past Norman couldn't help but notice that the room was much bigger and brighter than his own. It was so unfair. Then he noticed the editing machine. It was brand new; it was the Rolls Royce of editing machines, a Hollywood Moviola. Norman was so jealous he felt sick. After he had gone through the fire doors at the end of the corridor he paused before he started up the stairs. A thrilling idea was forming in his mind. He leant against the wall and lit one of his smelly cigarettes. He felt like Bogart or Alan Ladd in a Warner Brothers revenge movie. Norman Marks, ace cutter, deserved an ace machine and he was damned well going to get one. He started up the stairs now but there was a different swing to his step, he was confident, he was a man who was in charge of his own destiny, a man with a plan. Like most things in Norman Marks' life, it wasn't a particularly good plan, but it was his. Adam Tyler had one of the best editing machines in the BBC and Norman wanted to use it. Adam hardly ever worked the weekends, as he was devoted to his sons. Therefore if Norman came in at the weekend he could draw the key to Adam Tyler's room and work there. As long as he was careful to tidy up no one would ever know.

The rest of the week passed in blissful peace for the neighbouring editors as Norman postponed work on the music sequence and merely tinkered away cutting some interviews down to length. He was saving himself for a major effort at the weekend. He wondered if he should let his long suffering assistant in on the plan but quickly decided against it. He even had a vague suspicion that it might have been the assistant who had stirred up all those stupid complaints about the racket caused by the music sequence. There was just one danger. Norman wanted to be absolutely sure that Adam Tyler had no intention of working over the weekend and so he hit on another devious scheme in order to find out. At knocking off time on Friday Norman lurked at the bottom of the back stairs and looked down the corridor towards Adam's room. When the great man came out and started locking up Norman sauntered up the corridor, as casually as excitement let him and bid Adam a cheery "Hello. Got any plans for the weekend mate?"

Adam Tyler was rather surprised by both the encounter and the question. He rather feared that Norman might be about to invite him to some frightful party. Thank God he had the perfect excuse.

"Oh yes indeed; the boys and I are off down to Devon to-morrow for a holiday. It's half-term, so I am taking next week off."

"Oh, lovely." said Norman. "I hope you have good weather." a strange glint came into his eyes.

The idea, which had half entered Norman's mind during his encounter with Adam gradually came to fruition during the course of the evening until, as he was in bed and drifting off to sleep, the plan, in all its cunning detail, flooded into his consciousness. It would truly be 'a deed without a name'. Norman had heard that expression before, in some old play or other and it appealed to him. Most people would not have had much trouble finding a name for Norman's plan. 'Plain bloody daft' would have suited it well enough.

Anonymous or not the idea was this. Norman would not edit in Adam's room at all. If Adam was to be away all next week then the ideal thing to do would be to go into the studios over the weekend and shift the Moviola from Adam's room up to his own. He could then spend a blissful five days editing music sequences all day long and then move the machine back the following Saturday or Sunday. The part of the plan which took the longest to work out was how he would explain the sudden appearance of a 'top of the range' machine in his room when the other editors looked in. Norman knew that they were bound to as soon as he struck up, once more, with pom pom pom POM at full blast. The explanation, he thought, was the most brilliant part of his scheme and, like all brilliant solutions, it worked on several levels. Norman would tell his carping colleagues that as soon as the Front Office learned that his editing machine was only functioning at half volume they immediately took the decision to 'hire in' a new machine for him. The management were always very reluctant to hire equipment, because of the cost, and they only did it for the most prestigious programmes. So, in one sentence Norman could silence his critics with the story that the film editing manager jumped to the phone as soon as he knew about the faulty amplifier. 'Can't have you held up, you know Norman, your film is much too important.' That is what he would claim had been said. If only it were true, he thought, with some resentment. The one thing that might expose the awful truth would be if anyone should notice that the machine in Adam Tyler's room had gone missing, but they wouldn't. Adam was away all week so the door to his cutting room would remain firmly locked. What's more, if Norman held on to the key, it would stay locked. The plan was foolproof. With all the details in place he could finally relax and go to sleep. He stubbed out his *Disque Bleu* in the overflowing ash tray on his bedside table and started to drift off. What was the play that contained, 'A deed without a name?' It bothered him. He remembered that it had a lot of witches in it and something about fateful prophesies; then it came to him, of course....

'The Wizard of Oz.' He turned over and went to sleep.

Next morning Norman was up early. He had decided to supplement his usual breakfast, of coffee and a couple of fags, with some scrambled eggs on toast, after all there was a lot of work to be done. He was not quite sure exactly how heavy the Moviola would prove to be but it certainly wouldn't be light. The eggs would give him strength and he decided to have a third cigarette for extra courage.

As he walked across Ealing Green, towards the studios, he realised that he was a little bit nervous. 'What if the commissionaire questioned why he needed the keys for two different cutting rooms? Some of them could be right awkward bastards.' But he needn't have worried. The man on duty was not a regular at the film studios, he had been drafted in from Broadcasting House for weekend cover. Norman even had to tell him where the keys were kept. It couldn't have been easier. He passed the canteen and rather regretted that it was shut, as it always was at the weekend, for lack of trade. Still at least the studio was quiet; he wouldn't be disturbed.

A couple of minutes later, Norman was unlocking the door to Adam Tyler's cutting room. 'How the other half lives,' he thought as he glanced around. The room was twice as big as Norman's and newly painted. All the equipment was new, not just the Moviola. 'Just because the bugger has won a few Bafta's,' he thought, 'It's so unfair!' He looked, with envy, towards the beautiful, gleaming, green Moviola and steeled himself for the work in hand.

Now, to get some idea of the task with which Norman had landed himself, imagine an object about the size of three tea chests stacked on top of each other and to get some idea of its' weight imagine that the tea chests were packed full of bricks. Most sensible people would have had second thoughts at this point, but as we already know......

Manoeuvring the Moviola out of the room to the bottom of the stairs was not too much trouble as it was fitted with sturdy, lockable, wheels. It was the prospect of schlepping it up four flights of stairs that might have daunted a lesser mortal. Norman decided to pause for a 'fag break' before tackling the serious business of the day. He tried to fill his mind with positive images. He recalled stories which he had read in the tabloids on slow news days: the seven year old boy who had held up a collapsing grand piano for half an hour in order to give his pet tortoise time enough to escape; or the young husband who, desperate to get his pregnant wife to hospital, had dug the family car out of a snow drift using an ice cream scoop. This was the mind-set that Norman needed, faith could move mountains and, even if faith didn't really have much to do with Norman's present problem, envy and vanity did and they were, surely, equally powerful.

The stairs from the ground to the second floor were arranged in four flights, with a half landing and a turn after each eight treads. At least there was a chance for a pause on the landings. Norman tried an experimental lift and staggered back. The hi-tech wheels on the Moviola had disguised its' true weight for now, as he tried to lift it, the machine might as well have been screwed to the floor. This was going to take some thought. The Moviola had handles on each side to enable it to be wheeled about but they were not much use for lifting. The main reason for this was because to get hold of both handles at once you had to spread your arms so wide that your face nearly touched the casing. With a bent back and bum sticking out the prospect of raising the Moviola off the floor seemed remote and there was every likelihood of getting stuck in that position and spending the rest of your days imperson- ating *'The Hunch back of Notre Dame'*. The truth was that this was supposed to be job for two people. It took about half an hour for Norman to devise a possible method of getting the machine up the stairs. He finally decided to stand on the third step with his back to the stairs and pull the Moviola up so that its' back wheels were resting on the first step. Then he went up one more step and pulled the machine up to step two. The process worked well enough for the first eight steps but as he started on the next flight he realised that he was tiring fast. The trouble was that, between landings, there could be no let-up of effort. It was hard enough wrenching the bloody thing up each step but he daren't relax for a second because he had to keep the Moviola in perfect balance. If it tilted too far away from him it was somersault back down the stairs to certain de- struction and if it tilted too far towards him it would crush him to the ground. When he finally got to the landing at the top of the first flight of stairs he was sweating like a bull and had started to turn an alarming shade of purple.

Still, at least he could have a pause; he was half way there and comforted himself that he had gained some experience. He certainly planned to have a good rest at the next half landing before his final assault to the summit. He wiped the sweat from his face and hitched his trousers back up. Then he did some stretch exercises to ease his aching muscles. He would have had another cigarette but there was only one left, so he decided to save it until the job was over. He took several deep breaths and started off again. Almost immediately Norman found the lifting to be even more difficult than before. The Moviola seemed to have developed a will of its own and to be actively fighting against him. The fact was that he was losing his strength. The wheels were also suffering from the constant banging from step to step and they had begun to seize up. Norman was getting into a very bad state; twice he nearly lost his grip and when he reached the half landing he was in a kind of stupor. Fearing that if he stopped now he would never have the energy to start again he didn't take the rest that he so badly needed but blundered on upwards crashing the editing machine brutally from step to step and straining every last drop of effort from his trembling, ageing frame. It was very fortunate that no one else had come into work that Saturday because the noise that Norman was now generating was truly extraordinary. Groans, grunts, roars and curses combined with rending metallic crashes. It sounded as though King Kong had signed up for work experience in an iron foundry.

When he realised that he was only three steps away from the top Norman decided to make one last huge effort and get the job finished. He gave one mighty tug which he hoped would jolt the Moviola to the top in one leap. It was unfortunate that, at this point, the wheels, which had been locked up for some time, suddenly ran free once more, so much less energy was required than Norman had reckoned. He gave a massive heave and the machine flew up the steps, hit Norman in the guts, and toppled over leaving him stuck underneath it. Norman realised that he had just suffered the fate that would have befallen the pet tortoise had the seven year old boy not intervened. 'Precocious little bugger,' he thought.

Norman lay there for some time unable to move, he had been badly winded. After a few minutes he tried to wiggle his toes and his fingers, on discovering that he was not entirely paralysed, he at last found the strength to push the Moviola up and roll out from under it. He immediately reached for that last cigarette but found that it had been crushed to powder in the accident. Norman realised that his attitude towards the Moviola had changed somewhat during the course of the morning. He no longer regarded it as the most desirable of all machines; he now hated the bloody thing. He would get it to his room as quickly as he could and then go home to lick his wounds. Indeed there were plenty of wounds to lick.

When Norman finally got back and eased himself into a hot bath he found that his body was bruised from his chest down to his knees, that the muscles in the back of his legs seemed to be on fire and that a pain in his lower spine varied from a morbid throbbing to violent stabs of agony. Fortunately he knew what to do. He smoked three cigarettes, he swallowed four paracetamol and a very large whisky and then he went to bed.

It was at about four o' clock the next morning that Norman woke up to discover that he had lost the ability to move. It had not been a good night. He had been experiencing the most awful dreams, probably as a result of the reaction between the whiskey and the pills. The dream, which he most clearly remembered, found him buried in a snow drift while a tortoise tried to dig him out, using an ice cream scoop. He awoke with a start just as the tortoise was telling a seven year old boy to get off his arse and come and lend a hand. Norman lay there, glad that it was only a dream; then he went to turn over, in order to get more comfortable, but he couldn't. His back had locked up. It stayed locked up all through Sunday and was hardly any better on Monday morning. There was nothing for it; he would have to phone in 'sick'.

For Bill, Norman's assistant, Monday morning was full of surprises. The first one was to discover that, for once, he had got into work before Norman. For the last four weeks he had always heard the dreaded Tchaikovsky thundering up the corridor towards him because Norman was so obsessed with the sequence that he had taken to coming in especially early. Today, even though he was ten minutes late, Bill could hear no music. That was odd. The second surprise came when he unlocked the cutting room door. Norman wasn't there but something astounding was, a brand new Moviola. There was only one course of action for Bill to take and he took it; he went straight to the canteen to think about it all over a coffee. He was just wondering whether to have a second cup when the film-editing manager came over to his table.

"Ah Bill, glad I found you, I wanted a word."

Bill braced himself for another lecture about poor time keeping but, as the manager continued, he was in for his third surprise.

"Norman has phoned in sick; he wrecked his back gardening over the weekend. Shouldn't have thought that the weather was good enough for gardening but there's no holding these horticultural nuts I suppose."

"No," said Bill, as he remembered that Norman lived in a mansion flat.

"The point is that your director would be quite happy for you to finish off the film. You'll have to work without an assistant for a few days, but I'll put you on editor's pay OK?"

"Yes, fine, thank you!" said Bill.

"Oh and I had decided to let Norman have Alan Tyler's Moviola so you'll have a good machine to work on. Alan reminded me on Friday that he was off on holiday and it was a hired one. We've paid for it until the end of the month so it would be stupid not to use it. I'll have the lads shift it up to you this morning."

"Well actually it's there already" said Bill.

"Blimey they're keen." The manager turned to leave. "Try not to play the music too loud, there's a good chap."

The manager needn't had worried. The first decision that the director and his new editor made was to ditch all the sequences that used Tchaikovsky.

Chapter 14.

<u>Young Groupies and Old Gropers.</u>

The reason why Norman was particularly pissed off by the saga of the Moviola was that he had not only wrecked his back, he had also, unwittingly, given his assistant his first big break and the ungrateful lout had used the opportunity to snub Norman by removing all the wonderful sequences which he had cut to music. 'Cut to buggery' was the director's opinion but until Norman went off 'sick' he had not had the courage to say so. What was so galling was the fact the Norman knew he had only himself to blame; he therefore decided to take the greatest advantage he could from his bad back and stay off work for as long as humanly possible. This, at least would be some form of compensation.

It is strange how often the festering finger of fate has a part to play in the lives of the uniquely untalented, for it was during Norman's long absence that a production requirement developed for which he seemed exactly suited. What is more it would enable the film editing manager to ship Norman off to television centre and work on a programme where the production staff knew less about film than they did about breeding whippets. Even Norman would seem like an asset to them. The programme was a new weekly roundup of pop music called *'Ready Steady Rock!'* and was based at television centre. It featured both established groups and also newcomers on their way up the charts. The studio was packed out with teenage pop fans and, with the emphasis on youth, it was presented by teenage disc jockeys, most of whom had at least thirty years of experience in the business.

The reason the show found that it had need of a film editor was because this was in an age before the pop video. *Ready Steady Rock!* was a live show and whilst up and coming groups would kill for a chance to appear on it, sometimes the legendary groups of the era would be on tour and unavailable. In such a case it soon seemed rather dull just to play the song and show the fans in the studio attempting to dance. It was embarrassing. For a while a group of professional dancers were provided as an alternative. They were leggy girls who simpered about in the disinterested manner that was considered 'trendy' at the time and they were equally embarrassing. Somebody in the production team then hit on an idea that was to prove the forerunner of the pop video. It was this idea that would involve Norman and eventually, inevitably, it was this idea that would prove to be the most embarrassing of all. It was this. Any time that a group had a song in the charts but were unable to appear in the show a film unit would be sent out to film them living their exciting lives and a fun sequence would be constructed using the song as its music track. When the idea was first explained to Norman, and he realised that he was to have an 'in' to the wonderful world of 'Pop music', he became seriously over excited. This after all was the early sixties; a period which even today is regarded as the high point of British pop. Norman could scarcely believe that he would be likely to meet many of the groups that were then known to every teenager in the land. Groups like 'The Slime', ' Tourettes', 'O.C.D.' 'Special Bus' or the famous all girl group 'Kay Wye and the Loubes'.

The problem was that there was absolutely no one in the production team who knew the first thing about film direction. The producer somehow convinced himself that as the sequences needed to be contemporary, cutting edge, perhaps even anarchic, it might prove an advantage to have them directed by novices unencumbered with textbook cinematic theory. Had they used first rate cameramen and editors it could have worked but that didn't happen. Instead the film department camera managers grabbed the opportunity to schedule this work for the small gang of untalented old shaggers who were almost impossible to allocate because experienced directors refused to work with them.

So that is how the project got underway, to be directed by nervous novices, photographed by curmudgeonly cameramen at the end of their inauspicious careers and then to be edited by Norman (daft as a brush) Marks. It will not surprise you to learn that the films were all frightful beyond belief and neither may it surprise you that they were hailed as a triumph. After all they were made for the light entertainment department where the rule was that as long as the public like it then it's great. And of course the teenage audience of *'Ready Steady Rock!'* adored the films. To watch their idols rushing about doing Zany, Wacky, Pop Starry things was just what they longed to see.

It didn't matter that the picture was often out of focus and the editing could have been better accomplished by a chimp; what was so exciting was to see stars like Frankie Spasm of Tourettes having uncoordinated fun in a fair ground or Kay Wye and the Loubes sliding seductively down the pole at Shepherd's Bush fire station. It was fresh. It was 'with it'. It was the very essence of 60's youth culture. It was toe-curlingly naff.

Norman took so long mucking about with the editing of the first of these films that he nearly missed the transmission. The Slime's song *'Time to change my baby.'* was at number two in the charts but the group was not available for the show. They had therefore been filmed riding around on bicycles made for two and then running along the beach at Brighton. There were also lots of close ups of them pulling funny faces at the camera, which would have found better use in an 'ad' for acne treatment.

'Ready Steady Rock!' went on air live from studio 8 on Thursday nights at seven thirty. Norman got the film to the telecine machine at seven thirty five and then rushed to the studio control gallery to tell them all was well. They knew that of, of course, because they could see the film's leader appear on the telecine monitor in front of them but

Norman relished the drama of being the man who delivered the goods in the nick of time.

Before the Television Centre was buggered about by accountancy-lead re-vamps it was a very well designed building, extremely practical and even elegant after the fashion of the sixties. There were two ways of accessing the studio control galleries, directly from the first floor or from the studio floor by a staircase on the studio wall. Norman decided to use the studio floor route, as this might give him a chance to brush shoulders with some real live pop idols. The show was well underway when he ignored the flashing red lights and entered the studio. The air was heavy with sweating adolescence and for a while nobody noticed the incongruous middle-aged man gawping on the side-lines. A gangling youth dressed in what appeared to be the National Dress of Kurdistan approached and Norman thrilled with the realisation that it was none other than Frankie Spasm of Tourettes.

"Ere mate do you work on the show?"

"Yes I do, I'm the, the, Film executive." Norman reckoned that such an important encounter was worth a lie.

"That's groovey mate, but where's the pisser?"

Norman was so excited that for a moment he was unable to speak. Thoughts rushed through his head about how envious others would be when he regaled them with the encounter, then he pulled himself together and directed

Frankie to the Gents. After that excitement he decided it was time to make his way up to the control gallery.

Half way up the steep flight of metal stairs Norman paused to look down on the sea of available teenagers on the floor beneath, all working desperately hard to look casual. It seemed to him that any of the girls who were still innocent were very keen to lose their virginity, almost as keen as was Norman himself. This notion was nothing but fantasy but it seemed like a fundamental truth for it ran through his veins with the fire that has burned within dirty old men since time immoral. A pause in the music snapped him back to reality and he rushed up the remaining steps and through the heavy, sound proofed, door that lead to the control gallery.

As the door swung slowly closed behind him Norman found himself in an, almost dreamlike, other world. The brightly lit cacophonous environment of the studio floor was instantly transformed into a softly illuminated car-peted area. The noise from the studio was completely eliminated by the soundproofing and only entered the hal-lowed control gallery through the studio's speaker system. It was thus easily held in check by a volume knob and. in times of real stress, could be silenced altogether, at the touch of a button.

For a moment Norman gazed in wonder at it all and re-gretted that, like so many 'film people' working in televi-sion, for him the world of the multi camera electronic stu-

dio was uncharted territory. He quickly pulled himself together as he realised that the important thing was for him
to look confident and at ease. The door through which he
had passed had opened on to an executive lounge area. It
was divided from the control area by a glass wall and another high tech door. The banks of television monitors
shone brightly through the glass and the studio director,
the vision mixer, the production secretary and some inde-
finable 'hangers on' all sat opposite the screens behind a
control desk bulging with switches faders and buttons. It
was geek heaven. Norman quickly worked out that there
was one monitor for every camera on the studio floor and
one transmission monitor showing the camera whose shot
was selected at any particular time. There were several
other screens of no obvious purpose and one which displayed the figure ten of a film leader. Norman thrilled with
the realisation that this was the screen that would display
the sequence that he had cut to Slime's current hit. He
was jolted back to reality by a voice that issued from the
darkest corner of the lounge.

"You look a bit lost, need any help?" Norman blinked as
the voice took on a shape of almost human form as a
heavily wrinkled, scruffy looking man emerged from a
large black leather chair and came towards him. The man
was so short that he had been hidden by the back of the
chair. He was now close to Norman and standing in one of
the few pools of light. 'My God,' thought Norman 'what a
scruffy bugger'.

"I'm Johnny Tudor, I'm the producer." The introduction came as shock because Norman, in common with all *'Ready Steady Rock!'*'s' viewers he had been deceived by Johnny's screen credit. It was Mr. Tudor's vain conceit to back his name credit with the silhouette image of a handsome young guy posing elegantly on a bar stool. Nothing could have been further from the truth. The 'image' was a man in his mid-twenties; Mr. Tudor was pushing fifty-five. The image was tall, Mr. Tudor was short. The 'image' had beautifully coiffured hair; Mr. Tudor's hair was long, straggly and looked, as though he had recently emerged from a drain. In short the fantasy on the credit was every body's idea of what a pop producer should look like whereas, in reality, Johnny looked more like the proprietor of a coconut shy.

Doing his best not to appear disappointed and trying to sound suitably 'groovy', Norman replied. "Hi Johnny I'm Norman, I'm the film editor. I just popped in to make sure that everything as Ok with sequence."

"Oh, pleased to meet you Norman and yes, the film is terrif! We ran it in the gallery a few minutes ago but you're just in time 'cos we will be playing it down to the punters in a minute or two. It's great man! I just loved the shots you put in upside down."

Norman was not aware that he had cut any shots in upside down, though it had happened before when he was working under pressure. As this was the first time he had been actually congratulated for making a cock-up he thought it wise to make the best of it.

"Oh well just an off the wall idea I had, Johnny."

"Well it's groovy man! You know Norman I think you are the man for us."

Norman did his best to look modest but his ample nostrils swelled with pride and he found it impossible to hold back a beaming smile. Even in the low light of the production lounge Johnny could not fail to notice how enormous and how nicotine stained Norman's teeth were. Combined with the distended nostrils they presented the overall impression of a cartoon horse and Johnny relaxed that there was now at least one male involved in the show who was even less sexually attractive than he was himself.

"Let's go through to the gallery," he suggested to Norman. "They are about to run the film."

The two of them went through yet another glass door and stood at the back of the control gallery. The wall on their left was also made of glass so it was possible to see all the activity on the studio floor beneath them. Norman noticed that it gave him a great sense of power, like a Greek God looking down on the world of insignificant mortals. He tried to a recall a similar scene in a film he had recently enjoyed. 'Ah, *Jason and the Juggernauts*!', that was it.'

"Eight more bars of song on camera 3 coming to Jamie on cam 2 for film intro." The production assistant's shrill voice caught Norman's attention. So his film sequence was going to be introduced by no less a celebrity than the famous disc jockey Jamie Servile, this really was fame at last. The song ended amid near hysteria from the girls on the dance floor and, just as predicted, the vision mixer cut to camera 2 and Jamie Servile's leering features appeared in unpleasant close up. "Cue Jamie, On 2 for fifteen seconds, run telecine." The commands in the gallery were coming thick and fast and all eyes were on Jamie.

"Yes guys and gals, that was the wonderful 'Tourettes' straight in at number five with the title track from their new album '*Let's Get Sectioned*'. Anyway, at number two this week is Slime with '*Time to change my baby*'. Slime can't be with us in the studio tonight so we sent our film unit down to Brighton to catch up with the crazy happenings in the groovy guys wacky week."

Despite all the authoritative commands from the production assistant the film had been run a few seconds late so at the end of his announcement Jamie Servile was left staring into the camera for an uncomfortably long pause, the grin on his face freezing into the sort of look you might expect to see on the face of a cryogenically preserved corpse. At last the final numbers on the film leader flashed through and the vision mixer was able to cut to the sequence. "On film for 2 minutes fifteen" said the floor manager to Jamie.

"What the fuck are those wankers doing up there?" replied the award winning role model for the nation's youth.

But no one took much notice for this was the moment for which Norman had been waiting; everyone in the studio and gallery alike were concentrating on his film.

As Johnny had predicted, it was a triumph. Had the footage been of anyone other than the members of a famous group it would have looked like a home movie made by the inmates of a home for the cerebrally challenged but this was a film featuring Slime and they could do no wrong. Riding tandem bicycles, making sand castles on Brighton beach, playing at being Toreadors with two members of the group as bull fighters and the other two rushing about with a pair of antlers pretending to be bulls was just so... so... Groovy! And all this before the surprise of the upside down close ups; when they hit the screen the burst of hysteria in the audience, especially from the girls, seemed to presage the imminent danger of an episode of mass incontinence.

Just before he was due to cut back from the film to the Studio the director noticed that several of the boys in the audience were standing on their heads to mimic what they had just seen on film and that two of the cameras were offering up 'upside down' close ups of the boys faces.

Johnny jumped in to allay any hesitation, "Go to those close ups before you cut to Jamie, and hey, can we make him upside down too?"

"I can invert the image." said the vision mixer. "Do it! Do it!" shouted the ageing executive, in an unusual burst of creativity.

So they mixed from the upside down shots on film to upside down shots in the studio and then cut to a big upside down close up of Jamie Servile.

"Well how's about that then boys and girls?" The disc jockey always resorted to his favourite and most redundant catch phrase when stuck for anything appropriate to say.

"Blimey," said Johnny, "Jamie looks about the same upside down as he does the right way up."

"Like a moron any way up." muttered the vision mixer under her breath.

Norman had done it, he had really made his mark on the 'number one' show for teenagers and felt very pleased with himself.

Just before he left the studio the production secretary came up to him.

"Johnny told me to give these," she said and pressed four tickets for next week's show into Norman's sweaty hand.

"Use them well, they are gold dust," she added mysteriously, "and give them back if you don't use them...but you will, I bet."

As the girl rushed back into the heady whirl of congratulations and farewells Norman pondered on what use he could make of the tickets. He didn't have to wait long for an answer.

"Was them tickets she gave yer mate?" Norman recognised the voice of Frankie Spasm and indeed, when he turned, he saw that the colourfully clad artiste had sidled up behind him.

"Yes, four for next week, some sort of reward because they liked the film, but God knows what I'll do with them."

"How much do you want for them then?"

"Oh they don't cost anything, the production give them away. Why don't you ask for some?"

"They only give them to the record company reps and the managers and people like you. They don't give 'em to us groups cos they know what we'll use them for."

Norman looked puzzled.

"To get the birds mate," his new friend explained. "The groupies will do anything to get their hands on tickets for the show."

An unpleasant light started to gleam in Norman's eyes. "You mean like show you their knickers." he said, trying, but failing, to sound relaxed and 'hip'.

"They'll show you a lot more than that mate. Look you give me those tickets and you can come to our dressing room; you'll soon see what I mean. Come down in about half an hour and bring a bottle of vodka with you, oh and a mars bar.'"Frankie gave Norman a leering wink and Norman gave Frankie the tickets; then Frankie was gone.

The next half an hour dragged past. Norman went to the club bar and bought a bottle of vodka and then to the coffee counter. Unfortunately they were out of mars bars so he bought a packet of Maltesers instead. 'At least they won't go hungry,' he thought to himself.

At last the half hour was up but Norman decided to wait an extra five minutes. Partly this was because he thought it would make him appear to be 'cool' and partly it was because he found the experience of waiting exciting in itself. But after four minutes he could stand it no longer and rushed from the bar.

The club bar at Television Centre was on the fourth floor; some dressing rooms were on the ground floor others were located in the basement. As he ran towards the lifts Norman began to doubt if he had correctly remembered the dressing number which Frankie had given him. He was pretty sure it was 125 in the blue area. Anyway he would go there first. He could always enquire at reception if the need arose. He reached the lifts in some sort of record time but both cars were on the ground floor. He was too impatient to wait so he decided to use the stairs. By the time he reached the basement he was sweating and some-what dishevelled. He wondered if he should pop into the gents and smarten himself up a bit but then determined that it would be best to find the dressing room first. He could then tidy up and make a suitably 'cool' entrance. He found signs to 'Blue Assembly' easily enough and then saw dressing room 110 on his left. OK, all he had to do was to keep going until he came to 125. He pushed on. 118, 119, 120 and then 130; what the hell had happened to the missing ten dressing rooms and who was the bloody idiot who had numbered the rooms?

The main block at Television Centre is circular; as long as you are on the right the floor you should be able to find any room as long as you keep going. So that is was Nor-man did, indeed he ran the circumference of the basement corridor three times in an increasing state of nervous anxi-ety. It was only as he passed room 110 for the third time that he saw a sign pointing down a side corridor; ' Blue As-sembly spur dressing rooms 121-129'.

"Bloody architects Bloody extensions, Bloody Hell!"

He shot down the corridor with athletic grace of a rampag-ing rhino and thundered to halt outside dressing room 125. Determined not to lose his presence of mind he paused for a moment to sort himself out. He wiped the sweat from his face, hitched up his trousers and smoothed out the creases in his knitted yellow cardigan. Right, this was it; ready for anything. He knocked at the door. Norman's surprise when it simply swung open was considerable but nothing like the surprise that was caused by what he saw. Right there in front of him was…. a completely empty room; grubby, untidy even slightly smelly but definitely empty. "What a bastard." Norman voiced his thoughts out loud. He sank down on to one the spectacularly uncomfortable chairs with which the dressing rooms were all amply supplied and he stared bleakly at a smouldering ashtray. After a minute or two he started to munch on the Maltesers. A voice from behind him snapped Norman back to reality and he turned to see an extremely thin, extremely young girl framed in the doorway. She had long straggly blonde hair and was wearing a purple miniskirt and a green sparkly boob tube. Her red leather stiletto boots only served to exaggerate the skinniness of her legs and her make- up was a mélange of the world of ancient Egypt with that of the circus clown. She was, thought Norman, 'sex on legs'.

"Here mister are you the bloke what does the films?"

"Yes that's me,"

"Frankie said that you gave us some tickets"

"Yes I did."

"He said I should stay behind to say thank you, said you'd like to see my knickers."

"Oh well, I'm not really sure if…" Norman could hardly believe what he found himself saying. Why was he backing off? Why be coy? Of course he wanted to see the girl's knickers, he had nearly given himself a heart attack rushing about to find the dressing room for that very purpose.

"Look, I haven't got all bleeding day; do you want me show you my knickers or not?"

Norman came to senses, "Of course I do," he said, flaring his nostrils as sexily as he knew how.'

"Well they're on the floor over there."

She pointed and Norman looked down to see a pair of very skimpy panties lying amongst a confusion of Mars bar wrappers. He paused for a moment to comprehend the significance of the sordid collage and, when he finally glanced back towards the door, the girl was gone.

Chapter 15.

<u>The Wages of Sin.</u>

As Norman lay in bed that night he tried to work out what lessons he could learn from the experiences of such an eventful day. At length he decided they were these:

1. He was a brilliant film editor whose great gifts had at last found an outlet.

2. He had been unlucky in his sex life but if he cultivated friendship with the pop groups he would now be able to satisfy his smouldering sexual prowess.

But both conclusions were false. It was not the voice of experience that was echoing in his head it but the sirens of self-delusion. He had never shown any talent at all as a film editor and the sequence that had been so highly praised that day was an appalling piece of ephemeral tat. The people who made *'Ready Steady Rock!'* spent their lives enthusing about witless drivel so, of course, the film had been much to their liking. It was also a delusion to imagine that hordes of pop groups would welcome Norman to their orgies but here was the snare waiting to spring. Norman had access to tickets for the show. He just needed to be more assertive. If the groups wanted to get their grubby hands on Norman's tickets they would have to agree to let Norman have his grubby way with a few of their groupies. He sure wasn't going to fall for any of Frankie Spasm's tricks again. He turned over in his bed and sighed in contentment as he drifted off to sleep. Norman was about to take his first steps down the primrose path to perdition.

There was no film required for the following week's show. The willowy dancers who, until recently, had always been used to fill in when a group could not appear had been very pissed off by being replaced with film the previous week and they feared being made redundant. They all had a moan at Johnny Tudor and he decided to take the line of least resistance and use the girls again. Jamie Servile had also not liked the film much. It had received the biggest cheer of the evening and that was always his prerogative. It was certainly important to keep Jamie happy. He was a prince amongst the band of repugnant, unremarkable pre-senters who BBC entertainment producers held in rever-ence. It might be wise to keep Servile happy until someone equally anodyne could be found to replace him.

The production manager for the show tried to persuade Johnny that they could save some money by cancelling the film editing booking until they had another film to make but when the film editing manager pointed out that if they did so there was no guarantee that they could have Nor-man back again they quickly changed their minds. Of course the editing manager was bluffing, it was almost im-possible to find work for Norman but Norman had been going around boasting about how delighted the production had been with his film so the editing manager reckoned that it was a bluff worth playing. As things turned out Johnny Tudor was sure that he had made the right decision.

For a week Norman had nothing to do and that suited him just fine. He tidied the cutting room and spent a lot of time dropping in to chat with other editors. He was largely truthful when recounting the success of his film sequence but his version of events in Frankie Spasm's dressing room was complete fiction. Furthermore it was a fiction that no one, except Norman, wished to hear. In the revised version, dressing room 125 had not been empty when Norman arrived but, rather, the scene of an orgy the excesses of which might well have astonished Caligula. Three girls for every boy and naked, except for one who was wearing red leather boots. All of them were high on a cocktail of vodka and Maltesers. Frankie Spasm and the other lads in Tourettes were delighted when Norman arrived because they were becoming exhausted but all was well because Norman proved to have the potency of a donkey in an oyster bar. Even so he only managed to satisfy the sex- crazed groupies by employing techniques that he had learned on National Service from a sergeant in the medical corps.

Nobody believed a word of it but after telling the tale three or four times, Norman began to believe it himself. After all it might have happened like that and at some point in the near future he would make damn sure that it did. He learned from the production office that the show only ever used studio six or studio eight and he therefore decided to get to know exactly where all the dressing rooms for those studios were located. He certainly didn't want to be caught out again by that perverse numbering system so he stalked the relevant corridors until he knew their every secret. The truth was that it also gave him a strange thrill to imagine the time when he might be heading for a particular dressing room to take part in an orgy for real.

Norman therefore decided that even though there was to be no film in the next programme he would never the less hang around for the transmission. It would prove to Johnny Tudor that he was really interested in the show, he could charge it up as overtime but most important of all, he might be able to scrounge a few more tickets.

For the followers of the hit parade the next edition of 'Ready Steady Rock!' was something of a milestone. Frankie Spasm and Tourettes had slipped from number five to number eleven, so they would not be appearing. A new group, Ricky Zit and the Pustules, had jumped straight in at number four with 'Squeeze it Baby.' but the most sensational news of all was that Slime had gone to number one. It was their first time at the top of the charts and it seemed almost incredible that they had knocked Charlie Stash and the Pushers from first place. Their Ballad, 'The Wrong Kind of Snow', had been number one for the last five weeks and had shown no sign of fading. Now they were down at number five and their manager, Bernie Lines, was not a happy man. The gossip was that Slime's success had a lot to do with the fantastic film in last week's show. Bernie thought he was being very cunning by claiming that his group were unavailable for the current show as this might mean they would have a film made too. When he heard that this wasn't happening and that *'The Wrong Kind of Snow'* was to be a studio dance routine, he blew a gasket.

Matters were made worse by the fact that the dance routine that week was quite dreadful. The choreographer and the girls were desperately under rehearsed because they had been moonlighting on a detergent commercial and in any case the song itself was not suited for dance. The lyric was full of teenage angst, motorbike crashes and sex in a graveyard. The story concluded in a drying out clinic so, from the choreographer's point of view, there was not a lot to justify the use of 'jump splits', 'jazz hands' or 'spirit fingers'.

Sensing trouble, the studio floor manager had detailed two of his assistants to prevent Bernie Lines gaining access to the studio during transmission. Bernie therefore had to suffer the indignity of watching the show on a monitor in the public viewing area whilst trembling with impotent rage as the dancers mooched uncertainly around the set. The best thing about the routine was that no one actually fell over; the worst thing was that it might have been more entertaining had they done so.

In the control gallery, no one was aware that a storm was brewing. The choreographer, a young woman called Click Formby, breathed a sigh of relief and then turned to Johnny who was standing at the back next to Norman. Click was one of those TV people who are always simply bursting with confidence and mediocrity.

"Well what did you think of it then boss?" she said. It was more of a challenge than a question and Johnny hesitated for a moment.

"Well Click, baby," he said, "It was certainly...something else."

"Cos it sure wasn't dance," muttered the vision mixer. Johnny turned to his film editor.

"Now Norman matey, have a good look at this next group; we may well be doing a film with them for next week's show."

Sensing that the tentacles of redundancy might emerge from the woodwork at any second, Click Formby decided to head for the exit. She looked back and flashed her most charming smile at Johnny and her most daggered look towards Norman.

"See you guys," she chirped and was gone.

"Sexy Lady, clever too" said Norman displaying the fine judgement that had made him the editor he was.

"Now watch this Norman," said Johnny, "this is a group that is going places."

With a chord loud enough to vaporise the sound desk's most powerful limiter, Ricky Zit and the Pustules erupted on to the screen in their television debut.

When he introduced the song Jamie Servile had promised the viewers that they would have never heard anything like it and, indeed, most people would have been thankful that they hadn't. *'Squeeze it Baby'* was not so much a song as a musical act of indecent exposure. The lyric contained little more than lead singer Ricky Zit screaming *'Squeeze it Baby, Squeeze it'* whilst apparently trying to force a microphone far enough down his throat to rendezvous with his tonsils. The endless repetition of the same four chords seemed to be bringing the ginger haired youth on rhythm guitar to the brink of orgasm whilst the skinny young man on bass kept jabbing the end of the instrument into his genitals in manner that suggested he was hell bent on either auto castration or self-circumcision. The drummer was not so much into self- harm but simply engaged in the total destruction of his kit.

When the song finally shuddered to halt there was a moment of silence before the thunderous ovation. All the teenagers in the studio that night were convinced that they were in the presence of genius as for the adults, well they had all been in show business long enough to know when to succumb to self-delusion. So genius it was, by popular consent.

Johnny turned to Norman

"Jeeze, they are going to be mega. We'll need a film maybe two."

Doing his best to look cool and dependable Norman lit one of his malodorous *Gitanes* and flashed a wide nicotine stained grin. For the second time in a week he felt hugely important.

After Ricky Zit, the rest of the show was a bit of an anti-climax, even though it contained the top three of the week. Hanging on in there a number three was Kay Wye with *'Unprotected Love'* then, up from six last week and now at number two was *'Some Boys Like It'* from The Priesthood. When at last it was time for Slime to sing *'Time to change my baby'* it really felt that the party was over. Last week the song had featured a fun packed film, this week, performed live by the group in the studio, it all seemed rather tired.

"That won't be at the top next week I betcha," said Johnny.

"Well if Ricky Zit is number one we've got a problem because I hear that they might be booked for a week in Hamburg." Tina, the efficient production secretary, was proving her worth.

"Then we've gotta get a film made and quick," snapped Johnny.

"Can we keep the chat down please? Ok… stand by to cue Jamie for the wrap up… stand by end roller and music." The studio director had put up with enough distractions and had decided, belatedly, to assert himself.

It wasn't long before the show was over and the end credit roller was running, unsteadily, up the screen. Johnny Tudor's deceptive credit settled mid screen and then the director faded to black and handed the airwaves back to the presentation department. The instant that the red light went off Bernie Lines charged into the gallery raving about his group being sold up the river. He headed straight for Johnny but, as he did so, he pushed past Tina who had started to dish out next week's tickets. A lot of them fell to the floor and Norman instantly stepped forward to help the young lady pick them up.

"Thanks Norman. It is good to know that there are a few gentlemen left." and then as she counted the tickets she went on to say, "sorry I can't let you have any for next week we seem to be a bit short. The record companies must have taken more than usual."

"That's OK sweetie," said Norman, courteous to a fault.

After helping Tina there seemed no point in hanging around the gallery. Johnny was preoccupied with Bernie Lines.

"Charlie Stash and the Pushers are as big as it gets and if they don't deserve a film, no bugger does!" Norman heard Bernie's ranting but he took little notice of it as he headed out and down the stairs to the studio floor. He was pleased that Tina thought he was gentleman and even happier that he had managed to steal six of her tickets. This week he'd make sure they paid a dividend.

A lot of the excited kids in the audience were hanging around, trying not to be ushered out before they had got a few autographs from their idols. Norman sauntered among them looking benevolent. He was feeling much more 'part of it all' than he had done last week.

Now all he had to do was select the right group of girls and discover just how much his tickets were really worth. Suddenly Norman was finding it hard to look sophisticated and casual, he was getting desperate and it showed. A cackle of coarse laughter brought his attention to a group of girls at the far end of the studio. There were five of them, all quite sexy though the sobriquet 'common as muck' would have flattered them.

'They'll do', thought Norman but just before he made his move he was tapped on the shoulder.

"Sorry to bother you mate but are you Norman Marks?"

"Yes that's me."

"Well I'm Arch Angel. I'm the singer with Slime."

"Oh yes, of course you are. How's it going then Arch mate?"

"Well pretty good Norman and all thanks to your film we reckon."

Norman looked modestly down his nose, which was some considerable distance. The singer continued enthusiastically.

"Look man if you'd like to pop down to our dressing room we're having a get together with a few fans to celebrate making it to number one. After that well go on to my flat and do it all over again only noisier. Come to that too if you like."

"Thanks, I'd love to."

"See you down there in about ten minutes then, room 125. Do you know how to find it?"

"Sure do." came the confident reply.

Glad to have the decision made for him Norman ran out past the group of noisy girls and headed straight up to the fourth floor bar. He had a large scotch for confidence and then he bought a bottle of vodka from the off licence. The Mars bars were back in stock so he bought four of them for good measure. Ten minutes later he was outside dressing room 125. He could hear a lot of fun and laughter coming from within and several of the voices were young girls. Slime were certainly going to prove better news Frankie Spasm and the tossing Tourettes. Norman knocked on the door. Arch opened it and asked him in.

'This is Norman everybody! This is man who edited our film." There was a chorus of "Hey man that was great," and "Give us kiss darling." largely coming from people of the appropriate sex. Arch took charge.

"Well now that Norman's here we can really get things going. Becky turn the lights down. Ok everybody let's get down to it."

Norman could feel a sweat breaking out on his forehead. It was going to happen at last; this was to be his first orgy. What was the best thing to do? The girl beside him had sunk on her knees so Norman decided to follow her down there.

"Right everybody." said Arch, "I'll start us off." Norman looked in breathless anticipation as Arch fumbled with the front of his jeans and then his jaw dropped when Arch pulled out a bible.

"Lord, dear Lord, hear our prayer as tonight we thank you for the great joy you have brought to us all. Let this faithful group of your worshippers keep ever close to the paths of righteousness and let us never succumb to the temptations of the flesh."

"Bugger that for a lark," thought Norman and he could feel that the Mars bars were melting in his trouser pocket.

Norman was late into the studio next morning. It had really been the most awful night. His knees were sore from hours of praying and his hands were sore from excessive banging on a tambourine. The only interesting part of it had been to see inside Arch Angels flat and get some idea of how much money pop stars had to spend. White carpets, leather and chrome furniture, hugely expensive hi-fi gear and a fridge that was bigger than Norman's spare bedroom. The evening may have been disappointing in its' total lack of sex but it had been a revelation of the life style that was possible if only you had the money. Norman determined that somehow, some way, he would get himself into the league.

Wild schemes about how to make shed loads of cash were echoing around Norman's head as he approached his cutting room that morning. In fact he was so wrapped up in his thoughts that he failed to notice the urgent ringing of the cutting room phone until he had put the key in the door. Finally he snapped back into action. "My God.' I 'm late! That might be Johnny, Oh bugger this key." At last he got the key to turn in the lock and he rushed to pick up the phone. He calmed himself. *"Ready Steady Rock!'* cutting room, this is Norman Marks how can I help you?"

"Norm, this is Johnny. Get yourself up the office right away Ok. I've a job for you, one you might like."

The speed at which Norman left his cutting room and headed for the lift was in distinct contrast with the leisurely pace at which he had arrived. He was at the lift doors in seconds and waited impatiently for it to arrive. It was no mean distance from the cutting rooms in the East

Tower of TV centre to the seventh floor of the main building, where Johnny's office was located, but Norman covered it in record time. Again he remembered to pause outside the office door and smarten himself up before making his version of a 'cool' entrance.

"Ah Norman, come in baby, sit down if you can find a chair." Johnny Tudor was in 'busy executive' mode "Take that one; you can chuck that crap on the floor." The great producer indicated a chair on which was a pile of about forty discs. "They're what came in today from the record companies, they'll all be shit."

"How do you know?"

"Anything that is any good is brought in by an A&R man and handed over at the end of a good lunch. Anyway I haven't called you in to give you a lesson in record plugging. I want to know if you have any plans for the next couple of days."

"Well nothing until I get some film to edit."

"Well that is just the point; we need someone to direct a film of Ricky Zit doing that crazy number you heard last night. I've had to send Marcus off to film with Charlie Stash. It's a waste of time because the number is sliding out of the charts but I couldn't afford to piss off Bernie Lines any more. He is a powerful man in the industry, he doesn't just manage Charlie Stash and the Pushers, he handles Cold Turkey, The Shakes, and Mogadon as well OCD, so we have to keep him happy. But what we really need is a film to back *'Squeeze it Baby'* for next week's show. It is sure to be heading up the charts, it may even be at number one and we now know for sure that Ricky Zit and the Pustules are going to Hamburg for a week. They leave on Friday so you've got two days. We need that film Norman."

Only four hours later Norman found himself on the Kettering express out of St Pancras. He was heading for Bedford, which was the train's first stop. Frantic phone calls form the *'Ready Steady Rock!'* production office had established that Ricky Zit and his group were due to appear in a pop concert at the Granada Bedford the next day so the plan was for Norman to film them in and around the town on the day of the concert and, if necessary on the next day as well; before the boys set out for Hamburg. Ricky and the Zits were staying in the Bridge Hotel, which had rather come down in the world since World War II when it had often played host to the likes of Sir Henry Wood. Production secretary Tina had booked Norman into the same hostelry and the plan was for him to rendezvous with the film crew in the Hotel reception area at nine the next morning. It was all such terribly short notice that Norman had no idea of who the Cameraman would be and even less of an idea about what he was going to direct the boys to do. However Norman might have been low on intelligence and lacking in talent but he was certainly not short of self-confidence. Even he had observed that in the world of TV pop the only danger for a charlatan was to be exposed by someone of real talent. The law of averages rendered the risk negligible. No, he would shoot a film, he didn't know what would be in it but it would be Groovy and Zany and 'off the wall' and he would be highly praised for the achievement. It was with these confident thoughts that Norman descended from a rather ancient taxi and entered the faded splendour of the Bridge Hotel Bedford.

The experience of checking in proved to somewhat disappointing. Norman had anticipated that a buzz of excitement might have met his announcement that he was 'Norman Marks, BBC Television' but the woman at the desk could not have been less interested; in fact on receiving the news she became almost hostile.

"Are you anything to do with those yobs in the Bunyan Suite?"

"Are they a pop group?"

"That might be one description for them, I suppose."

"Well I am here to make a film with them."

"My God what do we pay our licence for? Anyway I'll put you in the suite next to theirs; nobody else will want it, that's for sure."

It was with mixed emotions that Norman followed the ancient hall porter to the equally ancient lift. He had been given a whole suite to himself, something that he had never experienced before. It was also great to have his bags carried for him. Apart from the feeling it gave of being an important person it also helped his back, which had never really recovered from the Moviola incident. They reached the room and the porter opened the door. He put Norman's suit case down on a table next to wardrobe and then he turned on the lights, as if to prove that they were actually working. Then he coughed. Norman handed him half a crown and porter shuffled out muttering something under his breath.

Norman had just sunk on to the bed for twenty minutes 'shut eye' when a thunderous crash from the suite next door brought him back to reality. There was a second great thud and a lot of loutish laughter mingled with girlish shrieks and giggles of a very unladylike nature.

Norman was suddenly wide-awake and certain in the realisation that he was nearer to an orgy than he had ever been before. There was one taking place in the next room. Moments later he was knocking on the Ricky Zit's door.

"Bugger off, we're busy," came the aggressive response.

"And we ain't got nuffink on neither" added another voice.

"Not to worry, I 'm Norman. I'm here to direct the film for you tomorrow, I just wanted to say hello and maybe chat over some ideas."

"Well at the mo mate the only idea we're be interested in is how four guys can shag five girls at once."

Part of Norman felt that he should be shocked by such an immoral riddle; but part of him, and the increasingly larger part, was excited. He wondered if he should dash back to his room and clean his teeth but decided simply to push ahead.

"Well it might be a good idea to even out the odds." he suggested.

"What do you mean?"

"Let me in and I'll show you."

"You a raver then?"

"Guess so." From behind the door there came another burst of coarse laughter and some shuffling about then Norman heard the key turn. The door opened just enough for a girl's head to peep out. The girl blinked at Norman in a mixture of amazement and horror. Norman responded by flaring his ample nostrils, in his habitual, mistaken, belief that it made him look sexy. The girl sighed and then shouted back into the room.

"Sharon I think this one better be for you; it'll be alright, just take your glasses off."

Oscar Wilde once remarked that the one thing worse than not getting your heart's desire was to actually get it and if Norman was to be honest he would have to admit, if only to himself, that the events of the following few hours were to prove very disappointing. In the orgies of his sexual fantasies Norman was ever the potent, desirable and masterful lover. The other participants were always beautiful, lustful, compliant and above all odourless. The reality of the orgy could not have been further from his ideal imagining. Norman entered the room and the girl locked the door behind him. It was helpful that the curtains were drawn and only one dim bedside light was on. Even so, as his eyes became used to the gloom, Norman could see that, whilst he might at last be able to experience group sex, it was likely to prove an uphill struggle. Ricky Zit was lying in the middle of a very large bed and there were three girls on the bed with him. All of them were naked and they were sharing a bag of sherbet lemons. Whether this was a novel part of foreplay or post coital relaxation Norman was at a loss to decide but he had no hesitation in recognising that Ricky and his lovers all belonged to that type of human being who look very much more sexy with their clothes on. The same held true for the gyrating forms on the second bed. Norman could see very little of the girls involved as they were completely hidden from view by two other members of the Pustules who were lying on top of them. From the extreme whiteness and multiple freckles of one pair of thrusting buttocks Norman knew that they must belong to the ginger youth on rhythm guitar but it was not so easy so decide if the other rutting rump was that of the drummer or the bass player but then Norman noticed an extremely thin youth sitting in an arm chair. This had to be the bass player. He was the only person in the room, other than Norman who was not entirely naked.

Even so, he had stripped down to his underpants. He was staring down at his crotch and looking very dejected. Norman remembered the frantic instrumental stabbings to which the lad had subjected his genitals during the recent performance and concluded that it was likely that the boy's bollocks were still in post- traumatic stress. However, for Norman, the most disturbing thing about this sullen seated figure was his underwear because it was high fashion and obviously very expensive. Norman realised that as soon as he undressed one of many embarrassing revelations would be his sad and sagging underclothes. They were clean (years of maternal indoctrination of the dangers of being knocked down in the street and arriving at A&E in soiled knickers had insured that Norman never ventured out in any underwear that was less than spotless) but cleanliness, in this situation, was not the issue. It was in the style of Norman's vest and pants that humiliation lay lurking, for they were mini-combinations. That is woollen vest and shorts made in one piece and looking like something usually only seen on bawdy seaside postcards. He had bought them in the closing down sale of a very old fashioned gentleman's outfitters and now very much regretted the decision.

"Well are you going to join in or not mate? Don't just stand there ogling, it's a right turn off." Ricky Zit was becoming assertive.

"Of course I'm joining in, that's why I'm here." As the words left him, Norman saw his salvation on the other side

251

of the room. It was an old fashioned screen of the type much favoured in bedroom farces and restoration comedy. He could conceal his passion freezing underwear from the world if he undressed behind the screen. He made a dash for cover. It was Sod's law that in his haste to undress Norman managed to get the zip on his trousers jammed. He therefore took a lot longer strip than might be expected. He had started to sweat again and he was feeling a strange mixture of fear and arousal. At last the zip loosened. Norman got his trousers off but then, as he pulled his shirt over his head, he was to discover the quality of dressing screens that had made them such a favourite with the writers of bedroom farces. That is their ability to fold up and fall over with a malevolence of their own.

After the struggle with his trousers, Norman used much more force than was necessary to pull off his shirt and, in so doing, he hit the screen in the exact spot that was required to send it into 'auto-fold' mode. There was a loud crash, a cloud of dust and Norman stood revealed in the full horror of his World War I undies.

"Blimey look at Granddad!"

"Last of the red hot lovers."

"I never knew you could get knickers on the National Health."

Norman had to endure a torrent of cruel jibes before he was able to continue undressing; but of course all was lost. The moment for ecstasy withered and all hope of night of steaming passion, worthy of the Karma Sutra was reduced to the level of a sweaty knee tremble in a shop doorway. Yes, Norman had some sex that night but it wasn't what he had hoped for. It was like being invited to a banquet and being served Pot Noodles. In fact it wasn't long before he wished that he was back in his own room and in bed alone. Orgies were all very well as a fantasy but the reality of trying to make love to a girl while some sweaty male foot was being pressed against your face and then later discovering that the girl you thought you were shagging was having a fag by the window and that for the last hour you had actually been humping her unattractive friend was disillusioning, disappointing and even perhaps disgusting. Still he hadn't had sex for a very long time and so he shagged he-roically onwards through the night; frequently aided by an assortment of substances, which Ricky encouraged him to sniff up his nose, shove down his throat or rub onto his dick. These potions certainly increased Norman's stamina but they also befuddled his brain so that after a few hours he was not sure if he was snorting something that he should have rubbed on his willy and vice versa. Come the dawn he was completely exhausted and in no condition to face a hard day's film direction.

There was a distinct chill in the atmosphere when Norman arrived in reception next morning. The crew had arrived on time at nine o'clock despite the most horrendous battle through traffic jams along the route from West London to Bedford. They were not best pleased to hang around for Norman, who finally staggered out of the lift at ten fifteen.

"Sorry I'm late guys, it was a hell of a night." He hoped that this excuse would at least make him sound like a trendy member of the world of Pop.

"Oh that's alright," replied the cameraman. "I mean, we only had to drive here from West London but you must have had a hell of time battling your way here all the way from the third floor." Norman was not sure if that was irony or sarcasm, perhaps it was neither; any way it was best ignored.

"We are here to shoot a film with Ricky Zit and the Pus-tules. It's for next week's *Ready Steady Rock!*"

"Your life must be one long thrill." This time it was the sound recordist who was doing little to diffuse the tension.

"It can get pretty groovy at times," said Norman.

The cameraman gave him a look that would have silenced a lesser man or at any rate silenced a man with an ounce of sensitivity; but Norman continued

"Guess you want to know what will be filming?"

"If you think it would help" came the reply.

"Well Ricky Zit and the pustules are heading for number one this week but they can't be on the show because of a previous booking"

"In the drying out clinic?" suggested the recordist.

"Very droll" said Norman, looking as executive as his knitted cardigan allowed.

"They are in Hamburg for a week starting tomorrow so we need to film a sequence which will go with their song when it is played on the show next Thursday."

"Is that *Squeeze it baby, Squeeze it?*" asked the assistant cameraman. He was young, about 23, and Norman sensed that he might have at last found an ally amongst the crew.

"That's the one," said Norman and tried to look both important and avuncular to the enthusiastic youth.

"So what are you going to get them to do?" It was the cameraman again.

"Well as the song is called *'Squeeze it Baby* I thought it would be fun it we filmed them..."

"Squeezing into a phone booth, a mini car, a lift, a boat on the river," interrupted the sound recordist.

"Well yes." said Norman, "How did you guess?"

"I'm the seventh son of a seventh son, the whole family are gifted with second sight and with it comes the mysterious ability to predict the fucking obvious".

"First things first", said the cameraman, "How long is the song?"

"'bout four minutes'"Norman replied.

"Well we are going to have to shift if we are going to film enough footage of them making tits of themselves before knocking off time." What the cameraman said was certainly true, if somewhat unhelpful, Norman thought.

"And we can't film with them after four thirty." added Norman.

"Why not?"

"They've got to do a run through and sound check at the Granada, ready for tonight's concert."

"Well we best get started then, so what I suggest is..." The cameraman's comment was interrupted by a peel of girlish laughter coming from the vicinity of the lift. It wasn't that vein of laughter, as described in Victorian novels, which sounds like the tinkle of crystal glass. It was female, for sure, but it sounded more like a crate of beer bottles being chucked down a slag heap. Norman recognised it as the sound of his recent sleeping partners in full cry.

''ere, Norm," said the leading lovely, "Ricky says to tell you that he's feeling like shit so would it be ok to abandon the filming."

"No it bloody well wouldn't. Hang on fellahs I'll have to go and sort this out." With that Norman headed back up the stairs.

"Good to be working with professionals," said the camera-man.

"And great to really feel wanted," added he recordist.

The cameraman turned to his assistant. "Have we got any fast stock in the car, Dave?"

"Three rolls of 800 left over from last week's job," Dave replied, "but surely they'll want this filmed in colour?"

"Maybe," mused the cameraman, "But I've got an idea that might well bail us all out of the shit and get us all home by a reasonable hour."

Chapter 16.

A Surprise Encounter.

Ken Davis, the cameraman was, in fact, not quite as miserable a man as Norman had first assumed. Like so many film cameraman, he was a frustrated director and he now saw a chance to take over the shoot. Of course Norman would have to go along with the idea, but as the minutes ticked away and all that could be heard from the rooms above was Norman and Ricky Zit arguing in increasingly obscene circles, Ken felt pretty confident that his solution to the problem of 'what to film?' would be gratefully accepted.

"Back in a minute, folks," he said and went upstairs to find Norman.

Ken Davis' plan was practical enough. He suggested that there was simply not enough time before the four o' clock band call to film enough material to illustrate the whole song; so why not film four simple 'squeeze it' sequences (the boys with a group of girls in a lift, the boys with a group of girls in a phone box) and then shoot the lads performing their song at the band call. The on stage stuff would have to be in black and white because of the lack of light, but intercut with the colour 'squeeze it' shots might look almost trendy.

At first Norman wasn't sure, not because it wasn't a good idea, simply because it wasn't his idea. So Ken explained to Ricky Zit that if they didn't hang about they could get all the squeeze it shots in the can by lunch time and then the group could have a couple of hours sleep before the band call at 4p.m. That was the clincher. Ricky Zit and the Pustules went for it like a shot, so Norman went along with the plan too. It wasn't his idea and that really rankled with him but then, as he thought about it, he had to admit that as he hadn't got any plan himself Ken's idea was worth a try. In any case, if the film worked no one need know it wasn't another of Norman's great 'off the wall' ideas.

At last the filming got underway. Norman bribed the hotel manager to let them use the lift for half an hour so the first location was not exactly an effort for the exhausted pop stars to reach. There was a phone booth immediately outside the hotel so that, conveniently, provided the second location.

Two separate incidents at the first two locations had the strange effect of bringing Ricky Zit and the Pustules to a closer relationship with Ken and Crew whilst simultaneously distancing Norman from all of them. It was quickly noticeable that as the hangovers of the previous night wore off, the effect of last night's drugs wore off and the effect of this morning's drugs wore on, the group became much easier to work with and indeed almost jolly. The lift sequence was easy enough to conceive. The group all squeezed into the life together with all the girls who had 'slept over' in the hotel room. It was Dave the camera assistant who suggest that it would funnier if the sequence was to' build' and it would also be easy enough to film. His idea was this: the lift doors open to reveal the lads in the lift, not much room but just about ok. The doors shut and open again to reveal the boys but this time there is a whole lot of luggage in there with them; the doors close when they open for the third time the girls are in there too and it is really crowded.

"What about the fourth time?" asked Norman rather sarcastically, "There are four *'Squeeze Its'* in each chorus remember. He was glad to be able to make some small attempt to regain his authority, it seemed to him that the whole day was no longer under his control.

"Oh just close the doors and don't open them until we say we're ready," said Ricky. "Will give you something to laugh about."

When the doors opened on the final tableau Ken laughed so much he nearly lost control of the camera. Norman was dumb-struck. Ricky had persuaded the girls to strip down to their panties and three of the group were naked, their genitals artistically concealed behind bits of luggage here or a girls leg there. As for Ricky, only his head and shoulder were on show, the rest of him hidden behind a girl laying on top of one the suit cases.

"Exactly what in the name of thunder is going on here?" The crew's laughter was stilled by a voice of terrifying authority. They all turned to see the large figure of a red faced man in his sixties, sports jacket, grey flannels, very much a golf club member.

"Now, before I call the police, I should very much like to know who is in charge here?"

Norman hesitated for a moment, but there was no question that he was and he certainly couldn't afford to lose anymore face with his cast and crew.

"I am Norman Marks, BBC film Director for *'Ready Steady Rock!'*, now what on earth do you want to call the police about?"

"If you can't guess then I'll tell you. I have been waiting on the top floor for more than half an hour for the lift to come, when I finally decide to walk down the eight flights of stairs I find that the lift has been commandeered for the purpose of shooting a pornographic film."

"Oh come now," said Norman, "I'm sorry if we inconvenienced you but this isn't pornography; it is just a comic sequence for next Thursday's programme. Besides, why didn't you walk down the stairs sooner?"

"If you could but tear your gaze from this orgy which you purport to be directing, you might have noticed that the reason I was reluctant to descend that many stairs is that I have wooden leg."

"Oh, well I am sorry", said Norman.'

"We all are," Ken added for moral support.

"I lost my right leg at Monte Casino," came the old soldier's proudly cold reply.

"Blimey, that was a hell of bet," said Ricky somewhat tactlessly.

"Monte Casino, you depressingly ignorant hooligan, is not a gambling house! It was in fact, the site of one of the bloodiest battles of the Second World War."

"Actually general, I did sort of know that 'cos my dad was in the eighth army so he was there too. I just thought you needed to lighten up a bit."

"My God," thought Ken, "this kid is more than just a spotty face."

Unfortunately Rick's attempt to lighten the argument was unsuccessful. The man did not lighten up at all; instead his face became even redder and it looked as if only a heart attack could actually prevent him from bursting into flames.

"So this is the thanks my generation gets for all the sacrifices we made as we gave our lives and limbs for the freedom of the world?"

"Oh, if you want us to say thank you then of course we will," Ricky was still trying to be conciliatory.

"I don't want your thanks."

"The trouble is that your idea of freedom and ours ain't the same, that's the trouble with freedom it doesn't come with an escape clause." Ricky was suddenly revealing an intelligence that was usually dulled by an excess of decibels and dope.

"Young man I am not entirely acquainted with details of the International Declaration of Human Rights, but I am reasonably confident that that the right to perform acts of group fornication in a public lift is not listed amongst them."

The argument was now getting beyond Norman and was also taking up a lot of time, he decided to intervene.

"Well let's agree on that then, we are sorry to have inconvenienced you, sir, but we really must get on. If you fancy a coffee please charge one up to our account." Norman smiled in a way which he hoped made him look swathe, executive and assertive; it didn't.

"I spurn your hospitality, sir, just as I despise you; now let me pass." With that the infuriated old soldier shoved past Norman and in so doing managed to swing the end his artificial of leg sharply into one of Norman's shins. Of course it might have been an accident.

"Oh Fuck!" screamed Norman, sounding less suave than before and by the time the violent pain had subsided, and

Norman was able to declare that it was time to change location, the self-righteous old uniped was seated comfortably in the hotel drawing room, where noticing the exorbitant cost of a late breakfast, he compromised the standards of a life time, ordered the most expensive one and charged it to Norman's account.

As planned, the next location was the phone booth opposite the hotel. It didn't take very long to get set up and be ready to start filming; the problem was 'what to film?' The guys and gals squeezed into the booth, obviously, but after that, unlike the lift sequence, it didn't really offer much potential to develop. In the end they decided to the best they could with shots of faces pressed hard against the glass pane of the booth, arms and legs sticking out of the door, Ricky on the phone with a pair of feet sticking over his shoulders; it was Ok but they needed more.

"Pity we can't do a shot panning over everyone in the booth all squashed up in odd positions but all on the phone, I mean each with their own phone handset.' Ken was being creative again and Norman hated it. Norman was just about to dismiss the idea as 'lovely but impossible as we haven't got the props for it,' when the bass player, he of the designer underwear and damaged genitals, spoke up.

"There's a *bric a brac* shop just round the corner, I was in there yesterday looking for classic 78's. Anyway he's got a few old phones for sale. Bung him a fiver and I'm sure he'd let us borrow them."

Before Norman could come in with a patronising put down Ricky was in there. "That's great Danny, you get round there and see if you can get them. Anyway I'm dying for a pee, OK to take five, Norm?"

"Yes OK, but only five minutes everyone." Norman hated being called Norm almost as much as he hated the fact that everyone seemed to be having ideas except him but at least Ricky asked permission before calling for a break and, what was more, he seemed to be enjoying making the film. In fact when Norman thought more closely he realised that things were not going too badly at all, in fact, apart from the throbbing pain from his shin, everything was fine.

A few minute later Danny was back carrying a box which contained three old standard phones and a candlestick one.

"He's an OK bloke," said Danny. "Asked us to be careful with them especially this old funny one," he pointed out the candlestick phone. "Worth a bit," he said.

"They sure are," it was Ron the sound recordist. "Tell you what, when we finish here I'll take them back and make him an offer for it."

"Sure" said Danny.

"You film lot ain't 'alf weird," said the gangliest of the girls.

"And recordists are the weirdest of the lot," said Ken.

"Tell you another thing the blokes got in his shop," said Danny, "a huge old fashioned mangle like you'd see in a museum."

"Well?" said Norman'.

"Well don't you get it?" said Danny. "Squeeze it ...Mangle, we could do some stuff with us squeezing funny things through a mangle. We need another sequence and it's just round the corner."

"Fine that's our next location, then," said Norman realising that it was necessary to appear enthusiastic, "But come on folks we've got one more shot to do here first, so back in the phone booth all of you." His voice trailed away as he turned to see what everyone else had already noticed - the phone booth was no longer vacant. It had been occupied by a large woman, of fearsome aspect, who was engaged in a heated conversation. It seemed that she would never leave the booth; but only half an later the cast and crew were moving location once more, to the shop which had the mangle, having completed their final shot of the phone booth sequence ; boys and girls crammed in tight and all speaking on different phones. Ken said it looked very funny and Ricky was delighted with it too. Norman might well have been more enthusiastic about it had he not gained a large bump on the head to add to the pain in his shin. This, second injury, was received when the large lady hit him over the head with her umbrella. Three times he had, impatiently, opened the door of the booth and asked her how much longer she would be. As she was Polish, and hadn't got a very strong grasp of English, she had completely misunderstood Norman when, at the third attempt, he had offered her five quid for her time.

It was, therefore, with some trepidation that the injured director approached the mangle sequence; unlike his cast and crew, who were now getting on well together. Neither group had been expecting to enjoy the day but now they were sharing jokes and ideas and generally having a good time. If they were honest the group were enjoying the fact that, whilst they were still working, they were doing so without enduring 90 decibels in each ear'ole. It all made for a pleasant change. As for Ken Davis and his crew; they had been expecting a ghastly day of being buggered about by a gang of drugged up spotty oiks whilst being directed by an ineffectual twerp. Well, the group was spotty, but for the time being they were not drugged up and they were certainly proving to be very co-operative and even creative. Norman, of course, was exactly what the crew expected but he was so easily side-lined that it wasn't really a problem.

"Well there it is," said Danny as they arrived at the *bric a brac* shop. He pointed to a huge Edwardian cast iron mangle.

"Blimey", said Ken, "that's a monster. Great, eh Norman?"

"Oh yes groovy." said Norman, but he didn't sound very convinced. The truth was that having already suffered a kick in the shins and crack on the head he was wondering if the 'rule of three' principal was going to apply. He couldn't help but remember the lyrics of the old song. Norman never had had his bollocks in a mangle and he was determined that he would complete directing the next sequence without adding that particular sensation to his catalogue of life's unusual experiences.

"Is it OK to move the mangle out into your yard?" Ken asked the shop keeper. "It is all a bit cramped in here."

"Fine but do be careful, it weighs a ton." Reggie Cowell, the shop keeper was proving to be a real darling, and loved the idea of having a TV crew in his shop.

"It'll be fine with three of us lifting," said Reg, "Then I'll put the kettle on. I expect you could all do with a cup of tea?"

"That would be lovely," said Norman, "and you wouldn't happen to have a couple of aspirins?"

The tea and biscuits that Reggie provided were very welcome; Norman had hoped that the break in operations might give him a chance to think of, at least, something that they might do with the damn mangle. So far every idea they had filmed that day had been someone else's idea but twenty minutes soon passed, the cups and plates were being collected up and Norman had still no ideas in his head at all. He tried a despicable ploy.

"Well I have a few wacky ideas about what we can do with this baby," he said confidently tapping the mangle, "but I don't want to be selfish. If any of you have thought of anything well, let's hear it and I'll see if we can use it." A glance passed between Ken and, recordist, Ron but Norman was too busy trying to look executive to notice.

"How about we are squeezing at lot of funny old underwear through the mangle?" This idea came from Tracy, the girl who Norman had thought he was shagging the night before only to realise that she was having a fag break on the other side of the room.

"Well I suppose we could do that," said Norman, "But where would be get funny underwear from at short notice?" The instant that the words had left his lips he regretted what he had said.

"Well, there's your undies for a start Norman. Blimey you don't get much funnier than them."

"How come you've seen Norman's undies?" Ken asked with a smirk.

"Well there was a bit of confusion last night," Norman stammered, "I went into the wrong the room."

"Well for someone who went into the wrong room you didn't half stay for a bleeding long while."

"The truth is, Ken," said Ricky, "the truth is, that last night we had a gang bang."

"Only Norman didn't know if he was coming or going," Tracy added, somewhat vindictively.

"You bastards," yelled Norman in genuine rage." I thought that we had all agreed to keep that quiet."

"I don't remember that anyone was particularly quiet," said Danny, "especially not you Norm."

"I…,I…, You…, You…," Norman stood there spluttering and the more he spluttered the more obvious it became that Tracy and the others were telling the unvarnished truth. Why Norman should not want Ken and the crew to know about the seedy events of the previous night, Norman didn't quite know himself; but he didn't and he was determined to look innocent if at all possible.

"It's a damned lie." said Norman and he turned towards Danny. It was the turn that proved to be his undoing because Norman had not realised just how close his genitals were to the substantial winding handle of the mangle. It was long, it was made of oak and it was now heading towards Norman's bollocks at thirty miles an hour. The impact was to have a dramatic effect on the rest of the day. Norman let out a bellow and sank to his knees as a red mist swirled before his eyes.

"Oh my Goodness," said Reggie the shop keeper, "you'd best come with me." And so it was that while Norman sat upstairs on Reggie's comfortable sofa, drinking tea, Ken and Ricky got on with directing and shooting the mangle sequence. Luckily Reggie was able to supply a range of comic under garments which he had gathered over a life time of house clearances, quite why he had kept them all was a bit of a puzzle but it would have been churlish to ask. The important thing was that Reg was able to supply all the props they needed and tiny bras were filmed being fed into one side of the mangle while huge ones, of Zeppelin proportions, emerged from the other side.

It was, by now, about a half past two so Ken suggested that they took a break. Ricky and the lads could have a bit of a rest before the band call at 4p.m. and the crew could have a breather too. Norman was told of the plan and agreed to meet them all at the Granada cinema.

'Do you think they'll let us film there?'" he anxiously enquired of Ken.

"I bet if you bung the manger twenty quid he'd let you graze sheep in the foyer." came the somewhat world weary reply.

At 3.30 Reggie, ever delighted to be of assistance, gave Norman a lift in his car to the Granada cinema. It was about a mile from the shop at the other side of town. In the car it took no time at all but for Norman to have walked that distance after his most recent injury would have been no easy matter. Norman did his best to seem interested in the running commentary which Reg felt obliged to deliver as they drove up the high street of the old market town. The statue of John Howard to their left, 'Who the fuck was he?' thought Norman; the Medieval buildings which the council planned to demolish next year to make room for some much need office space, until finally they turned right, opposite a statue of John Bunyan . Then the impressive edifice that was 'The Granada Bedford' came into view. As Norman got out of the car he suddenly felt very insecure. What if the manager told him to get stuffed? He couldn't face yet another humiliation. He stood there for a moment trying to work out what to say, when a small miracle occurred. As Reggie drew away a rather tatty old-fashioned charabanc pulled into the parking space. Writing on the side of the vehicle proclaimed the legend 'The Sister Snatch Shelter for the Very, Very Vulnerable'. The conveyance was being driven by a determined looking Nun, probably Sister Snatch herself. Her passengers were all rather sad and dowdy looking girls aged between about thirteen and sixteen, all that is except for one, because as the girls disembarked Norman noticed a person whom he had last seen in the *'Ready Steady Rock!'* studio; yes indeed, pressing himself generously into this clutch of excited maidens was none other than the celebrity disc jockey Jamie Servile.

Chapter 17.

<u>Acts of Charity.</u>

The frenzy of interest generated by the unannounced arrival of Jamie Servile was, in fact, to prove to be of great assistance to Norman. The jocular eccentric had hardly placed one foot in the Granada's foyer before the manger emerged from his office and started toadying around the charismatic Mr. Servile in a manner which would have done credit to a masochist at a sadist's convention. The man was so wrapped up in his determination to please that he paid little attention to Norman's request for permission to film and, thinking that Norman must be part of the Servile entourage, granted permission without further thought.

The truth was that Jamie Servile was on the scrounge. He hoped to lay his hands on thirty tickets for the concert. Sister Snatch explained to the manager that 'dear Jamie' was up from London 'on one of his charity visits to the shelter' when he spotted that there was a pop concert billed for that very evening at the Granada. He had promised the girls that he would use his influence to get them in for free. This put cinema manager, Fred Remnant, in a real dilemma.

"Oh this is awful, Jamie, really awful," Fred whined, "but the house tonight is sold out with at least seventy kids hoping for returns." This news came as a blow to Jamie as he was hoping for a few returns himself. He kept smiling but a look of malice came into his eyes and he tried to put pressure on the unfortunate Mr. Remnant.

"Oh well now Mr. Boss man, we know you're in charge, don't we girls? Oh yes you're the boss man alright but we can't have Jamie disappointing the girls now can we?"

Ricky and the group who had been setting up on stage heard a lot of loud conversation and giggling coming the foyer and decided to investigate so they left the auditorium and looked into the foyer. As soon as he clapped eyes on them Jamie Servile calculated his chances.

"Well how's about that then young ladies?" he leered, "this is Mr. Ricky and his group. They are the stars of the show and I reckon that if your uncle Jamie says he'll compere the tonight's concert for free, they'll find you some tickets alright. After all *'Squeeze it Baby, Squeeze it'*, is at number one this week but how long it stays at number one is anyone guess, eh guys ? That sort of thing all depends on how many plugs Uncle Jamie gives it on his radio show, doesn't it guys?" Again, the egregious smile on Servile's, less than lovely, face seemed less truthful than the sinister glint in his lupine eyes.

"Any chance of some comps?" Ricky asked, but poor Mr. Remnant could only repeat what he had already told the manipulative Jamie Servile.

Ricky realised he was in a spot. Ironically the last he thing he wanted was for Jamie Servile to present the show. The group was top of the charts and the Granada was sold out, they didn't need any other attractions to put bums on seats. Besides Ricky couldn't stand Servile, but the veiled threat to blacklist the group on radio had not gone un-heeded. Ricky needed a' let out'.

At this point Ken and the crew arrived and started to carry in the camera equipment; Ricky noticed that the girls seemed very excited to see to see all the film gear as it emerged from its' shiny silver cases

"Well, perhaps if they can't come to the concert, the girls might like to stay and see Norman film the band call?" he suggested.

For a moment Jamie looked sour, but the suggestion was greeted by so much excitement from the girls that he quickly decided to go along with the idea.

"Of course we will have to ask our director's permission," said Ricky with a look of appeal and a wink towards Norman.

Norman, who had been feeling very side lined by events was delighted to be suddenly centre stage and taking a huge draw from his *disque bleu* and brushing the ash from his cardy, smiled his most toothy grin. "Well Ricky, if the young ladies promise to be very good and to do just what they are told, then I think I can allow that." Ricky exchanged another wink, this time to Ken.

"Oh it's Mr. BBC man, how's about that then ladies, Mr. BBC man will let you watch him film Ricky and his group, maybe you'll get into the film too."

"I'm sure we can fix that," said Norman, flaring his nostrils and feeling that something like status was returning to him at last.

While Ken and the crew got the gear set up in the auditorium Norman accepted Cyril Remnant's invitation for a drink in the manager's office. Sister Snatch joined them and proved to be no shrinking violet when it came to downing generous quantities of the amber liquid.

Cyril was disappointed that Jamie didn't also join them but the considerate D.J. said that he would be happy to show the girls some interesting things back stage.

As Cyril's whisky oiled the wheels of conversation, Norman plucked up the courage to ask how Jamie Servile had become involved with the Sister's home for the very, very, vulnerable. In a lilting brogue the good sister told the astonishing tale of Jamie Servile's acts of charity.

"Oh, to be sure the man is practically a Saint," she enthused, "It is not just my shelter he supports but dozens of homes up and down the country. There's the Father O'Fiddler Lodging for Lapsed Lolitas in Liverpool and the Malcolm MacMaul Bothy for Boys in Bother... oh there are lots of others. I wrote to him three years ago, asking if he would come and open our annual fete and, bless him, he did, so he did. The fete only raised a few hundred pounds but Jamie said, then and there that if I was to let him visit the girls on a regular basis he would do his damndest to get it up."

"And has he?" asked Norman.

"Oh that he has for sure, there's a tidy little sum in our bank account these days."

"How does he get on with the girls?" It was Norman again, trying to sound as innocent as he could.

"Oh, for sure he's been a marvellous influence. I had three really difficult young madams. They were all hell bent on getting in to show business or some such nonsense, but Jamie made them see sense, it only took a couple of private meetings with him for them to completely change their minds. Now two of them want to join the police force and the third one plans to become a martial arts instructor."

Ken put his head around the door. "We're ready for a take Norman, I've set up a close up of Ricky, I thought you'd want to do the whole song through once like that then, if they go through it again I can go hand held and grab shots of the others."

"Absolutely," said Norman who was feeling much better for Fred's whisky.

"After that, if there's time I'd like a couple of shots of the Sister's young ladies cheering and screaming."

"No problem governor" said Ken. "My God," thought Norman, "This is becoming like a real film shoot."

So the last part of the day's filming went off easily enough. Ricky and group went through the song twice which enabled Ken to follow his plan. The group's second song was not very different from their 'Hit' so, while Ricky and the gang were rehearsing Norman asked Ken to get what shots he could of drums being clouted and guitars being abused. He was pretty sure that images like that could easily be cut into *'Squeeze it Baby'* and no one would notice the deception. Now all the remained before Norman called 'Wrap' was to get a few shots of Sister Snatch's girls screaming and waving in true groupie fashion. The trouble was that six of the girls were nowhere to be found and, strange to relate, neither was Jamie. At last a stage hand heard some muffled cries coming from an old costume hamper back stage. Jamie had apparently suggest that he and the girls play a game of seeing how many of them could fit inside the hamper but they had got trapped when a stage hand had dumped a load of unwanted drapes on the top of it. Most of the girls didn't seem too upset though two seemed more ruffled than the others. The most surprising thing was that, for some inexplicable reason, Jamie Servile seemed to be developing a black eye. With everyone at last assembled it didn't take long to knock off a few shots of the frenzied fans. Norman even remembered to ask Ken to hold the camera upside down for few close ups, explaining what a hit the effect had been when he first used it on *'Ready Steady Rock!'*

Norman found that he was almost sad to announce, "Well everyone I guess that's a wrap."

It had all gone better than he had expected had certainly better than he deserved. Ken thanked Ricky, Ricky thanked Ken; everybody expressed the hope that they might work together again soon. "If we have to make another film for the programme Norman, the lads and I want you to direct it."

"That's great Ricky" said Norman "I'd love to."

"And we must have Ken and his crew too." Ricky added, 'Cos that way,' he thought, 'we will make the film just the way I want it.'

280

Chapter 18.

<u>Breaking Bread.</u>

Ron, the sound recordist, planned to drive back to London up the A6 .This took him straight past the Bridge Hotel and Norman was able to cadge a lift.

"Funny how Jamie got that black eye," said Norman, as they set off.

"Hilarious I reckon," said Ron.

"No" Norman continued, "mean I don't understand how it happened. Still if you play silly games with a bunch of giggling girls I suppose anything is possible."

"And that's what he was counting on," said Ron.

"Any rate he decided not to *compère* the concert, he couldn't appear on stage with a shiner."

"I don't suppose that news broke Ricky's heart." said Ron. "Well here we are Norman, the Bridge Hotel, door to door service. I hope the film works out OK. See you around mate."

Norman watched as the unit car drove off towards Luton and he wondered what to do for the rest of the evening. He could just pay the bill and head back home to London, it was only half past six and there was a seven thirty five express from Bedford to St Pancras; on the other hand he hadn't got any food in at his flat and the injuries of the day were persuading him that a hot bath would be a very good idea, especially if followed by a meal in the Hotel restaurant. It was supposed to be pretty good. The only trouble was that he didn't feel like eating alone. As he entered the hotel reception he had an idea; Reggie Cowell. He hadn't wanted any money for allowing them to film with the mangle and he was obviously very star struck by having a film unit in his shop. He would make an ideal dinner guest. Norman could charge it all up to hospitality expenses and Reggie would lend a keen ear to all Norman's stories about his glamorous career at the BBC. It would be perfect; Norman could exaggerate and invent as much as he liked and Reggie would believe every word of it.

Norman took a bath almost immediately after he got back to his room, he was tired and still aching from the various injuries he had received during the day. He lay in the hot water and gradually felt the pains ease a little. Then he started to regret asking Reggie for dinner. Why ever did he think that was good idea? Surely this would have been a great time to find some wide eyed groupie and seduce her over a romantic meal taken in the Bridge Hotel's fading splendours. But now he had spoiled all that, he had asked bloody Reggie. A stabbing pain in his genitals suddenly reminded him of the encounter with the mangle handle and then he thought that, perhaps, he had made the right decision after all.

The truth was that he was very sore and in no condition to face another session like last night's orgy. No, Reggie it would be, and a lot of boastful lies from Norman about his hugely glamorous career and prodigious sex life.

He towelled himself dry and then dressed in, what he imagined was, his 'executive look' outfit. This was smart sober brown suit and contrasting, loudly coloured, yellow shirt with a green silk tie. Norman had seen some of the senior journalists on the late night current affairs show wear similar schmutter and he was convinced that he looked exactly the part in his version of the ensemble. As you will have guessed, he was badly mistaken for, in Norman's case, the suit was some-what past it's best and the shirt and tie not only clashed horrendously with each other they also clashed with Norman's sallow skin colour and his large yellow teeth. The overall effect was revolting but Norman was convinced that the dissonance between the suit shirt and tie looked the very essence of 'Media hip.'

He applied rather less Aramis after shave than usual for fear that Reggie might think he was a poof, but even so, he was more liberal with it than was prudent.

At a quarter to eight Norman headed for the bar, where he had asked Reggie to meet him. In fact when he arrived in reception Norman found Reggie standing in the middle of the hallway looking rather lost. He was wearing a suit which, though of much better quality than Norman's, was obviously not his own. Presumably, Norman thought, it was another of Reggie's house clearing trophies. The biggest 'give away' was the fact that the trousers were too short and Reggie's choice of white silk socks unfortunately emphasised the sad fact. Both men were convinced that they had dressed up well for the occasion whereas, in fact, a costume designer would have been proud to come up with two such outfits for a production of *'Guys and Dolls'*.

Norman had decided that as every expense that night would be charged to the BBC so he did not hesitate to buy the first round. While Reggie found a comfortable spot in a discreet alcove Norman went up to the bar. There he was more than a little surprised to find Sister Snatch in the company of an overweight Catholic priest. Norman had never been much of a judge of character but simply looking at the prelate was enough to make him feel uneasy. Tiny bright blue eyes peered out of a bloated red face that brought to Norman's mind the image of a scrubbed pig. However it would not do to appear to be impolite.

"Good evening, Sister," said Norman, "What a pleasant surprise. "Oh 'tis the man from the BBC, to be sure it is," came the saintly sister's smiling reply.

"And this is Father Cummings, our local Parish priest," she added, indicating the pig in the cassock.

"Delighted to meet you, Father," said Norman. "Now can I buy you a drink?"

"Well that would be most kind" said Father Cummings, "A pint of Guinness and a Campari soda please."

284

"Bar-man", said Norman, sounding as 'executive cool' as he could. "I'd like two gin and tonics, a pint of Guinness and a Campari soda, thank you."

Norman paid for the drinks and then made his excuses. "Now please forgive me but I must re-join my friend Reggie Cowell; he was incredibly helpful with our filming today so I am buying him supper."

"Oh don't mind us," said sister Snatch, taking a large slurp of her Guinness, we are just here for a little celebration of our own. We don't drink here every night you know!"

Norman laughed politely. "What is the celebration?" he enquired.

"Oh that lovely man Jamie Servile has just donated £4000 to the new orphanage shower rooms." The lilting voice of Father Cummings seemed strangely at odds with his appearance. "'Jamie's joining us here later, just as soon as he gets out of A&E. He injured his eye backstage at the cinema, you know."

"Oh yes, indeed," said Norman, "Well good luck with it all," and he moved across the room to join Reggie.

The small talk exchanged between Norman and Reggie over their gin and tonics did not really provide promise of a fascinating evening to come. Reggie was all too keen to talk about his past life, living with his mother and coping with her loss. She had run their business very much as a respectable antique shop but after her death Reggie found it increasingly difficult to find enough real antiques and so the *bric a brac* end of the market gradually took over.

He had seemingly endless tales of the odd things he found during his house clearing exploits. For a moment Norman's interest was roused by the hope that some items of salacious naughtiness were about to spice up the tale but, with revelation that principal among these items were the old phone and the mangle used in the film, Norman's interest took a distinct dive and he was much relieved when the waiter arrived to announce that their table was ready. As they crossed the bar and entered the dining room Norman resolved that as soon as they had started into the first course he would take over the conversation and steer it towards his fictitious sexual encounters. Norman was confident that his stories would be much more interesting; they would not be about doting mothers, old fashioned telephones, and cast-iron mangles but about leggy girls in red leather boots, knickers on dressing room floors and alternative uses for Mars Bars. Most importantly, they would be about him.

Half way through the first course Norman felt the moment had arrived.

"Reggie, you seem to be a bit smitten by the world of television, would you be interested in hearing a few bits of 'behind the scenes' gossip?"

"Oh yes Norman, I certainly would but just before that could you answer one question for me?"

"Of course I will, if I can," said Norman sinking back in his chair with a patronising smile.

He took a bet with himself about which question it would be; "What is the clapper board for? What does a Grips do? What is a Matt shot?" He had just settled on the riddle of the clapper board when Reggie asked his actual question.

"Tell me Norman, do you believe in the redemption of world by our Lord Jesus Christ?"

To say that you could have heard a pin drop would be un-truthful. What you could hear drop was the spoon with which Norman was eating his prawn cocktail. He dropped both it and it's' contents all down his green silk tie. Several answers of a decidedly un-Christian nature came into his mind but he managed to suppress them.

"Or to put it another way," Reggie continued, "have you ever felt that you have been saved?"

"Oh yes," Norman replied, "quite recently, as a matter of fact."

From that point on the evening held no pleasure for Nor-man whatsoever. Reggie on the other hand seemed to be-come increasingly possessed with the fires of evangelism and, well before the dessert trolley had made its' sticky ap-pearance, he had held Norman spell bound with his disser-tation on how Saint Paul's second letter to the Corinthians could provide invaluable guidance in the running of a house clearing business. A look gradually came into Norman's eyes which Reggie believed could be the dawn of new spirituality. In truth it was the onset of catatonic boredom which was so chronic as to lead to Norman considering self-harm with some of the cutlery. He was therefore much relieved when riotous gales of laughter announced the arrival of Sister Snatch, Father Cummings and Jamie Servile. They were pushing their luck, as it was well past the kitchen's closing time but of course Jamie's celebrity, as well as his life- long commitment to charitable deeds,

ensured that they received full and obsequious service. Indeed, the nasty black eye he had just had treated at the local hospital only occurred as a result of his good-hearted playfulness with the girls from Sister Snatch's hostel.

"Just my luck," thought Norman, "I am stuck here with this religious nutter while, just across the room, two religious pros are having a great time with a famous celebrity."

In that moment, with half his mind numbed by Reggie's mindless wittering and the other half stimulated by his envy of Jamie Servile's celebrity, Norman made a decision. Somehow he was going to make a lot of money and enjoy a celebrity life style himself.

Chapter 19.

<u>Anxious Moments.</u>

In those distant golden days of the mid-1960s, a BBC director could claim first class travel on the railway. Most young directors travelled second class and pocketed the difference, but on that fine spring morning in 1967 Norman was feeling extravagant and, besides, he wasn't exactly young anymore. He settled into a comfortable, slightly faded, first class compartment which he shared with three self-important business men in slightly faded suits. The swinging sixties had still not conquered the senior staff of the city so Norman was only faintly amused by their umbrellas and bowler hats. He congratulated himself on how much better his job was than theirs but he wondered how much more they earned than he did. He spent the seventy five minutes it took the train to travel from Bedford Midland Road Station to St. Pancras pondering the point. His recent experiences with the world of Pop music had focused his mind on one important goal. He wanted to become rich; not comfortably wealthy, no, stinking rich. The more he thought about it the more determined he became and one thing he was sure of, he would not let wealth drive him into balmy religious pursuits like he had witnessed at Arch Angel's flat; neither would he be insanely generous with it, like Jamie Servile. No, Norman's wealth would be strictly for him and would be spent on life of indulgence. He had decided on that for sure as the train pulled in under the mucky wrought iron and glass canopy of St Pancras there was only one point on which he remained uncertain,

"How the hell was he going to make that sort of money?"

Norman was still deep in thought when he changed on to the central line at Oxford circus for a tube train to White City; but suddenly he was snapped out of his reverie by jolly voice.

"ello Norm, how's it going mate?" Norman looked blankly at the weaselled little man who was crushed in beside him before, with some effort, he remembered who it was.

"Good Lord it's Bert Tyke isn't it?" he asked.

"Sure is," replied the weasel, "Long time no see eh, any rate Norm mate, how's tricks?"

"Oh fine thanks," said Norman, "I'm a director with the BBC now."

"Oh that's good, but I'd heard you were a film editor."

"Well I do I bit of both. I work on *Ready Steady Rock!*"

"Very interesting," said Bert, and Norman thought that he noticed a glint come into the eyes of his old time colleague.

Norman had seen that glint before. It was many years ago when Norman had got his first job as second assistant projectionist at a second class cinema in Watford, the Essoldo. Bert Tyke had been the first assistant and when the chief projectionist was off duty Bert had taught Norman some of the less legitimate tricks of the trade. The most useful of which was how to make the change overs between the reels of a feature film several minutes before the actual end of the reel. This practice could reduce the running time of an overlong film by as much as 15minutes and ensure that the projectionist did not miss the last bus home.

"The punters never notice and I've not seen a film yet that didn't benefit from being a bit shorter." Norman remembered Bert's very words and also the glint he had in his eye as he said them. Bert had changed a bit with the years, he had become more grey and shrivelled, but that glint had remained the same.

"So you've done alright for yourself since the old Essoldo days then" said Bert, more as a statement than a question.

"I suppose you could say that" said Norman trying to strike the right posture between modesty and pride. "But how about you, Bert? You look pretty successful yourself."

He didn't, in fact, but Norman was anxious not to be patronising.

"Oh I'm doing alright, you know, Norm."

"Chief projectionist somewhere now I bet?" said Norman, being very patronising indeed.

"Lord no, I gave up that mugs game when the old Essoldo closed, I'm in opticals now, you know, special effects. Got me own little firm in Acton."

"How did you get in that line?" asked Norman, genuinely impressed.

"Well bit of chance I suppose. I got a job at the Rank film laboratories, when the poor old Essoldo finally went under. I started as a projectionist, of course, running the rush prints and stuff. Then a vacancy came up in the optical department. I went for it and got it. Good old geezer ran the show, Fred Silk, he taught me a lot, titles wipes, mixes, speed ups, slow downs, freeze frames, any optical trick you could think of, Fred knew how to do it; but then the poor old sod had a stroke and had to give up."

"So you took over?"

"Did I fuck! No, the bloody management got in some creep form another lab to run the department. He couldn't stand me and I couldn't stand him. He was all for change; wanted to throw out all Fred's wonderful old machines and buy in a whole range of new kit. Eventually he persuaded the management to go ahead, it cost a fortune. When I heard that all the old gear was going for scrap I bunged the driver twenty quid and told him to deliver it all to my uncle's garage. About a month later I had it all up and running again and a month after that I was doing more business than Mr. Smart Arse back at the labs.'

"Sounds like a good move," said Norman, genuinely impressed. "Well here we are White City, this is my stop."

"We should meet for a drink sometime Norm, here's my card, and remember if you ever need any trick effects in a hurry then I'm you man."

"Sure will!" and, tucking Bert's card into his wallet, Norman got off the train.

It was, by now, about 10.30 a.m. but there was still a large number of BBC employees leaving the White City station and heading for the Television Centre, a short walk away, up Wood Lane. Some of this crowd would be shift workers but still a lot were mangers, whose hours were strictly 9.30 to 5.30. However it had long been the custom for senior office staff to start work an hour later and compensate by leaving an hour earlier.

Norman stopped at the zebra crossing. Wood Lane was always heavy with traffic and drivers were very reluctant to stop because the army of people waiting to cross held up the traffic for five or ten minutes at a time. Eventually the traffic lights up the road turned red so the motorists realised they had a wait on their hands anyway and reluctantly stopped to let a tide of the Nation's most gifted programme makers safely across. In its midst was Norman, still dreaming of a wealthy future. It was the blast from an impatient car horn that shook him out of his reverie and had the unpleasant effect of shifting his thoughts in an unsettling direction.

"Had he shot enough footage?" *Squeeze it Baby Squeeze it'*, had three verses and four choruses. The verses were covered by the black and white coverage of the stage performance in the Granada Cinema; but what about the' *Squeeze it'* choruses? There was the lift sequence, the phone booth sequence, the mangle sequence and, and.......And bugger all else!' Norman could see the sweet smell of success turning to dust before his eyes in a terrible flurry of mixed metaphors.

He was in something of a sweat by the time he had reached the large white iron gates of TV Centre. Partly because he was now in a hurry to see the rushes of yesterday's filming, partly because he was now in a state of anxiety and partly because he was suddenly aware of the weight of his overnight bag. When he noticed who was on security duty at the gate his heart sank even lower, for it was George, the one armed commissionaire. George had been with the BBC since 1943.He had lost his right arm at Dunkirk and with it his ability to be courteous to anyone who he felt it safe to bully. As a consequence senior Managers talked of him as 'Good Old George' and enjoyed his fawning obsequiousness; whereas ordinary members of the BBC staff thought of him as an insufferably obstructive, one armed, old bastard. In other words George was 'a character'. Norman reached the gate.

"Where do you think you're going?" It was George at his most aggressive.

"I'm going to work," said Norman. "I work here."

"Well I ain't never seen you before."

"I can't help that," said Norman, "It doesn't alter the fact that I work here."

"Don't get insulting with me."

"I'm not getting insulting, I'm simply stating a fact."

"Smart arse eh? What have you got in the bag?"

"A change of clothes, it's an over- night bag.''

"Well that settles it, there's no sleeping on BBC premises, so you can piss off."

"I'm not going to sleep here. I stayed in a hotel last night on BBC business."

"Don't believe you."

"I work for' *Ready Steady Rock!*', and if you phone the pro-duction office they'll identify me."

Nowadays it is hard to believe that, in 1967, it would be another twelve years before the BBC issued identity cards to all its' staff but that was the case and it was this absurd situation that allowed commissionaires, like George, to gain such huge amounts of job satisfaction.

"*Ready Steady Rock!* Is that a new show?"

"Yes it is, been going a month now."

"Can you get me some tickets?"

"If you like but is very much a show for teenagers, pop music, you know."

"Oh that's alright sir, I can give them to my church's youth club."

"Oh well in that case, I'm sure I can get you some tickets."

"Thank you very much, sir. Sorry about the confusion, but I have my job to do, you understand?"

"Oh yes of course," said Norman and he set off towards his cutting room in the east tower, wondering if George was as much of a pain in the arse for the Church as he was at the BBC. Meanwhile George was wondering just how much money he could make by flogging tickets for *'Ready Steady Rock!'* on the black market.

Norman dropped his suit case in his cutting room and then went down to the projection area to see if his rushes from yesterday's filming had come back from the processing laboratories. He was in luck - they had and the Film Operations Manager was just about to view them. This was regular procedure. Every programme category, that used film, had its' own FOM who allocated film crews and film editors to the show and who viewed all the rushes when they came in from the labs. Norman went into the viewing theatre just as the projectionist was lacing up the film which he had shot yesterday.

"Oh hello Norman, good you're just in time. Everything go OK?" The FOM was a man called Fred Chapman, a rather crumpled looking man, in an ill-fitting suit. He smoked even more than did Norman and the theatre was heavy with full-tar fumes.

"Oh it all went smoothly, thanks," said Norman.

"Cameraman OK?"

"Well the crew was a bit awkward at first, but I soon won them round," "Good, good, well let's have a look at what they got for you, then; OK projection, run please." Fred sat his heavy frame back into his chair and lit yet another un-tipped coffin nail.

The film started to run and soon Norman was relieved to hear a few chuckles ruttling up from the depths of Fred's considerable bulk. The first of the nude shots in the lift hit the screen.

"My God Norm, I hope you've got a take which is a bit less revealing than that."

"Oh yes there are a couple more."

"You dirty old bastard." said Fred.

Well actually, the fact that they all got naked was not my idea; it was Ricky's, he's the leader of the group.'

"Oh, a raver then is he?"

"He is a bit, yes."

Fred took a drag on his cigarette as the second 'take' came on screen.

"Oh that's better," he said, "can't see any naughty bits on that one."

"That's why we did a second take."

"You know, if this group is going to be as famous as you say they are, you ought to make sure the labs send you the negative back as soon as you've made the show print . The scandal rags would pay a load to have that nude shot on the front page."

"Guess you're right," said Norman, wondering just how unprincipled he could allow himself to become.

Thirty minutes later, having viewed all the rushes, Norman was heading back to his cutting room on the second floor. He had the cans of film under his arm together with a transfer of the record of *'Squeeze it Baby'* which had been put on to magnetic film, for him, in the sound suite. With this track laced into the sound path of his editing machine he could match up the pictures for another cinematic triumph. As he approached the cutting room door he felt more and more uncomfortable because he was now quite certain that he had only got enough images for three verses and choruses, whereas the record repeated that last chorus. No doubt about it, he was in a jam.

By mid-day he had matched up some of the shots of the lads on stage with the record track and cut some of the lift shots together. They worked pretty well and he would have been excited by it all were it not for the problem of what to do about the final chorus. Just as he was about to light another *disque bleu* the door opened and Johnny Tudor hurried in.

"Hello Norman mate' how did it go? I hope it's good. The record has gone shooting up the charts, just like we said it would. Believe me, darlin', this group is going to be mega, mega. mega. Oh is this it?" Johnny sat himself down at the Steenbeck editing machine and switched on.

"Hang about,' said Norman, I only started cutting about an hour ago, you won't get much on idea from what's on there."

Some very grainy black and white images of the group on stage at the Granada came up on the Steenbeck screen.

"Hey what's all this, man?" said Johnny somewhat aggressively, "The show is in colour, now, you know."

"Of course I know," Norman replied, "But Black and White is trendy in Pop, ever since the Beatles made '*A Hard Days' Night*' and, anyway, it is only the verses that will be in black and white; every time we get to a chorus it will go into colour with stuff like this. Norman quickly laced up some of the phone box footage and ran it on the machine.

"Oh I see, I see, groovy, groovy man," said a much relieved Johnny, "I should never have doubted you. Well, got to dash Jamie Servile wants to see me about bringing in some special guests to the next show. Keep up the good work, Matey, and remember this one has got to be the bestest ever, cos Ricky Zit and the Pustules are 'where it's at', man. They are going Astral!" With that Johnny shot out of the room and back into the creative miasma that was television centre. Norman breathed a sigh of relief but he was sweating slightly, perspiration brought on by worry. What the hell was he going to do about the last bloody chorus? He dug in his inside pocket for the crumpled pack of *disque bleus* and his fingers touched on something other than the malodorous ciggies; it was a card, it was Bert Tyke's card. 'Bert Tyke, Opticals and Cinematic Effects.' Norman thought hard for a moment, then he reached for the phone.

Chapter 20.

<u>Coining It.</u>

The Globe Inn, Brentford, stood in Boston Park Road. This had once been a thorough-fare with several shops and good passing trade but since the widening of the A4 it had become a run down *cul de sac*. The Pub itself was a substantial building in the Edwardian, no nonsense, tradition of Public house architecture but now, like all the other buildings in the street, it looked neglected and definitely in need of a lick of paint. The shops were now all boarded up and several buildings had been demolished leaving spaces which were fenced off with tall corrugated iron sheets behind which large unkempt Alsatian dogs barked and planned their revenge on humanity. As Norman walked down Boston Park Road toward the pub he wondered why ever Bert Tyke had chosen this particular pub for their rendezvous. He also wondered what on earth those tatty corrugated sheets concealed that required such vigilant canine protection.' Whatever it is I bet it isn't legal' he thought to himself as he passed the last of the fences and reached the door of the saloon bar.

Once inside Norman found that he could relax. The grim exterior belied the welcoming atmosphere of the Globe. It certainly wasn't grand but the furniture was comfortable;

a few leather sofas, but mainly bentwood chairs set around three legged cast iron 'Britannia' tables. The theme of the pub seemed to be boxing. There were many old photos of long forgotten champions and pre-war posters advertising bouts involving such legends as Johnny Curly, Benny Lynch and Don Cockell. 'Who the fuck were they?' thought Norman as he sat down at a table, near the door, and took the first sip of his pint. The beer was good and the landlord, a big bruiser of a man, had been friendly enough. Perhaps the evening might prove to be enjoyable? After a couple more swigs Norman got to thinking. Bert had already agreed to make a whole host of opticals in double quick time to eke out the lack of footage for the last verse of *'Squeeze it baby'*. It was a desperate ploy, but then Norman was desperate and the solution on which he had decided was to make the last verse a montage of shots from the previous three verses but to liven them up with a lot of optical trickery. Freeze frames, reverse printing, speed ups, shots bursting out from the middle of the screen to replace the image already there. In fact any trick that Bert might be able to create in the limited time available. Bert had already pointed out that the schedule was very tight, but he had agreed to go ahead. So why this mysterious meeting and why pick such an obscure location for it? 'I hope to God he's not going to rat out,' Norman muttered into his beer.

"Hello Norm, sorry I'm a bit late, can I get you another?" Norman nodded as he was snapped back to normality by Bert's whirlwind entrance.

"Evening Derek, I'll have the usual please and the same again for my mate."

"Why hello stranger," said the large landlord. "Good to see you again Bert, how's tricks?"

"Oh mustn't grumble, mustn't grumble, thanks Derek and have one yourself," said Bert as George handed him his drinks.

"Don't mind if I do, Bert, thanks. You are a scholar and a gentleman"

'Wrong on both counts' thought Norman as Bert carried the drinks to his table.

"This your local then?" Norman enquired as Bert settled himself into his chair.

"Used to be before I moved Chiswick" Bert replied.

"Funny sort of place," said Norman. "More like the East End."

"Yeah guess it is a bit: friendly though and nicely off the beaten track, good place for sorting out a deal, if you know what I mean?"

"Not sure that I do," said Norman. "What have you in mind?"

"Well you know all these opticals you want in a hurry?"

"Oh fuck Bert, you're not going to let me down?"

"Calm down Norm, of course not, you know me, anything for a mate."

"Well what then?"

"Well you want an awful lot of stuff and in a real hurry. I'm going to have stop work on some of my other clients work until I've finished yours."

"I guess so," said Norman, still uncertain about where the conversation was going.

"The trouble is that the BBC don't pay extra for fast service, they just pay the labs a flat rate, as you know, and a piss poor rate at that."

"Yes I know, but there's not much I can do about that is there? After all Bert, it's still a hell of a large order."

"Very true Norm, very true; my point is: would the programme notice if it was even larger?"

"What do you mean?"

"Listen up mate. The production people know sod all about film, right?"

"Right."

"And they think the sun shines out of your arse?"

"Well they are happy with what I've done for them so far, yes"

"Well here's what we do. I go ahead and make all your opticals but you tear up the original order and send me in a blank one that's dated and signed. You get the trick footage you need and the Beeb gets a bill for a few hundred quid more than the job is actually worth. Got it?"

"Well I don't know..."

"Say I overcharge by three hundred quid; I get one fifty and so do you, just like old times eh mate?"

"Well I'm not sure,"said Norman after a pause. "I really need some time to think it over."

"And time is the one thing you ain't got much of, matey," said Bert sounding slightly threatening for the first time that evening. "I would hate to have to let you down with your opticals."

Norman lit a comforting *disque bleu*. Suddenly he was back at the Essoldo, Watford, with Bert firmly in control.

"Ok then Bert, it's a deal, but I must have the opticals back by Wednesday at the absolute latest."

"Don't worry my boy, your uncle Bert won't let you down."

'For a bung of a hundred and fifty quid, I don't suppose he will,' thought Norman, but he was wise enough to say nothing.

For the next couple of days Norman had the devil's own job to keep the production staff out of his cutting room.

He had enough sense to realise that they would have no ability to imagine what the completed sequence would look, once Bert's opticals had been included into the final cut. In truth, Norman hadn't got much idea either but at least he knew what a freeze frame was and how reverse printing a shot could make almost any action look funny. Besides, Norman was counting on holding out showing the film to anyone until the last moment and if possible not letting a soul see it until it was played to the audience on Thursday's show. A studio full of screaming teenage kids would go mad for the film simply because it contained wacky shots of Ricky and the Pustules. Good bad or indifferent, there was no reason why the sequence shouldn't be another huge hit and by keeping Johnny Tudor and his team in suspense the sheer relief they would feel, after being presented with something even half competent, would very much assist Norman in maintaining his reputation as the genius film maker with his finger on the pop pulse of youth. It was and anxious time for all concerned, especially for Norman because he knew only too well that the inflated bill which Bert Tyke would send would be paid without a murmur if the film was a hit but there might be some awkward questions to answer if it was a flop.

By mid-day on Wednesday Norman was feeling pretty desperate. He had been down to the film dispatch office three times already to see if the opticals had arrived and he had left numerous instructions about how important they were and how he must be contacted the moment they arrived. The truth, as we know, is that Norman was certainly not the most gifted or fastest of film editors. The trick effects ultimately had to be cut into the final version of the sequence so that Norman could send it off for negative cutting and show printing overnight. The dead line for all that was about 8 pm.

At 2pm Norman's cutting room phone rang and the lad in film dispatch told him that a taxi had just arrived with two small cans of film for him. "That'll be them!" he shouted and nearly tripped over as he rushed for the stairs which lead down to film despatch, on the first floor.

"Sign here, please, Norman," said the lad in film dispatch. "Two 400ft cans from Bert Tyke Film Effects; can't remember ever having anything from them before."

"No," said Norman hurriedly. "They don't usually do work for the Beeb, commercials mostly, first rate outfit."

"And pricey too I bet." said the lad who seemed to know rather more about the film making process than Norman would have wished.

"Get what you pay for" snapped Norman as he dashed back to his cutting room.

The *'Ready, Steady, Rock'* production office was in even more chaos than usual that afternoon. There was always a lot of pressure for a weekly show on the day before 'studio day but with' *Ready, Steady, Rock'* it was worse. Sometimes the top groups would pull out at the last moment, sometimes a group, who had seemed to be going no-where, would zoom up the charts overnight. The group' OCD' had already phoned in ten times already to check their dressing room number and make sure that it had a minimum of two wash basins and Bernie Lines had ranted down Johnny Tudor's phone for twenty minutes. According to Bernie, the film which Marcus had made for Charlie Stash and the Pushers was 'a load of shit' and he was not best pleased when an exasperated Johnny Tudor said that in that case it must have suited the song quite well. Bernie huffed and puffed and threatened but he was badly shaken. No TV producer had ever been brave enough to speak to him like that before, he could see his power base slipping away. He must ensure that one of his groups had a number one hit in the very near future. There were two ways of achieving this; one was to find a good song (never very easy). The other was to screw the opposition and this was a tactic of which Bernie had some considerable experience.

As an exhausted Johnny finally managed to hang up on Bernie Lines he realised that he had still seen hardly anything at all of Norman's film. As predicted, Ricky Zit was now at number one and still climbing. The film had better be bloody marvellous. He was just about to go over to Norman's cutting room when the phone rang again and John heard the irritating staccato of Jamie Servile's Liverpudlian twang.

"Hello there Jamie, and how's my favourite D. J?" Johnny Tudor had been in show business long enough to be able to lie with convincing sincerity. Unfortunately on this occasion the strategy backfired somewhat as it only served to encourage Servile in his extravagant demands. He had phoned to remind Johnny that he needed 17 guest passes for tomorrows show. Sister Snatch, her mother superior and fifteen of the girls in their care would be arriving by coach. That issue had now already been dealt with but now Servile was demanding two extra dressing rooms, for the party, adjacent to his own.

"The girls will need somewhere to slip out of their uniforms," he explained to his disinterested producer, "and it would be good to have another room for meditation and prayer." Johnny Tudor was puzzled by this. Why couldn't the girls arrive already dressed in their party clothes and was there really a need for the extra room? He decided to console himself that Jamie Servile knew more about teenage girls' meditations than he did and probably more about maidens' prayers too.

"Ok Jamie, we'll fix two more rooms, must dash, see you tomorrow mate, bye."

In the cutting room Norman's, nicotine stained, fingers rushed with unusual speed over the lace up path of the Steenbeck editing machine. The roll of film which Bert Tyke had sent him was encouragingly large, Norman only hoped that it contained some images that would save the film. Norman checked the lace up, he didn't want any rip ups, then he paused; half out of fear and half out of an enjoyment of the frisson of anticipation, he decided to light up a *Disque Bleu* and take at least three puffs before he leant back in his chair and switched the machine to 'run'.

It took only a few seconds before he was puffing out smoke like a dragon, such was his excitement at the images before him. Bert Tyke had certainly done a wonderful job. Shots from the mangle sequence had been speed up and run forwards and backwards to great comic effect, shots in the phone box scene were compressed into a small ball and then sprang out again full size to reveal a new shot and shots of Ricky on stage at the Granada would suddenly burst into a sparkle of stars which, in their turn, became the faces of the other members of the group. Bert Tyke was obviously a genius and, what was even better, all the credit would go to Norman.

Chapter 21.

Drama Backstage.

As Johnny Tudor left Television Centre, that evening, he was not in the best of moods.

The day had not gone well for him. He'd had had a row with Bernie Lines, been mucked about by Jamie Servile but, most worrying of all, he had not been able to see the final cut of Norman's film version of' *Squeeze it Baby'*. Norman had already sent the cutting copy off for an overnight neg cut and print by the time Johnny had finally found time to go over to the cutting room. Jonny had pretended he understood when Norman banged on about 'Lab deadlines' and 'catching the night bath', but in truth, he hadn't the faintest idea what his film editor was talking about. Still Norman had insisted that everybody would love the film and that it would be the grooviest sequence the Beeb had ever transmitted. Johnny could only hope that this was even half true. Besides, Norman had not let him down in the past and though he looked faintly crazed and always exuded a rather unpleasant aroma of B.O. infused with strong French tobacco, Norman still had Johnny's confidence. After all, Johnny Tudor prided himself that he was no mean judge of men, he had sensed hidden depths in Jamie Servile's character long before Jamie had devoted himself to broadening the experiences of disadvantaged children. As he thought on he realised that in their different ways both Jamie Servile and Norman Marks were admirable characters; eccentric maybe, but fundamentally good hearted, decent and honest as the day is long.

As Norman headed for home, that same evening, he too was deep in thought. He had no doubt that the film would be a hit. Ricky Zit and the Pustules were becoming bigger every day. You couldn't open a tabloid newspaper or walk onto an underground station without seeing huge photographs of them surrounded by beautiful girls. Head-lines like 'Ricky Rocks 'em for Sex' or 'A tight Squeeze for our Ricky' provided a good indication that Norman's film would go down a storm in the studio. No it wasn't a fear of failure that was worrying Norman it was a fear of what would happen when Bill Tyke sent in his account. There was no doubt that the trick optical footage Tyke had supplied was quite brilliant, but that was a worry in itself. Even at the proper rate the cost of those effects would be astronomic, once Bert had doubled the charge it would be beyond belief, 'belief 'being the word which worried Norman most of all. He was glad to be heading for home.

As soon as he got back to his flat Norman poured himself a large gin and tonic. It had been a hard day, first the anxious wait for Bert's effects to arrive and then working under pressure to get them matched up to the music and cut into the final version of the film in time to catch the lab deadline. Still, now he could relax. Just one more call to the labs, perhaps, to make sure they had received the film and that the show print would be ready by tomorrow morning? Yes he would do that, then he could enjoy supper; something special to night he thought A Fray Bentos steak and kidney pie, with some frozen peas and instant mash. He had just finished a reassuring conservation with the contact man at the film laboratory and was reading the instructions on the Fray Bentos tin when the phone rang.

"Hi Norm mate, did you like em?" It was Bert Tyke.

"Oh hello there Bert yes I loved them, absolutely loved them. I've only just this minute got home and I was just about to phone you." lied Norman with conviction.

"They'll cost a bit mind you."

"Yes I realise that, any idea how much?"

"Well, what with inter-negs, high contrast matts not to mention printer time I guess about £1500, so let's settle for £2000, that's £250 each OK?"

"That's one hell of a bill, Bert."

"What's the matter Norm, don't you want to make a bit of cash?"

"Course I do but I don't want to be fired either."

"Look Norman we had a deal and if you're going to rat out now...." Bert Tyke was becoming aggressive.

If necessity can be the mother of invention, the same is equally true of desperation and indeed it was the latter which suddenly gave Norman the first inspired idea he had had in a long while.

"Calm down, Bert, I'm not ratting out, I am just thinking things through. You know how tight arsed the Beeb is about lab costs. If you send in a bill for £2000 they'll pay it, sure they will, but they'll have my guts for garters and put your firm on the black list."

"You never said anything about black lists when we met in the pub."

"I hadn't thought it through, then but I have now and I have had an idea; a bloody good one too."

"Well?"

"You say the actual cost of the opticals is £1500?"

"That's right"

"Well send in a bill for £1300."

"What?"

"Didn't you ever hear of a sprat to catch a mackerel? Look, after they see this film I'm bloody certain they will want me to shoot more films for the programme."

"With trick effects at two hundred quid less than cost I'm not bloody surprised. Get stuffed Norman."

"Hear me out, for God sake. I've told you before the production know the square root of fuck all about film making."

"So?"

Well if I make the next three or four films using hardly any optical effects at all, but use a lot of whip pans and tricks we can do on location, they won't know the difference. You do a hundred pounds worth of work and send in a bill four hundred and no one will suspect a thing. For some films you can send in a bill which has involved no work for you at all.

"I see, yes it's not a bad idea."

"The payments office won't get suspicious, they might even start encouraging other editors to use your services, but for every film I direct and edit we will each clear a couple of hundred quid."

There was a brief pause while Bert Tyke thought over the scheme.

"Ok Norm, you're on."

"Great, and tomorrow, when everyone is having an orgasm about your trick footage I'll be able to tell them how brilliant you are and how little you charge."

"And how clever you were to find me?"

"But of course."

315

Norman slept better that night than he had done for ages. The fact that he had managed to defuse the potential time bomb of Bert's bill was certainly one event that contributed to his deep slumber, the other was the bottle of Bordeaux-style Romanian merlot blend which he had downed with the Fray Bentos pie. He certainly felt refreshed when he awoke on Thursday morning and, after a breakfast of strong instant coffee and three ciggies, he set off for Television centre with a spring in his step.

Another BBC employee who journeyed cheerfully to work that morning was George, the one armed Commissionaire. He had volunteered to work a double shift that day but it was not the thought of the overtime that made George so cheerful ; it was the opportunities the new show *'Ready Steady Rock!'* offered for uncooperative obstruction. Lots of new Pop groups, their managers and roadies, all a bit nervous about their first time at the BBC, could therefore be easily intimidated by George's unique brand of unhelpful bloody mindedness. The fact that they all arrived in large limos helped too, making it possible to create the most spectacular traffic jams in the vicinity of the white gates of Tele Centre. Last week George had managed to grind most of Wood Lane to halt by eleven thirty; this week he was hoping to beat his record and bring Shepherd's Bush Green to a complete stand- still.

When Norman arrived for work at 9.40 George had been on duty for more than an hour and had already managed to create a traffic jam which stretched southwards back down Wood Lane as far as the junction with the Uxbridge road.

"You promised me some tickets."

"I haven't forgotten, I'll get you some today for next week's show."

"Well don't forget OK!" Norman couldn't help thinking how much happier George would have been if he had been born in East Germany but he said no more, hurried past, and headed across the executive car park towards main reception. A frantic beeping of horns caused him to turn and, to his surprise, he saw that it came from a very tatty coach which was trying to turn into the gates and making a terrible mess of things. George had stopped it much too late for it to be able to swing clearly into the entrance so, now that he had at last decided to let it through, the coach was having to back out into the road, adding to the congestion and confusion which was worsening by the minute. This was one of George's more sophisticated tactics and was working even better than usual as the driver was extremely inexperienced. Norman suddenly realised that he had seen that ancient vehicle before. It was Sister Snatch delivering her precious cargo of Jamie Servile's teenage guests for their exciting day of celebrity experience. Norman had about fifteen minutes before his film was due to arrive at film dispatch and he had intended to go grab a coffee in the' Blue Assembly' area outside the *Ready Steady Rock* studio. However the entertainment being provided by Sister Snatch's increasingly desperate attempts to negotiate a route through the gates was more than he could resist. He checked his watch and reckoned he could easily give it another five minutes and then go directly to film dispatch in the East Tower. The antics at the gate were really too good to miss. The problem could have been easily solved if George would only open the second of the two white gates; but that would be too simple and be contrary to every principle of bloody-mindedness in which he so fervently believed. The poor Sister, at the wheel, was reaching exhaustion point as she heaved the huge steering wheel of the ancient bus left and right. Her chief difficulty, apart from George's refusal to open the second gate was the build-up of traffic behind her. There was only about a yard of space between the back of the bus and the front of the nearest car behind it. It seemed to be an impossible task.

Then common sense reared its noble head. The door at the back of the coach swung open and a very large Nun stepped out and strode purposefully towards the second gate.

"Hey you can't open that, that's strictly for scenery lorries only!" George was at his most assertive.

"Well you can go to the devil you ghastly little gnome," came the saintly reply. "Now get out of my way unless you want to help me open the gate and save yourself from the fires of damnation." It was one of the most impressive confrontations Norman had ever witnessed and, as a crushed George helped the oversized sister to open the second gate, he decided it was time to go and collect his film. Yet he was puzzled; there was something familiar about that Nun but Norman felt sure he hadn't ever met her before.

In studio 6 the camera crew for *'Ready Steady Rock!'* were preparing themselves for another exciting day at the cutting edge of British Pop. The chief camera man, Ron, was reading a home improvements magazine and Dave, on camera three was trying to solve the telegraph crossword. The only member of the crew who seemed at all stimulated by the imminent prospect of eight hours of deafening cacophony was Terry, the youngest member of the team. Terry was a cable basher, and it was his job to see that the camera's heavy cables did not become entangled as they moved around the studio floor. Ron looked up from his magazine, just to check that the camera line up was proceeding on time. In the days before such adjustments became automated there was a period of about forty five minutes each day when the five electronic studio cameras were adjusted and matched for colour balance and exposure. Ron wondered why anyone should worry about such niceties on a Pop music show. The whole set would be flooded with every coloured light in the grid, so camera matching didn't actually matter a damn. Still engineering regulations had to be fulfilled. At ten thirty, sharp, the floor manager called, "Cameras please," and the crew immediately approached the inelegant, weighty, cameras which they would be shoving around the studio floor for the next eight hours.

At about that same time Sister Snatch finally found a place to park in one of the service roads that encircled TV Centre. The search for a space had been almost as stressful as the manoeuvring that had been required to get through the gates. By the time the coach finally came to a rest the girls on board had very definitely had enough and were longing to disembark. One or two of them had probably noticed the sign which said, 'Scenery Lorry Access, No parking at any time'; but Sister Snatch hadn't seen it and the girls were certainly not going to say anything that might cause further delay. They quickly formed up into a 'crocodile' and with Sister Snatch leading and the large Nun forming the rear guard they set off to find studio six. As they passed the entrance to East Tower who should they bump into but Norman? The film had arrived safely, he had checked it, marked it up for the studio and was heading over to deliver it to telecine. Sister Snatch recognised him at once and was grateful to have met with a familiar face.

"Why look girls, sure if it isn't the gentleman who directed the fillum." Norman was amused by her old Irish charm and flared his nostrils appreciatively.

"Now did it all come out alright for you?"

"Oh yes indeed Sister, I have it right here, I'm just taking it over to telecine now." Norman allowed himself a moment to enjoy her confusion. "A telecine is the machine which sends the pictures on the film to the studio," he explained, with restrained condescension.

"Oh well glory be, and there was me thinking that was a projector."

"Well in a sort of a way it is; but a very specialised one."

"Oh I see" said Sister, but she didn't really. "I was wondering; could you be showing us the way to studio six?"

"But of course, dear lady. Just follow me, I can take you there and then pop up to telecine afterwards, there's no rush, they won't be needing the film for a while yet."

"Sure tis a Godsend you are to be sure. Now say thank you girls."

"Thank you kindly sir." said the girls in chorus as they all dipped in a slight curtsey. Was there the faintest tinge of sarcasm in their tone? Norman assured himself that there was not.

In the gallery of studio six Johnny Tudor was definitely stressed, more stressed than usual at the start of a show recording day. Charlie Stash and the Pushers were threatening to pull out, so were OCD. The songs of both groups were slipping in the charts, so normally Johnny wouldn't have cared that much. But Ricky Zit and the Pustules, at number one, could not appear either. With that number of absentees the show was in danger of becoming a terrible disappointment for the viewers. Charlie Stash and OCD were both managed by Bernie Lines. Johnny felt sure that Bernie was hitting back after their row on the phone, yesterday.

"Joan, ask telecine if there is any sign of that bloody film yet." The production assistant jumped to her producer's command. "I want to see it as soon as they've got it laced up OK?"

"Right oh, Johnny and I've got Bernie Lines on the green phone, says he wants an urgent word."

"Ok, Ok, better see what he wants I suppose. Thanks Joan."

"Hi Johnny, show's looking a bit thin for tonight I guess?"

"Oh Hello Bernie, thanks for taking an interest."

"Well I just wondered if there was anything I could do to help?"

"What, after pulling your two top groups, you mean?"

"Now look Johnny, that's not fair. I didn't pull them, it's not me. OCD were pissed off last time because there were only four towels in the dressing room, when they had asked for four dozen and Charlie Stash won't forgive you for sending the B. team to make their promo film."

"Oh I see, and there was me thinking you were playing power games, Bernie."

Joan, who had been talking urgently on another phone slipped a piece of paper to Johnny, it read, 'Kaye Wye sends her love but says sorry she can't help you out, she is recording a new number with the Loubes tonight.'

"Bugger," said Johnny under his breath.

"What was that?"

"Oh sorry, Bernie, just some news in about studio guests." (Johnny could think quickly, when it mattered.)

"Is bloody Jamie Servile landing you with another bunch of waifs, then?"

"Er, yes part of his charity work." Johnny's heart sank even further, he had forgotten about the group which Servile had taken upon himself to invite to the show.

"Pity that there won't be much of a show for them to see then."

"So Bernie, how do you think you might get your lads to appear after all?"

"Ah, now you're talking sense mate. Well OCD are easy, just make sure that there are at least two dozen bars of soap in the dressing room and a shit load of white, and they must be white, towels. Charlie Stash will take a bit more persuading, but if you promised to have that hot shot film man make a movie for their new single, I think that would sort it."

"OK Bernie, you're on, have them here as soon as poss. OK? God knows we are far enough behind already."

"I'll do my best, Oh and make sure they get star dressing rooms OK?"

"Will do."

"Nice to do business with you Mr. Tudor, see yers later, bye."

Johnny put the phone down with a sigh. "Thank God that's settled. Right, Joan it's back to square one with the running order and we'll need some more star dressing rooms. Get on to it, will you love?"

"I'll call facilities right now because the studios are pretty busy today. Oh look the film has arrived." Joan pointed to the telecine monitor where the number 10 on the film leader had just appeared.

"Maybe we might have a show after all, " said Johnny. "Get them to run it right now please."

As he left the telecine, having delivered the film personally to the operative, Norman was feeling very pleased with himself because he had also found the time to deliver Sister Snatch and her charges into the safe hands of the Floor Assistant. He was Nick, a slightly camp young man, in charge of taking performers to their dressing rooms and calling them to the studio when required. It was not usual for visitors to be given dressing rooms, but Nick was getting used to the fact that working on *'Ready Steady Rock!'* was full of surprises. When he consulted his list it was all there in black and white. The four oldest girls were to be in dressing room Blue 4, Jamie Servile was next door in Blue 5 and all the other girls were next to that in the larger room Blue 6. Sister Snatch and her colleague had been allocated room 123 in the basement, some distance from the studio and therefore much quieter and more suitable for prayer and contemplation. Norman thanked Nick and said goodbye to the young ladies, assuring them that he would see them later. As he resumed his journey to telecine he glanced out of a window and saw Jamie Servile getting out of his Rolls. As usual he was smoking a huge cigar but Norman was puzzled by another item which Servile took from the car. It was quite big and shiny, but before Norman could see exactly what it was Jamie Servile had slipped it under his jacket; surely it couldn't be a gun? Norman hurried about his business.

In the control gallery of studio six the film had just come to its frenzied climax. Johnny slumped back in his chair. "Well what did we make of that then loves?" Years of experience in television production had taught him never to express an opinion without first determining the consensus.

"The kids will love it," said Joan, "but it was a bit naughty."

"That sequence in the lift you mean?"

"Yes, that was a bit saucy for six o'clock air time."

"What do you think Norman?" Johnny turned to the man himself, who had just entered the gallery.

"You might have waited for me."

"Never mind that, we were just wondering if the scenes in the lift were a bit too sexy,"

"Oh just because it looks like that they've got no clothes on?"

"Well... yes."

"Oh no I think that's fine. You can't see any naughty bits, I made sure of that; besides it was Ricky's idea and he would be well pissed off if you cut it."

"Ricky's idea you say? Oh well I guess it's alright then." Johnny felt the pleasant sensation of responsibility slipping away from him and into a fog of muddled accountability. Norman was crestfallen. "Well is that all you've got say about it? Don't you think that the kids'll go mad about it?"

"Oh yes .sure Norman, it's great, great; now Joan, any news about those dressing rooms?"

"I'll get on to them again." and, as Joan reached for the red phone, a belittled Norman headed for the Blue Assembly snack bar to nurse his disappointment.

It took Norman three cigarettes, two cups of coffee and a doughnut before he felt like facing the *'Ready Steady Rock!'* production team again. All that effort, all that worry and all those special effects and the buggers scarcely had a good word to say about it. He wished, now, that he hadn't bothered to persuade Bert Tyke to reduce the bill for optical effects and he resolved that, next time, he would take them for every last penny. The caffeine and nicotine were just beginning to have some cheering effects when he noticed one of Sister Snatch's girls heading towards him.

"Hello mister, so are we in your film then, I mean, you didn't cut us out?" It was Sharon, one of the senior girls who had been keen to go into show business, before meeting Jamie Servile.

"Oh No, you're in it all right, don't worry about that."

"Oh great, well we'll all cheer like mad when they run it on the show.'

'Yes you do that," said Norman." I'm sure Ricky and the lads would be really happy if you did that."

"You think so, honest?"

"Of course, we made the film because they can't appear' live' on the show tonight; so you make sure you cheer to let them know that you think they're the tops."

"OK .Mister, you're on."

"That might make that ungrateful bugger Johnny Tudor think twice anyway," thought Norman, and he felt his confidence beginning to return.

"So do you know a lot of pop stars then?' Sharon sounded little more than half interested and Norman decided to be honest, for once.

"Well not really, I've only just joined the show but I've met a few good groups, I suppose."

"Like who?"

"Like Frankie Spasm, and Arch Angel, of 'The Slime."

"They're Ok I suppose, I think Ricky Zit is better though, don't you?"

"Ricky is certainly no fool, I'll say that for him."

"What about the D.J.'s, do you know any of them?" Norman's usual response to Sharon's question would have been to lie and claim that he was pals with all of them, but something about her demeanour made him give an honest answer, for a change.

"Well I don't really know any of them yet because I've only been working on the programme for a couple of weeks. I met Jamie Servile when we were on location, but you girls must know him a lot better than I do."

"Yeah, we know him alright, you should count yourself lucky mister," and with that somewhat disquieting remark Sharon drifted off in the direction of her dressing room. Norman found himself wondering what on earth she could have meant. Servile was certainly an odd character, according to Sister Snatch, he was a latter day Saint; and yet what was the mysterious object that Norman had seen him slip under his coat, perhaps it was a gun after all?

Back in the gallery the problems of the day were not getting any easier for Johnny Tudor. Joan put down the phone and turned towards him with some unwelcome news.

"Bookings can't give us any more star dressing rooms; the studios are really busy today. They have a couple available in the basement so I've taken them, Ok Johnny?"

"Oh my God, we can't put Charlie Stash and OCD into second rate dressing rooms; Bernie Lines will go berserk."

"What about if we shifted the girls?"

"Girls?"

"Yes, Jamie's little special guests. They have three dressing rooms, two next his on the ground floor and a big one in the basemen."

"My God however did that happen?"

"You agreed it with him."

"Did I? Well yes we'll have to shift them."

"He'll not like it."

Johnny thought for a moment. "Well we won't tell him. Once he is on the studio floor I'll keep him really busy until lunch time: I'll even make the ultimate sacrifice and take him for lunch in the 'waitress service'. We'll get the girls to change rooms before Bernie's lot arrive. Get the floor assistant up here now and I'll brief him. If we are careful and keep Jamie busy all day, we'll get away with it."

"Right ho Mr. Tudor, you're the boss."

"I sometimes wonder."

Now it was Nick, the floor assistant's, turn to feel stressed. Usually the floor assistant's job was very routine, almost boring, that is what Nick liked about it, but now he found himself involved in a real intrigue. Johnny had told him to get Jamie Servile to the studio as soon as possible.

"Tell him we want to try out some new special lighting, or something, tell him anything just get the bugger into the studio and as soon as he's there I'll keep him busy. That'll be your cue to shift the girls downstairs. Then all we have to do is keep the girls away from him until after the recording. Ok? Good lad .we're depending on you." If Johnny Tudor thought that these last words would encourage Nick to give of his best he was mistaken. Nick hated being depended on, it always entailed stress and usually the only stress his job involved was when he was working on a drama with a lot of bloody minded extras. Stars could be hysterical awkward bastards, of course, but when those sorts of rows occurred Nick had learned to shrink into the background and leave it to the production manager, or the producer, to rush in, on a tide of regret and insincere flattery, and calm things down. So now he was lumbered. He had to get Jamie into the studio, much earlier than was usual and then persuade the girls to decamp to much less salubrious accommodation. He was so deep in thought that he nearly bumped into Norman, who was just moving away from the till, having bought a third cup of coffee.

"Oh I'm sorry." said the distracted Nick.

'That's Ok, no bones broken: you should calm down a bit, though, mate. These buggers aren't worth rushing around for."

"You're telling me." said Nick and then told Norman the intricacies of the situation.

"And the trouble is I really need to be in reception. If I'm in the basement sheepherding those blasted kids there won't be anyone to sort out the Pushers and OCD when they arrive, and they're due soon."

Norman felt a sudden urge to be noble, and also saw a sudden opportunity to chat to Sharon again. "I could help out if you like. The girls know me, we used them in Ricky Zit's film. You take Jamie to the studio and then go and wait for the other lot. I'll take the girls down to their new dressing rooms."

"Would you really? That's great, thanks. Now I'd better go and get the great Mr. Servile, and remember, he mustn't know a word about this, at least until after the show."

It crossed Norman's mind whether he should mention the fact that Jamie might be carrying a gun, but Nick seemed stressed enough and, in any case, Norman couldn't be certain. He put down his coffee and followed Nick towards Jamie Servile's dressing room. As they got near to the door Norman held back. He hoped that Nick would think that he was being tactful, but his actual motive was cowardice. Norman reckoned that an angry Jamie Servile would not make for a pleasant encounter. Nick reached the door and was just about to knock when he stopped and listened; he paused then beckoned Norman to join him and gestured for him to listen too. Norman did so. The sounds that they heard were unusual to say the least and consisted of heavy breathing, assorted creaking and frequent grunting.

"What the fuck is he doing?" Nick mouthed to Norman.

"I've no idea" replied Norman in a whispered lie, because he had all sorts of ideas; but none of them was to prove to be as bizarre as the truth.

"Oh well here goes…" Nick rapped sharply at the door while Norman backed off and hid behind an adjacent pillar. There was a clatter as something hit the floor and then all the mysterious noises stopped; next there came an aggressive shout from within the room.

"What do you want?"

"It's the floor assistant Mr. Servile. The producer would like you to go to the studio immediately."

"Well I can't. I'm having a…having a shower." Whatever Jamie Servile had been having Nick was pretty damned certain it wasn't a shower but he was duty bound to persist.

"I am sorry if it is inconvenient but Mr. Tudor was very insistent that I should return with you."

"Sodding Hell, give us a minute." There were some more strange sounds from the room which included the sound of sweeping and then finally Jamie Servile opened the door just wide enough to be able to slither out. He was red faced and agitated.

"This is a right bloody nuisance, that's what this is. I'm never called to the studio before mid-day."

"I'm sorry Mr. Servile I'm just doing what I've been told." Nick thought he heard the cheerful joker of the pop world mutter, "Snivelling little job's worth" as he turned to lock the dressing door, but he choose to ignore it.

"This way sir."

"I know the bloody way young man."

As they approached Norman had to slide around the pillar to remain out of sight but he was able to keep them in view once they had passed him and were walking away. When Nick and Servile came to the first set of heavy swing doors that formed the entrance to the studio Jamie Servile pulled a handkerchief from his pocket to stifle a sneeze. As he did so his dressing room key fell to the floor. What with negotiating the doors and coping with the sneeze Jamie didn't notice, but Norman did. He was just about to call after them when the heavy first doors of the studio entry area swung closed. Norman hurried forward and picked up the keys. He thought for a couple of seconds and decided the priority was to get the girls relocated; he could give Jamie Servile back his key later, at a time when he it might be possible to chat and add the famous DJ to his burgeoning list of celebrity friends.

Chapter 22.

<u>Strange Habits.</u>

When he got back to Servile's dressing room Norman found Sharon outside with her ear pressed to the door. She stood up hastily at Norman's approach and tried to look casual. She didn't succeed.

"Hello, whatever are you up to?" asked Norman in a counterfeit fatherly tone.

"Well to be honest, mister, the girls and me, we was wondering what the bloody hell's been going on. That Jamie wasn't half making some funny noises."

"Yes I heard them too, but he's not there now, he's been called to the studio."

"Oh so that's why it stopped."

"Reckon so."

"You're sure he ain't in there."

"Certain, I saw him go."

"Right." Sharon gingerly tried the door handle. "Bugger, he's locked it."

"Of course he's locked it."

"I really wanted to find out what he was up to."

"Well to be honest I'd love to know too." Norman took a half pace closer to the school girl. "Can you keep a secret Sharon?" She backed away from him and her eyes narrowed with suspicion.

"Depends what it is."

"I've got the key to that door."

"You never."

"I have, Jamie dropped it by accident, I picked it up, but I've not given it back to him yet."

"You naughty old man."

"Well yes I am, but less of the 'old' please young lady." Norman puckered his lips in an attempt to look sophisticated and sexy. With a flourish he produced the key.

"Shall we?''

"Yes, let's."

''It really is very naughty."

"Oh get on with it."

Shaking slightly with the excitement of the moment, Norman tried, and failed to fit the key into the lock.

"It doesn't bloody fit."

"We had trouble with ours, they go in upside down."

"Oh, OK." Sharon was right; the key turned in the lock and for moment they stood stock still outside room. Then, like a pair of experienced robbers, they slipped silently inside.

Norman shut the door quietly behind them.

"I don't like this at all, let's be quick."

"Yer sure, Blimey what's that?" Sharon pointed to a strange looking metal object sticking out from under a copy of the Radio Time with Jamie Servile's picture on the front cover. He was grinning and giving a thumbs up sign; it was an un-nerving image in the circumstances. Norman realised that he had seen the mystery object before, it was the thing he had thought might be a gun.

"Blimey it's a brace and bit."

"A what?"

"It's a sort of old fashioned drill. Carpenters use them for drilling really large holes."

"Oh so that's it!" Sharon stiffened and stood very tall, her eyes narrowed again and darted around the room.

"I don't understand." Norman was genuinely confused. Glancing around the walls Sharon failed to see what she was looking for but when she turned her attention to the

skirting board she immediately saw something that justified her suspicions; it was a small pile of plaster dust. An
attempt had been made to sweep it up, but it had not
been a very thorough job. Norman and Sharon's eyes met
and he followed her gaze from the dust on the floor to half
way up the wall where there hung a gilt framed picture of
the' Black and White Minstrels' taken during their recent
triumphant tour of South Africa. Sharon walked up to the
picture and took it from the wall immediately revealing a
large hole presumably drilled by the brace and bit. It had
not quite penetrated the full thickness of the wall but it
was very nearly through to the girls' dressing room next
door. Norman looked puzzled, but Sharon had no doubts
about the significance of the hole.

"Dirty old bastard." she said. "Right, either he moves
dressing rooms, or we do." Norman could hardly believe
his luck, here was a chance to get the girls quickly into
their new rooms and to appear to be an influential man of
action in the process.

"Leave it me, young lady. You get all the girls together in
reception and I'll arrange new dressing room for you. It
won't be easy, the studio is pretty full today, but I have
some friends in high places, I think I'll be able to fix it."

"Suppose we better put the picture back."

"Yes, then let's out of here, It's a big bastard isn't it?"

"Yeah."

"I wonder why he's drilling the hole so low?"

"You really don't get it do yer? It's at knicker height, silly!"

In their basement dressing room Sister Snatch and her mysterious large companion were using the time until they were required to chaperone the girls into the studio by filling their minds with religious enigmas. The Bishop had suggested various topics worthy of quiet contemplation. Top of the list was the early Saxon sacred poem, *'The Dream of the Rood.'* The Bishop had recently been troubled by a spate of *'Rood Dreams'* and was hoping to gain some helpful advice. In fact, for the moment, neither of the sisters were involved in much contemplation. Sister Snatch had taken off her heavy leather boots and was sitting with her feet up on the dressing table whilst reading *'The Racing Times.'* Her companion was engrossed in a well-thumbed copy of a Vatican publication *'Salvation through Pain'*, the history of torture during the Spanish Inquisition. A fly on the wall onlooker might well have been disquieted by the fact that the reader occasionally flinched, paused, and then hurriedly scribbled notes into a jotter pad; the more severe the facial flinch the more intensely determined the scribbling seemed to be.

"Would you be liking a cup of coffee?" Sister Snatch enquired of her friend. "I'm getting sick of just sitting here, and I think I'd be able to find our way back to that cafe area."

"Yes I'd like a coffee."

"Come on then."

"Could you bring me one back? To be honest I 'd really like to get out of this clobber for a while ; honestly I don't know how you put up with it day in day out." and with that the large Nun pulled off her wimple to reveal the bloated red features of Father Cummings. Sister Snatch looked at him for a moment.

"I don't know why you ever wanted to dress up in like that in the first place."

"I'm sure the BBC would not have let us share a dressing room if I had come as a priest."

"Stuff and nonsense, they wouldn't give a tinker's cuss; even if I'd said I wanted to share a dressing room with a male protestant."

In the studio Johnny Tudor was having difficulty holding Jamie Servile's attention for long enough to allow Nick sufficient time to shepherd the girls to their new dressing rooms. Servile was simply not interested in the prospect of a new set, or a change of transmission time. Both of these were inventions but Johnny had to think of some reason for having called Jamie away.

"Well if that's all you want to tell me, I'm going back to my room, there's ... there's things I want to be getting on with." Tudor looked anxiously towards the studio door. Nick had promised him that he would put his head around the door and give a 'thumbs up' when the coast was clear.

There was no sign of him; Servile started to leave. Under pressure Johnny came up with a better ploy.

"Oh there's one more thing Jamie, the powers that be have suggested that we might get a couple of other presenters to share the show with you." This announcement had the desired effect, Jamie stopped in his tracks.

"What? Like who?"

Well they are very keen to find another vehicle for that trendy girl Janice Rhodes-Sweeper.'

"Another vehicle, another vehicle? Well an ambulance would be good start: get her to hospital and have her fucking teeth fixed. Present a show? She can hardly fucking speak with that gob full of tusks."

"I'm only telling you what the front office have told me"

"You said a couple of new people; who's the other one?"

"Toby Barnsley, from pirate radio. Nice jolly lad."

"All bloody teeth again, when he smiles it looks like the window display in a piano showroom."

Johnny noticed to, to his great relief that Nick was by the door and giving a 'thumbs up.'

"Well, it's only an idea at the moment, why don't we discuss over lunch in the waitress service?"

"You paying?"

"Of course."

"Alright then, seems we've got a lot to talk about."

As she mounted the stair case, in the direction of the Blue assembly coffee bar, Sister Snatch was surprised to see Norman coming in the opposite direction at the head of a column of her girls.

"Mercy me, where are you taking the girls now?"

"Oh their dressing rooms were a bit small so the producer asked me to move them to a couple of bigger rooms. But, don't worry, they are next to yours."

"Oh dear, Jamie was so looking forward to having them near him.''

"It'll be much better like this sister, honest." It was Sharon who spoke and she was at her most forceful.

"Oh well, if it has to be, it has to be, but I sometimes don't think you girls appreciate exactly how much Jamie Servile thinks about you all."

"Oh we do Sister, I can promise you that."

Norman sensed some tension in the air and decided to speed matters along.

"Well we better hurry along, I'll be needed in the studio again soon. See you in there, Sister and don't forget to cheer like mad when the girls appear on film." They all filed past the disapproving Sister who cast a daggers look a

Sharon. That girl was becoming too big for her brassiere, and no mistake.

In the car park Danny Anxious, the lead singer with OCD, was just about to return to his car for the third time to make sure it was locked, when he heard Nick's voice calling him.

"Hello there, Mr. Anxious? I'm Nick the floor assistant I've come to show you to your dressing room."

"Oh hello mate, thanks."

"Can I help you carry anything?" Nick could see that Danny was struggling to manage with his guitar case and large suit cover.

"Oh yes thanks mate. Just hang a minute will you." He juggled with the luggage to avoid putting it down on the ground and finally managed to pull a pair of white gloves from one of his pockets.

"Put these on first please mate. Anyway thanks a lot, my back has been bloody awful just recently."

"I think it will be easier if we go this way." said Nick indicating a less than obvious route. "There is some awful snarl up on the studio ring road, even the pavement is blocked"

"Blimey what has caused that?"

"It looks like some clapped out old bus has parked in the wrong place. It is probably a prop vehicle for studio one, they're doing a new drama set in a breaker's yard."

"Jesus, Mary and Joseph! Why did they want to go and move the girls into rooms right next to ours?" Father Cummings was not best pleased.

"I don't know'," said Sister Snatch, handing him his coffee. "That man who made the fillum said something about them needing a bigger room."

"Well that scuppers our plans then doesn't it? I mean there is only so much pain I can take without actually crying out and we can't afford the girls to hear what we are doing."

"I suppose I could go easy on you for a change?"

"No point in that, I have to really suffer if I am ever to have a chance of final salvation, the Bishop himself said so."

"Oh he's just a sadistic old pervert."

"Of course he is, that's how he got the job, but I really thought that this would be my one big chance to impress him. I mean to be able to confess to being tortured in the basement of BBC television centre, why he might have appointed me the headmaster of that new boy's school he hopes to open in Scotland.'

"Well perhaps the good Lord has had other ideas?"

"Maybe, but I haven't"

In the control gallery Johnny Tudor was feeling much re-lieved as they neared the end of their first run through of the show. OCD had performed well enough, but the fact that lead singer Danny Anxious was suffering from back ache had certainly put a downer on proceedings and would obviously need a good pep talk before the actual re-cording. Charlie Stash and the Pushers, however were a completely different kettle of fish. They gave their number 150%; indeed they were so impressive that Johnny Tudor felt tempted to place them last on the running order. This would be unprecedented as they were not number one in the charts. That honour fell to Ricky Zit and the Pustules, but they were not live on the show and were simply to be represented by Norman's film. It was a difficult decision. Johnny decided to wait and see what the audience reac-tion was to the film before he made up his mind. As this was only a run through the audience was only about half the size that it would be for the evening's recording of the show. However, crucially, sister Snatch's girls made up a large section of the audience for this rehearsal run. Nor-man need not have worried, Sharon did not let him down. When the film came on to the studio monitors the girls went crazy.

"Well that's game set and match, then," said Johnny Tu-dor. He turned to Norman who had been sitting anxiously beside him. "Well done mate, brilliant bit of film; no ques-tion we'll close the show with that."

"You really like it then? Only, earlier I thought you didn't rate it that much."

"Oh nonsense I loved it. It was just that I had a lot on my mind."

Norman was not the sharpest knife in the draw but even he was beginning to realise that Johnny Tudor had no critical judgement whatsoever. He totally depended on the view of the mob. It was his most important quality as a light entertainment producer.

"Ok that's it until the recording." Johnny was talking to the studio manager. "Let the kids go but hold on to Jamie and both the groups, I'm coming down to give a few notes."

"Jamie says he needs to go to his dressing room." The floor manager's answer put Johnny into panic mode.

"Oh God, if he goes now he'll realise that we've swapped the girls' dressing rooms; hold him there as long as you can OK? Now what the bloody hell do we do?" Johnny's question was to no one in particular, but Norman chose to pick up the challenge.

"Leave it with me, I think I can fix it." With that Norman rushed out of the control gallery and rushed down to the studio floor as fast as the steep stairs and his general lack of condition would allow. He mis-judged the last three steps and fell in an undignified heap onto the studio floor but all was not lost; he had landed at the feet of the lovely Sharon.

"Hello mister, you're in a hurry as usual."

"Yes I am, and I'll tell you why."

From his Ivory tower in the gallery Johnny was anxiously regarding the scene through the glass observation wall. He saw Norman dusting himself down whilst urgently talking to Sharon and then he saw Sharon nod her head and rush over to where Jamie Servile was cursing the floor manager for wasting his time. Sharon went up to the mega- star and suddenly the mood changed. Servile put his arm round Sharon and she snuggled up close. From a distant perspective this had the look of an affectionate encounter but, had Johnny Tudor been nearer, he could not have failed to notice the look of vengeful loathing in the young girl's eyes. Servile took Sharon's hand and lead her over to where 'The Pushers' were making some final equipment checks. Jamie Servile introduced Sharon to Charlie Stash and it was autographs all round. Sharon then whispered in Jamie's ear and he turned and made a leering remark to the group. He only took a moment, but when he turned back Sharon was gone.

She made it safely to the exit door but as she passed through into the Blue Assembly area Sharon was concerned about being pursued and she was looking over her shoulder. As a result she ran straight into the arm of George the, uni-dextrous, commissionaire.

"Here just you watch where you're going."

"Sorry mister."

"Ere, ain't you one of them girls that came in that clapped out old bus?"

"What if I am?"

"I want it shifted that's what. It's causing bloody chaos. I suppose you know where the driver is?"

"I might do."

Johnny Tudor reached the bottom of the stair case, rather more gracefully than Norman had done and went over to where the film editor was dusting himself down.

"Well done Norm, don't know how you did it but you seem to have delayed him a bit."

"Yes, well all part of the service I suppose." After all his recent adventures Norman was certainly feeling part of the team, he even might have been feeling exploited, if it wasn't for the fact that his scam with Bert Tyke stood to make him several thousands of pounds.

"Brace yourself Norman, Servile's heading straight for us."

"Right ho Mr. Tudor, but what should I say?"

"Anything, just delay him a bit." Jamie Servile hurried up to them, looking aggressive.

"Did the convent girls go out this way?"

"I'm not sure I didn't see them; did you see them Mr Tudor?" Norman thought that involving Johnny Tudor in the lie might make it more credible.

"Well no, Norman I can't say I did see them, they'll be around somewhere."

"Of course they'll be around somewhere but I want to know where. You can be a right bloody idiot, sometimes Johnny Tudor, you know that?"

Johnny felt an overwhelming urge to punch Jamie Servile on his amply proportioned nose but he was stopped, just in time, by the sight of Nick. The floor assistant had come up quietly behind Servile and was giving a discreet 'thumbs up'. Guessing that this could only mean the girls had made it safely to their new dressing rooms. Johnny determined to get rid of Servile as soon as possible and to tantalise him in the process.

"Oh, come to think of it think I heard one of them say that they had got so excited over Norman's film that they needed a shower. They must be heading for their dressing room"

"Did you like the film Jamie?" Norman inquired.

"Loved it, loved it Fab, Fab, Fab. See you later, gotta dash," and with that the over-sexed celeb rushed away.

There was a look of vengeful determination combined with suppressed glee on the face of Commissionaire

George as he advanced towards Sister Snatch's dressing room door. Sharon had identified the room some minutes before and George had already knocked insistently on the door. There had been no reply, yet George had definitely heard some frantic scuffling from inside; so this time he had armed himself with a security pass key. This time there would be no mucking about, that bloody tatty old bus needed shifting and George was the man to get it moved. He fitted the key in the lock, as quietly as his disability allowed, then he paused, drew breath and threw open the door.

"That bus of yours needs shifting and shifting right now!' was what George had planned to say but the sight which greeted him as he entered the room somewhat altered that to "Cor Blimey, what the fuck?" The vision that had skewed George from his purpose was the state of Father Cummings; for the holy man was gagged and tied to heavy metal coat stand in the middle of the room, he was naked apart from some extremely unflattering underpants, which looked as if they had been designed, if not actually made, before the dissolution of the monasteries. The good father's body was covered in bruises and welts. Before George could do anything to assist the saintly sufferer he had a fleeting glimpse of another figure reflected in the make- up mirror and coming up behind him. It was Sister Snatch, but she could not be easily identified as she too had changed her garments. What the mirror revealed was the hideous sight of Sister Snatch wearing jack boots, fish net tights and a voluminous black brassiere. The ensemble

351

was completed by a Nazi SS officer's cap which the good sister had been lucky enough to acquire, some years before, while holidaying in France at a Benedictine Monastery. The brothers were having a clear out and it had seemed churlish not to buy something from their jumble sale. However George had very little time to interpret these bizarre images before Sister Snatch hit him behind the ear with the handle of her bull whip (a second purchase from the monastery sale). The commissionaire saw a flash of light then fell heavily to floor. He put out an arm to break his fall but, unfortunately, it was the wrong arm. Strange to relate, when George's head hit the dressing floor both Father Cummings and Sister Snatch thought that they saw a flash of light too. Perhaps it was the release of metaphysical energy or even the intervention of the Holy Spirit? But, it was neither of these; it was Sharon, standing in the door way with a camera.

353

Drama and incident, that afternoon, were not just taking place in the second class basement dressing rooms. On the ground floor some of the rooms reserved for stars and V.I.Ps were also destined to become the setting for extraordinary events. As soon as Jamie Servile had returned to his room he could hear the shower running in the dressing room next door. Thanks to the exhaustive efforts of Johnny Tudor, Norman and Nick, Servile still believed that the room next door was occupied by some of the Convent Girls. The shower kept being turned on and off and every now and then he could hear low moans and whining noises. It was more than a compulsive voyeur could take and Servile grabbed his brace and bit and attacked the wall with a frenzy that only a frustrated kiddie fiddler could muster. He had already drilled a good way into the wall so surely it couldn't be long now before he broke through? Every time the next-door shower stopped Servile's heart almost stopped too, but then the shower started again so his spirits raised and urged him on to yet more desperate excavation.

In the next door dressing room the lead singer of OCD, Danny Anxious, was making every effort to alleviate his back pain. He was not entirely unhappy because the treatment which he had devised for the purpose fitted in well with his obsession for routine. He would shower for three minutes under cold water, then perform stretch exercises, pressed against the wall for three minutes and then have a hot shower for four minutes. He was not quite certain whether it was best to do the wall exercises again after the hot shower or to switch straight back to a cold one before continuing the cycle. This is what made it such a comfort for him as there was a lot to worry about and every excuse for starting again from the beginning. The one thing Danny was sure about, the one thing that his chiropractor always stressed, was that the harder you pushed yourself against the wall the better the relief of the back pain would be.'

Don't just push yourself against the wall Danny boy!' his practitioner would say,' Try and push yourself right into it!'

It was fate that decided that this is exactly what Danny Anxious was doing when Jamie Servile's drill broke through the remaining brick work. One second Danny was firmly pushing himself against the wall and relishing the relief of tension that was slowly, but surely reducing his discomfort; then, the next second, he felt the most agonising stabbing pain between his buttocks. He screamed ; looked down to see a mess of shattered plaster and brick dust on the floor and, for a moment, wondered if he might have suffered some terrible episode of gastric calamity, as yet unknown to medical science. Danny was familiar with the expression 'Shit a brick' but even in the most morbid depths of hypochondria he had never before imagined that it might be possible. In a state of near collapse he staggered to a chair and sat down more forcefully than was wise, considering the location of the injury which he had just suffered. He screamed again.

In the adjoining dressing room Jamie Servile was now in a state of excited panic. He was confused about exactly what was happening in 'the girls' room and was determined not to miss any of the salacious action. He rushed over to his hold-all and produced a long metal viewing tube. This was an optical instrument that provided a wide angle view. It was essential equipment for the serious voyeur. In his eagerness Servile pushed the viewing tube rather too quickly into the newly drilled hole. It disturbed a good deal more brick dust and it was this that caught the attention of the traumatised Danny Anxious. He was confused, puzzled and extremely angry. What on earth could it all mean? Well, one thing was certain; whatever was going on had done him serious injury. As a result of the actions of a lunatic in the next room he now had rectal haemorrhage to add to his list of afflictions. The wrath of the wounded beast arouse within him, he picked up a shoe and he struck Jamie Servile's viewing tube with all the force he could muster. Instantly there was a third cry of pain, but this time it came from the other side of the wall.

The double doors at the bottom of the stairs which led up to the Blue Assembly area opened furtively and the head of one the smallest of the Convent girls popped out. Carefully but quickly, she looked around and then gave the 'all clear' to her friends behind her. The doors now swung fully open and a six of the big girls came out. They were carrying the unconscious body of George. A little after them came Sister Snatch and Father Cummings, now dressed in their regular vestments, and they looked extremely uncomfortable. There was much mumbling of 'Hail Marys' and a great deal of furtive fumbling with rosaries.

"Right girls, put him down near the bottom of the stairs and lay him with the bump on his head next to a step'. Sharon was unquestionably in charge of the situation.

"Now untie one of his shoelaces."

"Why Sharon?"

"So they think he tripped over them, silly. Now hurry up, he's moaning; he'll come round in a minute."

Sister Snatch stepped forward. "Well done girls; now it's straight back to the coach. We're going home."

"Hang on Fish Face," said Sharon. "You just don't get it do you? We've just bailed you out of a huge pile of shit and we've got demands to be met."

"Demands, what Demands?"

"We want better food, new beds, new uniforms and no more visits from that creep Jamie Servile."

"Jesus, Mary and Joseph, Sharon Shorrocks, just who do you think you are?"

"I think I'm the owner of a photograph which will be on the front page of 'The News of the World ' next Sunday if you don't do exactly what we tell you from now on."

"This is Blackmail."

"Got it in one."

"Now Sharon, dear, listen to me." This was Father Cummings at his most oleaginous. He threw a meaningful glance to Sister Snatch

"We can agree to better food. We can even think about new beds and uniforms. But surely you can't really want to stop Mr. Servile's visits? To be sure, the man is practically a Saint."

There was a pause before Sharon answered. She circled the two devout servants of the Lord and then faced them and spoke in a clear but chilling tone.

"Listen you pair of toe rags, I used to think that you two were just wicked,... but you're not just wicked, you're fucking thick an' all. Now come on girls, up to the studio and cheer our film like mad."

Chapter 23.

<u>A Show to Remember.</u>

The recording of *'Ready Steady Rock!'* that night was certainly full of surprises.

Charlie Stash and the Pushers, who had been so fantastic at the dress run now seemed almost incapable of performing because they kept collapsing in fits of helpless laughter, every time they came in sight of Danny Anxious.

Nothing, it seemed, could stop them. On the other hand, Danny Anxious and OCD sang with a fervour which Johnny Tudor had never heard from him before.

"This is great," Johnny whispered to Norman. "I've never heard Danny make a sound like this."

"The boy seems to be singing from the bottom of his heart." said Norman displaying his uncanny knack for getting things half right. Danny's new intense sound had nothing to do with his heart but everything to do with his bottom, resulting, as it did, from the singer's recent sphincteral skewering with the drill bit.

Another surprise for the production team was that Jamie Servile insisted on presenting the show dressed as a pirate. Johnny was not particularly bothered by this, he was used to the presenter's eccentricities and thought of it merely as another attention grabbing gimmick.

He did wonder, though, as to why Servile had chosen to wear such an enormous eye-patch as part of the outfit. However no amount of pleading would persuade Mr. Servile to change the eye-patch for a smaller one.

Viewers, at home, were somewhat puzzled by the fact that some of the audience shots included a Catholic Priest and a Nun and that they seemed to be involved in a blazing row. When, later in the show, they were seen being chased from the studio by a one armed man of dishevelled appearance most fans of the programme simply put it down to the producer's fashionable taste for the absurd.

To Norman's great relief there could be no doubt that the highlight of the evening was the film he had made with Ricky Zit. Triumph would not be too strong a word. The kids in studio loved it. They went wild, shrieking hysterically at the mangle sequence and shouting out lots of 'ooh errs!' when they saw the saucy goings on in the lift.

"Well Norman, mate, that was great. I loved the special effects." Johnny Tudor smiled at Norman who was sitting beside him.

"They'll probably cost a bit." said Norman cautiously.

"Never mind, you have to pay for quality." said Johnny.

"That's what I hoped you'd say."

The film came to an end and the vision mixer cut to wide shot of the studio audience. The boys and girls were simply mad with excitement but it was the girls who were the most demonstrative. As if to show their love and appreciation for Jamie Servile a group of them, led by Sharon, picked him up and carried him shoulder high around the studio. It was a memorable image over which to run the end credits but somewhat unfortunate that, in their enthusiasm, the girls ran right under the heavy *'Ready Steady Rock!'* neon sign and the D.J was smacked painfully about the head, once on the nose, when the girls ran under the sign and once again when the sign swung back and cracked him on the back of the head.

Norman went home that night filled with the warm glow of success. His film had been a sensation and he was already booked to make another one for Charlie Stash and the Pushers. He also had the secret of making a lot of spare 'bubble' thanks to his shady deal with Bert Tyke. But it wasn't to be: and that was all because of a picture which appeared in the next Sunday's *'News of the World.'* It wasn't the photo which Sharon had taken in the dressing room, it was one that Bert Tyke had managed to lift from the negative he had of Ricky Zit in the lift. The explicit nude shot, which had not been used in the film. Bert Tyke had regretted letting Norman talk him out of sending in an inflated bill and decided on another ploy. Bert was paid a lot of money for the boot-leg print but his greed killed the goose that might have laid dozens of golden eggs. There was a copyright row and Bert Tyke's film effect services were immediately blacklisted, not just by the BBC but by all the other TV companies. Norman's chance to' get rich quick' vanished quicker than evidence in a trial for Police corruption.

He stayed with *'Ready Steady Rock!'* for another nine months, or so, and tried to make some extra money by fiddling expenses and selling tickets on the black market. He was found out and demoted back down to assistant film editor. He complained bitterly, went to the union, but in the end there was nothing he could do about it. The sad truth was that he should never have been made an editor in the first place.

Dame Fate had very different plans Jamie Servile. By the time he died, at the age of 84, Servile had been personally blessed by the Pope and honoured with a knighthood. He had also pressed his unwanted sexual attentions on more than 500 young people, many of whom were under the age of consent. To ease him down the glittering pathway towards fame and fortune he had always been able to rely on the sanctity and wisdom of the Roman Catholic Church and the perceptive judgement of popular opinion.

Chapter 24.

<u>Some Funny Men.</u>

I suppose the truth is that when I was working in the BBC TV's Light Entertainment Department I was too young to appreciate why it was that most of famous comedians, with whom I worked, were such a miserable load of buggers. There were exceptions: Harry Secombe and Les Dawson spring immediately to mind. Harry was the most generous hearted and appreciative man you could ever hope to meet. If things went wrong he would just laugh in one of his mad 'goon' voices and say, "Well I think we should all dress up as Gypsies." Even the most self-regarding and stressed out programme producer found it hard not to relax when Harry was the star of the show. Significantly he was just as courteous and encouraging to the junior members of the cast and crew as he was to the senior executives. Indeed he always seem tempted to deflate anyone who whose exalted position was inclining them towards delusions of grandeur. At a Light Entertainment Christmas party, to which only stars, BBC executives, and selected creeping sycophants were invited, Harry was introduced to the secretary of Paul Fox .Mr. Fox was then head of BBC1.

"Do you know Paul Fox's secretary?" said a voice.

"Oh does he?" said Harry.

Les Dawson was very similar. He was also a large man and surprisingly modest. The characteristic that Les shared with Harry (and which so few comedians possess) was a genuine regard for humanity. As well as taking pleasure from making people laugh, he did actually enjoy their company. Many famous comedians would shun the public bar, indeed any bar, of a pub; not so Harry or Les. If some over enthusiastic fan came up to them they seemed genuinely pleased to meet them and even if that fan was unwise enough to tell them a joke they would laugh heartily. That was certainly a rare quality: most comedians loath any company that dares to attempt humour in their august presence.

One of the most embarrassing misanthropes I encountered was Dick Emery. I worked as production manager on his TV shows in the mid-1970s. Dick had the reputation of being a 'difficult' artist but I didn't find that to be the case. He was testy, if he thought he was being mucked about, but as long he was comfortable on location he was not a problem. Once I discovered that he liked to have a nap during the lunch break I made sure that he always had a comfortable place to sleep nearby. Sometimes it was a hotel room, more usually a location caravan, it didn't matter as long as he could grab 20 minutes shut eye, and it transformed his mood. There were good reasons for Dick's need for a nap. For years he had lied about his age. When I joined in the show, in 1974, his publicity read 'Dick Emery, 59. he was still 'Dick Emery,59, when I left the show six years later and he had, in fact, been Dick Emery, '64' when

I joined in '74! The other reason he tired easily was that he frequently didn't get enough sleep. When we finished the day's filming at about 6p.m. Dick would get in his car and be driven to some Northern club. There he would do his 'spot' at midnight, pocket about £3500, and be driven back again. Sometimes he would be driven directly to the film location. I knew him well enough to know that he had no great love of performing; he was more of a gifted comic actor than a comedian, so I asked him why he did this to himself.

"I know the BBC doesn't pay you a fortune, Dick, but your fee is pretty good so why do you knacker yourself out with all these Northern club gigs?"

"Don't you understand, Mike, I didn't become a star until I was 55, I have a lot of catching up to do. The clubs pay well and they pay cash." He was into fast cars, motorbikes and sexy ladies. No wonder he needed his naps.

In the same way as he subtracted from his age it was rumoured that he reduced the number of women to whom he had been married. He confessed to having been married five times but the truth was quite possibly more. Seven was the generally accepted figure. I only ever met his last wife, a tall, elegant, ex dancer who had no intention of being cheated. Dick sometimes boasted that his previous numerous divorces hadn't cost him a penny, probably because they had all happened before he had become a big earner. His last wife 'Jo' was determined that wasn't going to happen to her. Dick, himself, was always on the look-out for a conquest, a dancer in one of his summer seaside shows or maybe an extra when we were filming. I remember once when we were on location in Oxfordshire a young boy was part of the cast and he was chaperoned by his mother .She was an attractive woman in her early thirties. Need I say more? Dick pulled her on the first night. He had to be careful because wife Jo, would often arrive unannounced at a film location and stay for a few days; but Dick had thought about that. He bought Jo a purple E type Jaguar. It was a lovely car apart from the awful colour but it was unique, that was the point, there was only one purple E type Jag. So if there was a purple jag in the car park it meant that Jo had arrived.

This ruse saved him on that Oxfordshire shoot. Dick came back from filming, immediately saw Jo's car and rushed into the hotel to greet her with drinks at the bar, before she had a chance to go up to his room. He always took his key with him so it was possible for his dresser to slip it to the boy's star shagging mother and she could get her stuff out of the room before Mrs Emery encamped. The purple E type earned its' price on that occasion alone.

The times I dreaded the most were when the script required us to film in public places: in the high street, at a railway station, in a park, or, worst of all, in a fair ground. This was simply because Dick's pathological loathing of the great British public would cause him to turn into a monster should he be approached by a cheery fan. And of course this happened often. After all at the peak of his fame in the mid-1970s, Dick Emery was a hugely popular comedian. His shows regularly gained audiences of 14 million. One Christmas special achieved 17 million. The public were therefore delighted to run across him being filmed in the street and would rush up for autographs or try to grab a snap shot. It was then that they had a nasty shock because instead of encountering the jolly, saucy man of a hundred comic characters they knew so well from their telly at home, they came face to face with a bad tempered, short, fat curmudgeon. Mr. Emery was at his worst if anyone should try to take a photo of him without first asking his permission. He thought this the height of rudeness and it never occurred to him that many people were probably just too shy to ask. I was told that he had been known to grab an offender's camera and rip the film out. Great for public relations and a calm atmosphere on location! I have to admit, though, that he was as good as his word because once, on location in Blackpool, I noticed an elderly man about to grab a picture. Thank God I spotted him before Dick did. I went up the man and warned him of Dick's 'photophobia'.

"He will be fine if you just ask him," I said, hoping to God this was true.

"But I don't like to ask him, " said the man, confirming what I had always believed to be the reason why people didn't ask. "Please do," I urged. "Just ask him and it will be fine."

When there was a break in the filming the shy man approached Dick and said, "Excuse me, Mr. Emery, may I take your photograph?"

The effect was electric. "Hold everything,"shouted the star. "Look everybody, at last we've found a real gentleman. Of course you may take my picture sir! Is that your wife? Take one of me and her together and then I'll get one of the crew to take one of the three of us." Dick posed with them for about five minutes. The couple went home devoted fans, and I breathed a sigh of relief.

It was on that same Blackpool location that I arrived ten minutes late one morning to find that disaster had struck. I can honestly say that it was the only time I was ever late on location, as the production manager you simply could not afford to be. In fact it was always a good idea to arrive at least thirty minutes before the crew call time, just to make sure that there were no last minute problems that needed sorting out. Well on that sunny morning during the heat wave of 1976 there were some problems, two very big ones. Gerald, the producer, was always keen to maximise the budget - if there was a cheap way of making it look as if we had spent a lot of money, without it costing much at all, he would grab it both hands. If they gave awards for coming in under budget he would have become a legend; but they don't. Anyway, we were filming in Blackpool because Dick was doing a summer season there. He was a the ABC theatre, Dickie Henderson was on the North Pier, and the Black and White Minstrels were at the Opera

House. The reason we were filming with Dick Emery during the day was that the BBC wanted his show available for their autumn schedule, and the only way we could get enough material filmed in time was to go to where Dick was already working and shoot the scenes on location. Dick was in Blackpool, so we went to Blackpool. It wasn't a very wise idea. Dick was always tired-out after his show in the evening and so was short tempered and seldom on his best form. He, quite naturally, insisted on short filming days, so he could at least have some shut eye between filming and performing at night so the whole project was, inevitably, not a very efficient use of resources. However there was one big saving we *could* make. With all those shows in town it was possible to cast small parts and extras from the actors and dancers who were in Blackpool for the season. In this way we could save on travel and accommodation fees. They were all equity members, they were all free during the day and were pleased to be able to pick up some additional 'bubble' at very little inconvenience. The other big show in Blackpool was the Tower Circus. When, in the late 19th century, the city fathers had built Blackpool Tower they took the decision to incorporate, not only a palatial ballroom, but a circus in its base, and a fine piece of Victorian engineering it turned out to be. Designed by Frank Matcham, the three ring circus had the facility to fill all rings with water to allow spectacular finales with fountains and lakes. I saw it, that year when we were on location, and will never forget it. When we were visiting the circus on a pre filming 'reccy', to see if any of the circus folk wanted to be extras, Gerald discovered that the elephant trainer took his animals to the beach for a swim every morning. The elephants loved it. They rushed into the sea and sprayed water over themselves and each other. It was much more enjoyable to watch them at play than gawp at them working on their act in the circus; riding huge bicycles and such like. The council granted their trainer permission to take the elephants onto the beach for reasons of animal welfare but, for reasons of public safety, the elephants had to be off the beach before 7.30 in the morning; long before the great British holiday public emerged from their B&Bs. Gerald could instantly see the possibility of getting some production value into the show at very little cost. If he could persuade the writers to come up with a sketch involving one of Dick's characters with the elephants then surely the trainer would agree to the idea for a very modest fee? After all the elephants would be on the beach anyway, so there would be no additional trouble for him. Fifty quid and he'd be happy. Like many of Gerald's money saving strategies, this one was flawed, to put it mildly .Firstly the writers didn't come up with anything very funny at all. This was no surprise as they had been washed up for several years. Secondly Herr Gudrich, the German elephant trainer, quite understandably, expected a full rate for the job. By the time Gerald had screwed down the fee as much as he could all good will between the production and the trainer had gone 'right up the trunks.' Eventually a deal was done and a date agreed, but of course the crew call had to be very early and Dick's call even earlier for makeup and costume. The Elephants were on the beach between six thirty and seven thirty in the morning. Gerald had an hour to film the sequence and was anxious that not a moment of precious time should be lost. For Dick to be ready for six thirty he would have to be in make up at five thirty, and you can imagine how keen I was to break that news to a 65 year old man who would have had been filming all the previous day and starred in a heavy show the previous night. Still it might be worth all the effort if the script writers came up with a cracking gag; and, true to form, they didn't.

It was this:

Shot of elephants with their trainer in the sea, Dick as his bovver boy character walks across the beach towards them;

Dick: Here Mister are those big dogs yours?

Trainer: Yes, but they're elephants.

Dick: Oh...'ere give us one!

And that was it. It would, surely, take all the resources of the studio sound department's library tapes of hysterical laughter to save that comic gem from the pit of ignominy into which it deserved to sink. Gerald insisted that it would 'work' and that it was 'gentle comedy'. Gentle Comedy being a euphemism, much favoured by Light Entertainment producers, when they were landed with a script that was about as amusing as an in-growing toe nail. Any rate, he accepted the script and I set about adding the Elephant sketch to our schedule. To my surprise Dick didn't seem to be bothered about the early start, he simply insisted that he would not be prepared to film in the afternoon that day as he would need to catch up with his sleep. He knew that this would infuriate Gerald and took no little pleasure from the fact. The one person who made a real fuss when the early call was announced was Bill the cameraman. I couldn't stand him and neither could anyone else on the crew. To say he was a very average cameraman would be a damning slur.... to average cameramen. He was one of those sad men who try to disguise their insecurity behind pompous bluster. Gerald liked Bill because he never argued with the director, but the flip side of that coin, of course, meant that he never offered any creative cinematic suggestions either. I didn't like Bill because I quickly realised that he had developed a legion of ways to shift the blame on the many occasions when he had cocked up and needed a retake.

'We'll have to go again, the mic came into shot.'

'We'll have to go again the actor didn't hit his mark.'

'We'll have to go again I can see the wig join when I zoom in.'

Bill had dozens of these up his sleeve for use when he had pulled focus too late, panned too soon, or even realised that he had forgotten to set the right exposure. A film cameraman, in decline, can often be bailed out by a supportive assistant, but Bill was too vain, or too stupid to realise that. He would frequently shift the blame for his own mistake onto the assistant and thus destroy any chance of co-operation. It was an unhappy situation. The day before the elephant scene had been particularly wearisome. It was exceptionally hot; remember this was 1976, the year of the great drought. Dick had been in a bad mood all day, probably because his wife had turned up unexpectedly and forced him to cancel his plans to seduce one of the dancers in his theatre show. Bill had been above averagely useless, Gerald had been above averagely irritating and the scene we were filming below averagely funny. By the time we came to 'wrap' I had had enough and I suggested to my assistant, Ken, that we might slip away and escape the crew for a while, drive into the country and find a pub were we could have a few pints, enjoy a quiet meal and forget the bloody Dick Emery show for one evening, at least.

It was a hot, still evening. They all were in the summer of 1976. We drove to a pretty hamlet, just inland from Blackpool and enjoyed a pint of good ale as we sat outside the pub and looked across the village green. I can still remember the sight of four or five ducks standing in the middle of a circle of dried, cracked mud. Before the drought this had been a pond and the ducks seemed confused and as anxious as everybody else for it to rain again soon. As long as it stayed dry for the next couple of days that is all I hoped for, and after that we would have completed our filming.

Ken and I finished our second pints and went into the pub's restaurant to eat. Ken and I had worked together on a lot of shows: *'Porridge'*, its' sequel ' *Going Straight'* as well as three series of with Dick Emery so we were good friends as well as being close colleagues. With the end of the filming in sight, it was a jolly evening. The food was excellent and, by the end of evening, I confess that I had had rather too much to drink. Ken had volunteered to drive and I took shameful advantage of his generosity. I was to pay for my indulgence the next morning.

When we got back to the hotel we bumped straight into Gerald. Where had we been? Had we forgotten that it was a very early start tomorrow? Had the artists and the crew been reminded about the early call? I was about to tell him to worry about doing his job and leave us to do ours but Ken, ever the diplomat, reassured him that everything was under control. We wished him goodnight and headed off to our rooms.

"Shall I bang on your door in the morning?" said Ken as I rather unsteadily unlocked my bedroom door.

"Might be a good idea," I said. "I think I might have had bit too much tonight."

"Yes, just a drop, probably. Good night."

That parting remark from Ken was as much as I remembered of that night until early the next morning when I groped for my watch, gazed at it in a stupor and then realised, to my horror that it was 6.45. Everybody involved in the filming had already left the hotel for the beach and for the one and only occasion in my time as a production manager I was going to be late on location. As I put my head under the cold tap and struggled into my clothes, I had a dim recollection of having heard some banging in a distant dream. That must have been Ken and he must have believed my grunted response to be a sign that I was awake. Of course I wasn't, I had been stirred a little and then plunged back into torpor. Oh well, no help for it now, I was late and that was that. I grabbed my brief case, checked that I had enough cash on me to pay the elephant trainer and rushed to find my car.

When I got to the location I parked behind the costume wagon and the first person I met was Derek, Dick's dresser.

"Hello Mike, you're running a bit late aren't you chuck?"

"Too bloody right I am, Derek. I got pissed last night, like a fool. Is everything OK?"

"Well dear, I only do frocks you know, but I get the impression that things could be going smoother."

That was enough to put me into a panic. Derek was one of those elegant and mild mannered middle aged gay men whose unflappable demeanour is often an asset to a show in times of crisis, but I knew that 'things could be going smoother' was Derek's coded camp for ' We are starring disaster in the face.'

"Is Dick alright?"

"Oh yes he's fine; he's over there, look; sitting on the wall. He's watching what's happening on the beach. I should have a cup of coffee if I were you Mike, dear. I don't think that there is a lot you can do at the moment."

"Thanks Derek, but I'd better see what's happening."

It was about 50 yards from the parked crew vehicles to where Dick was sitting, on the sea wall, at the edge of the promenade. As I came near to him my anxiety level shot up several indices as the air was split by an elephant's trumpet call, immediately followed by another, louder, and even more disturbing than the first. As was now near enough to see that Dick was shaking but I still couldn't see over the wall to the events on the beach. It took me a moment to realise that Dick was shaking, no doubt of that, but not from fear, as I had first thought, but from laugher. Indeed he had tears streaming down his face.

"Oh Mike, I'm so glad you're here. I wouldn't have wanted you to have missed this." I took a few steps closer and peered over the sea wall. What I saw was an image that remains with me to this day. Bill, the cameraman, had the arriflex camera in his arms with the tripod still attached. These were each a considerable weight but that didn't seem be preventing him from running as fast as his dumpy little legs could carry him. Behind him, and not very far behind, ran Gerald. Behind Gerald there ran two very angry elephants with their trunks pointing skywards and their tusks levelled for revenge. It was a moment before I realised that, for reasons best known to the human participants of this chase, they were all running round in a big circle. It was also evident that it was a circle of ever decreasing circumference and that it wouldn't be long before the pursuers caught up with the pursued. There was nothing I could do to help and yet I had to appear to be doing something. As Production Manager I was responsible for the safety of cast and crew. I could easily imagine the pompous voices of court of inquiry interrogating barristers.

"So tell us Mr. Crisp, what exactly you were doing when one of your colleagues was trampled to death by the first elephant and the other was impaled on the tusks of the second elephant?" I had to be seen to make some helpful gesture, however useless, simply so that I could plead mitigation. I ran across the sands in the direction of the unfolding drama as fast as I could, which wasn't all that fast as I have never been very athletic. It must be said that Gerald and Bill were running faster, but they had rather more incentive. I got as close to the stampeding pachyderms as prudence and my very limited degree of courage would allow, when suddenly I realised that Herr Gudrich, the trainer was standing right beside me. I couldn't imagine where he had sprung from. Perhaps he had been behind the break water having a pee? Considering the circumstances he seemed remarkably unconcerned.

"Morgen"

"Good Morning, Herr Gudrich."

"How are you?"

"I'm fine; I say Herr Gudrich can't you do something to stop the elephants?"

"Oh don't worry about the elephants, they are having fun."

"I'm not worrying about the elephants Herr Gudrich, I'm worrying about my friends."

"They too will be fine, if they stop running the elephants will stop chasing them."

"Yes but they don't know that and I think the cameraman is in danger of having a heart attack." At that moment Bill and Gerald rushed past on another circuit.

"It is possible." agreed Herr Gudrich and he paused just long enough to allow the elephants to thunder by.

"Now about my fee, we agreed £150 I think?"

I knew full well that whilst Herr Gudrich had asked for £150, Gerald had beaten him down to £75. I thought for a moment.

"In the circumstances, Herr Gudrich, I think it might be best if I paid you £200 and we had no more trouble from the elephants."

"It is good. *Helga ! Bertha ! Stoppen sie diesen augenblich!*." It was amazing; on hearing that shout Helga and Bertha immediately stopped their chase. It was if they were electric toys and they had been switched off. They looked at each other and, if elephants can look nonchalant, then that is what they looked, then they trotted off calmly into the sea. Bill put the camera down and then collapsed beside it gasping for breath; a red faced Gerald walked over to join me.

"My God Mike did you have anything to do with that?"

"Well a bit," I admitted.

"Whatever did you do?"

"Nothing much really; I just renegotiated the fee."

"So that was what it was all about .The bastard! What did you do, then, give him an extra fiver?"

"Something like that." I said.

As if to insure that I didn't become too insufferably smug, my preferred technique of buying the production out of trouble backfired badly a few days later. We had switched location and were now struggling to film in the delightful surroundings of the Blackpool seafront Fairground. There are several locations that present logistic nightmares for filming drama sequences: Railway stations, Airports, Racecourses are all up there in the 'avoid like the plague' category but Fairgrounds, too, have their own special place in the register of 'locations from hell'. In our case, the man who owned the fairground saw us coming. He knew that the script dictated that we should film in his tawdry pleasure dome so he realised that he could charge what he liked. Gerald argued and negotiated for days, if not weeks, but for once even he had met his match. We had to pay through the nose. However for this very considerable fee we were to be granted precisely... bugger all. Just the right to be there. It was expressly stated that if any stall holder thought that our presence was distracting from their trade, then we had to make it good with them on an individual basis. Of course these payments would be estimated in an entirely reasonably way, the straight forward

integrity and scrupulous honesty of fairground stall holders being one of their most renowned human qualities. In
short we were going to be well and truly stitched up and,
as production manager I had to steel myself to be fleeced
at every turn. I dreaded the approach of the first day of
the funfair sequence.

To prepare ourselves as much as possible Ken and I visited
the fair a couple of days before we were due to be filming
there. The idea was to get to know the layout of the place
and to try and find some stall holders who might be prepared to co- operate for a reasonable fee. We came away
not very convinced that we had succeeded but we had
fixed one important facility. This was a 'bolt hole' for Dick;
a private area where he could escape the general public
and relax between set ups. For the big make up and costume changes he would still need to return to his location
caravan, but Ken and I felt that it was a good idea to have
somewhere that he could 'vanish into' near at hand in order to escape the great British Public. We found a suitable
place behind the 'Hook the Ducks' stall. The woman who
ran it was happy to earn a bit of extra cash as it was never
a very popular stall. She would put in a comfy chair and a
table. It all seemed fine. At the time that we made the ar-
rangement I had no idea of just how useful this hiding
place would turn out to be.

The first morning of filming in the fairground went pretty
much as I had expected that it would. Dick was in a bad
mood, surrounded, as he was by crowds, of an unusually

moronic nature. The holiday making public, young couples, old couples, the halt, the lame, the cerebrally challenged, all wanted to crowd in on him for autographs and, the dreaded, photographs.

"Sorry I can't do autographs now, I'm working." that was an unusually polite reaction from our star.

"Nice work if you can get it 'eh Dickie boy?" some self-appointed jester remarked.

"It would be if you dropped dead." came the more typical response.

Gerald and Bill were in ostentatious 'conference' about the opening shot. They both entertained the fond hope that 'Joe Public' would be looking at them with envious eyes, thinking of them as men who had reached the peak of their profession in show business.

"Oh for Christ sake Gerald get on with it." came the desperate cry from Dick.

"With you in a minute, Dick." Gerald called back and then, so as to shift attention, I think, added, "Mike you really must get your lads to get the crowds back and to stop gawking."

"Doing our best Gerald." I replied and knowing, full well, that nothing short of the release of a pack of ravening wolves would have any effect on the crowd's behaviour.

After another twenty minutes of posturing about, Bill scanning the sky through his 'pan glass' to check if the contrast ratios were within limits and Gerald looking through his director's finder they decided on the opening set up. It certainly had cinematic possibilities. Dick as the 'Bovver Boy' again, would be seen in the distance walking towards the rifle range. The camera, itself, would be by the range but at the start of the shot the image would be framed by all sorts of twirling and spinning circus rides. As Dick wended his way towards the lens all sorts of exciting rides and fairground hardware would dip in and out of shot. Only as Dick got close would the camera pan with him and reveal the rifle range where the dialogue of the sketch would take place. It was in essence a good idea, but there were problems. The first was that any shot of that type requires a deal of rehearsal especially for focus pulling. As Dick gets nearer and nearer to camera the focus on him constantly changes and needs subtle adjustment until he reaches the final position. Focus pulling, as we have noted, was not Bill's strong suit.

As soon as we arrived on location I went straight to the rifle range and agreed a fee with the guy running it. I think we settled for £50. It all seemed amicable. I was, therefore, somewhat disconcerted that when, after Gerald and Bill's deliberations, we returned to place the camera, the man I had done the deal with was nowhere to be found and the stall was now in the charge of two unpleasant, greasy, youths. They had 'no idea ' of whom I had paid earlier and all I could do was to pay them all over again. I was

383

almost certain that the first man I had met, was their father. I had been taken to cleaners, in the best colourful tradition of 'show ground folk'

The other ride that I needed to 'square', for Gerald's grand establishing shot to work, was the foreground feature. This was one of those machines that look like a huge spider with jointed metal legs hinged into a central rotating unit. The passengers are locked into pods at the end of each leg, each pod holding about six people. When the ride is up to speed the central unit revolves the legs and the legs go up and down rising to a height of about sixteen feet above ground and then plummeting down again. As if this was not sufficient torture the 'pods ' also revolved, so their human content spent considerable periods of the ride upside down. It was the sort of thing that, personally, I would have avoided like seven plagues, but, of course it was a huge attraction for devil-may -care holiday makers. Now, as I say, the idea was for this monstrous device to twirl and dive in the foreground as Dick approached through the funfair. A great idea, but for...Bill. I had already learnt that the reason the elephants had first got out of control was that he had spent so bloody long getting the shot of them approaching the sea that, frustrated by forever being held back from their much -loved swim they took action in the only way an elephant can. (Well one of the only ways!). With the fair-ground shot it was, therefore, inevitable that we would have to suffer a deal of buggering about before we got the opening shot 'in the can'. After four attempts I was praying hard that Bill had got it when, just as Dick was about to pass the spinning spider the damn ride stopped and blocked him from view. The shot had to be declared NG.

"Oh really Mike, this is a very difficult shot you know, we can't have this happening all the time. Sort it out for God's sake!" This was Bill, at his most defensive aggressive. I could have hit him. We all knew full well that he had already screwed up three takes and that most decent cameramen would have managed it first time. It was sod's law that the damn ride happened stop in the middle of take four and what looked like being a good shot.

"Fine Bill, I'll see what I can do," I smiled through gritted teeth and headed off to tell Dick what was happening and to try to bribe the man running the spider ride.

I apologised to Dick and told him that we try for another take as soon as I had paid off spider man.'

"Oh don't worry too much darlin" said Dick. "The silly old bugger would have probably fucked it up anyway." I realised that, though he never said anything, Dick's opinion of our director of photography was quite as low as mine was.

"There is one good thing about this taking forever," Dick mused. "The public have got bored with us, hardly any' Brentfords' about now at all."

Brentford was the code word Dick always used when he spotted a member of the public who was about to press themselves on to his company. He could be chatting, apparently amiably with someone at the hotel bar but if I heard him bring the word Brentford into the conversation, then I knew that he needed rescuing and I would break in with an 'urgent phone call' that Dick needed to take.

As I looked around it was clear that Dick was right about the Brentfords in the fairground. The place had been groaning with them when we first arrived but now they had become bored with us and were seeking more genuine excitement in such delights as the dodgems, the waltzer, the big wheel and even the dreaded spider.

For a bung of £30, the Spider ride operator had agreed to keep the beast going until we had managed to get the shot that we were after. Bill continued to mess up, so I had to go back to the guy with another £30. After several other abortive attempts, with even Gerald beginning to doubt Bill's capabilities the spider ride man came up to me.

"Sorry Guv, but I really think I better stop the ride for a few minutes, now."

"Oh why now for God's sake?" snapped Bill, who had overheard the remark.

"Well it's like this. You've had my ride going non-stop for half an hour and the punters are only supposed to be in there for five minutes maximum."

"OH MY GOD. Why ever didn't you tell me before?" Of course I knew the answer. £60 was just too much temptation.

"Right listen everyone." I said, being forceful for once. We need to pack up the camera and hide it. We can put it in Dick's rest room; then we should all disperse and pretend to be just a part of the crowd."

"Whatever for?" said Bill.

"Didn't you hear what the man said? There have been people spinning about and turned upside down in that damn ride for 25 minutes, when 5 is the legal limit, and all because of us!"

When they get off, assuming any of them can still walk, we are likely to be lynched.

"Oh come now Mike I think that is being a bit dramatic, I think Bill will agree with me when I say..." but Gerald's *jejeune* optimism faded on his lips as the great spider wound to a halt and for the first time, for nearly thirty minutes, the motors fell silent and we could hear the groans of distress from within.

"Tell you what, everyone," said Gerald, "why don't we break for coffee and meet back here in, say, twenty minutes?"

The crew needed no further urging, but I felt a strange compulsion to stay and see just what fearful horrors we had inflicted on those unwitting pleasure seekers. I could be grand and say *'I felt responsible'*, which I kinda did and kinda didn't. I should have thought about the wisdom of keeping the bloody spider running for all that time, but the damned man who ran it might have mentioned it before he did. No, I just thought I'd better see that nobody actually suffered serious harm from the experience. I therefore queued up at a near-by hot dog stand and looked on in dreadful anticipation.

As one by one the 'pods' on the spider ride opened it became increasingly clear that, in some ways Gerald had been right. There was little danger of us being lynched because the shattered humanity that now crept back into the world was too confused to have thoughts above anything more than a blessed relief to be reunited with God's good earth.

I think that one of the most striking features of the sad vision that was unfolding before me was the unexpected array of colours. No one, it seemed, was the same colour that they had been when they had got on the ride. Bronzed healthy young couples were now ashen white. Black men and women, who had eagerly joined the ride with their jolly black children were now various shades of green and the few brave senior citizens amongst them, whatever their ethnic origin or skin type, had gone either bright red or dark purple. Inevitably vomit, too, had enhanced the rainbow palette of this tableau. Children had chucked up over parents, parents had chucked up over children and elderly men and women had chucked up over everybody. Hardly anybody in that sorry throng had managed to escape the ecumenical communion of projectile puke. I hung my head in shame and quietly consigned my hot dog to the nearest waste bin.

When I think back on that incident I realise how lucky I was that it occurred in the mid 1970's, before these frenzied days of 'compensation culture'. Nowadays people are much less stoic and a similar accident would doubtless result in the social services being summoned to the scene, community leaders would be pressed for advice and counselling for the victims provided by specialists in ' PTFFCS' (post traumatic funfair cock-up syndrome).

As it was, very little fuss was made by the unfortunate folk who had chanced to take that ride. It is possible, of course, that they didn't realise that their ride had been any different from the regular one. There is, after all, a type of person who visits a fun fair for the sort of experience that you would normally only suffer at the hands of the secret police in some torturing, totalitarian regime. Indeed as I looked on, that hot July morning, one boy who was wiping himself clean with his sun hat shouted to his sister, who had been too nervous, or too savvy, to have gone on the ride.

"You should have come on it, Lizzie, it was great. Everyone was sick, even the grown-ups!"

Within ten minutes of being released back into the community the last of the bespattered revellers had cleaned themselves off, with water from a nearby tap, staggered off into the further reaches of the fair ground. It certainly was different era then, innocent people had suffered, for no good reason but no one demanded redress and no sympathetic members of the public arrived at the scene with armfuls of cuddly toys or bouquets to mark the scene of tragedy with entirely pointless tributes. Perhaps they were more sensible times, the 1970s?

Chapter 25.

<u>Improperly Dressed.</u>

It was fortunate that Gerald passed some of the 'spider victims' on his way back from the coffee break as the unpleasant spectacle somewhat changed his attitude towards the rest of the day's filming. He now decided that the wisest plan was to keep the remaining filming as simple as possible and to get out of that damned fairground as quickly as possible. No one was more pleased to learn this than I was. No - one person was even more pleased: Dick was.

The rest of the Blackpool filming passed without further incident except for the saga of Gerald's missing trousers. This happened while we filming one of the last sequences on our schedule. Dick, as his old man character *'Lampwick'* was sitting in a deck chair on the beach. Next to him sat guest star, Mollie Sugden. I forget the precise burden of the sparkling dialogue but I think the sketch was supposed to end with the startlingly original notion that the tide should come in and wash away their picnic hamper. In order for this to happen the deck chairs naturally needed to be near the water's edge but there was three or four pages of dialogue to be performed before the hamper floated off. The prop men, who had experience of filming on beaches before, quite sensibly set the deck chairs at the top of the beach, above high water mark. They pointed out that as the tide was coming in we should shoot all the dialogue with the camera back to sea, then we could finally re-position for the tag with the hamper. Depending on how long it all took we might hardly need to move at all as the tide might well have reached us by then. This made perfect sense to everybody; everybody except Gerald and Bill. For God only knows what reason (probably simply because they hadn't thought of it) they rejected the idea. Bill had already set up the camera near the water's edge so the, very reluctantly the prop men moved the deck chairs up to join it. Of course the inevitable followed. We hadn't filmed one line of dialogue before it became necessary to move everything up the beach and start again. Even so, Bill insisted that we didn't move far from the sea's edge. We managed to film a couple of speeches and then, once again the water was lapping around the foot of the tripod. One of the prop men muttered something about 'Cnut' under his breath, but whether as a reference to the Viking King, or simply as a term of dyslexic abuse, I couldn't be certain. So we wasted a lot of time that morning being chased up the beach by the rising tide, only to end up in exactly the same place as the prop men had set the deck chairs at the start of the day. Fortunately the crew had arrived on location in beach wear, so the resultant paddling around was not too much of a problem for them. The two exceptions to this were, you've guessed it, Bill and Gerald. Bill had made some concession to the beach location and hot weather by wearing a pair of shorts. These were of the 'last days of the Raj' variety, the sort of voluminous things worn by scout masters in Ealing comedies. Bill completed his ensemble with long khaki socks and lace up brown brogues, neither of which benefitted from being soaked in salt water. Gerald, on the other hand, had eschewed beach clothing altogether and had gone in for the 'chair-man of the golf club' look; blazer, cravat and smart grey trousers. He looked elegant enough, at the start of the day, when he strode up to the water's edge and he and Bill made their first daft decision; but when it became obvious that *'Time and tide waiteth for no man',* he quickly regret-ted his choice of clothes. Indeed it wasn't long before he asked the wardrobe department if they had any shorts or swimming trunks that he might borrow until our session on the beach was over. They had; so during a break in the filming and in privacy of the costume caravan, he changed into this, more suitable, attire. His trousers and shoes, were already wet, so he left them in out in the sun to dry and asked one of the prop men to look after them. He looked elegant enough.

We broke for lunch later than planned, the buggering about chasing the tide up the beach had seen to that, but it was another hot day so many of the cast and crew spent their lunch time relaxing on the sands. That afternoon we were scheduled to film in the town centre and towards the end of the lunch break everybody changed out of their swim suits. Bill put on a pair of cavalry trousers and, luckily for him, his shoes and socks had dried out in the sun. Gerald too was fortunate with regard to his shoes socks but in the matter of his trousers he was not so lucky; they had gone missing, presumably stolen. For some reason he was absolutely convinced that this was a prank played on him by either Ken or me and no amount of denial on our part would persuade him otherwise. Indeed, he wasted so much time arguing with us that 'the joke was over' and that 'enough was enough' that there was no time left, before filming started again, in which he could get back to the hotel and put on another pair. I suppose I could have gone back and fetched him a pair myself; but I was so angry about being falsely accused that I let him stew.

At first, as we set up our afternoon sequence, Gerald didn't look particularly odd. He was dressed in swimming trunks in the high street, but he had a summer shirt on and, after all this was a seaside resort. Even his red socks and lace up shoes looked only, faintly, ridiculous. But then an odd thing happened. For the first time, in that long hot summer of drought, there came a hint of a change in the weather. It went cloudy and a strong chilly breeze came in from the sea. Everybody in the crew dashed back to their vehicles for pullovers and coats. Gerald went to his car and put on a smart new anorak. The result was startling because the anorak came down to just below his bottom so the effect was that of a man who had forgotten to put his trousers on. Now, if you were to walk down the street dressed like that a few heads might turn but, probably, very few people would take any notice. However if you try to direct a film unit in a high street full of onlookers and if you strut about with a loud hailer issuing instructions to cast, crew and the general public whilst looking like an absconder from the local mental hospital, then, frankly, you are asking for trouble.

"Alright everybody, stand by for a take. Those ladies and gentlemen in the back ground of our shot, could you clear please? Oh well, at least please don't stare at the camera."

"It's not the camera we're staring at mate."

"Oh Doris, hasn't that man got skinny little legs?"

"Mum why hasn't that man got any trousers on? Has he had an accident Mum, has he "um?''

Gerald had to suffer those sorts of remarks for the whole afternoon. Mind you the rest of us suffered too. Gerald was, understandably, plunged in a foul mood and filming took twice as long as it should have done because crowds of people gathered to watch the 'funny man who'd forgotten his trousers.' At the end of filming he left for his hotel without a word to any of us. His legs were going blue with cold and he was still convinced that I was involved in the mystery of the disappearing pantaloons. I always believed that the make-up girls were responsible for the prank and only, very recently, did Ken tell me that he was sure it was one of the prop men. The one whose advice about the incoming tide had been ignored and caused him no end of extra work. Gerald's disappearing trousers were the prop man's terrible revenge. Strange to tell, there was a 'silver lining' to all this. At the end of that afternoon's shoot, when I came to give Dick his call for the next day, I apologised for all the delays. I was surprised when our star told me that he hadn't had so much fun for ages.

Chapter 26.

A Fond Farewell.

A lot of people used to think that many of Dick Emery's sketches were in questionable taste. I don't really believe that. I think the truth is that most of them were in appalling taste, with the funniest ones often in the worst taste of all. The road race between the hearse and the hell's angel motorcyclist was one of finest examples of the genre. In this film sequence Dick played both the undertaker, driving the huge old fashioned Rolls Royce hearse, and the biker, riding a huge Harley Davidson. Dick was in his element when we shot the scene because he loved driving both powerful cars and powerful motor bikes. We had a good crew too, which included an excellent visual effects man. Bill was, again the cameraman and Gerald was directing, but on this occasion both of them were on good form. The sequence was this: A hearse is seen driving along a road, and at the wheel is Dick dressed as an old fashioned undertaker in frock coat and black top hat with a black *crêpe* band. For this part Dick also wore his comic protruding teeth, which the make-up department had specially made for him and which he used when playing parsons and such like stalwarts of religion. The hearse driver looks in his mirror and sees a yob on a motor bike determined to overtake, the undertaker is equally determined that he should not. A battle ensues in which, eventually both hearse and motor bike are screaming along overtaking each other, cutting each other up and generally driving like maniacs. Eventually the hearse ploughs around a bend the back of the vehicle springs open and the coffin flies out and lands in the village pond. It turned out to be one the best comic films we ever made for the show but, as you can imagine it was no easy thing to stage.

As production manager, my first job was to find a stretch of road where we could safely film the main part of the chase. With the hearse and the bike carving each other up and swerving all over the road this was likely to be no easy task especially as the 'on screen' vehicles would need to be preceded or followed by the camera car. There was no way we could film this on a public road. Old aerodromes or roads in the grounds of stately homes are often used for such scenes, but they always look a bit false and we wanted the chase to look as dangerous as possible, without actually putting anyone at risk. After about a week's research I got lucky. We discovered that the new Watford-Tring by-pass was soon to open. It was complete all but for a few signs and was due to open on the Monday. Our filming was scheduled to finish on the previous Friday, so there was a chance we might be able to use this new, as yet un-occupied, stretch of motor way. Maybe someone in the ministry of transport was a Dick Emery fan? I don't know, but to my amazement and great relief we got permission to film our chase on the new road. The 'men from the ministry' were even helpful enough to suggest where the crew should rendezvous. There was a roundabout at the Tring end of the new road and from this a new exit lead down to the by-pass. A barrier was in place until the official opening, but we could remove the barrier, gain access, and then replace the barrier. This we did, the access road became our base and we parked all the vehicles that were not going to appear on screen along the side of it. There was one comic outcome from all this. The coffin was not required in the hearse for all the shots. Some-times the back of the hearse needed to be empty to allow room for the camera crew when they were filming shots of the motor cycle passing and gesturing rudely to the driver. Indeed we had two coffins. One real one and one light weight mock up for the shots of the coffin flying out of the back. A number of motorists using the roundabout slowed down and gawped in amazement as they saw a hearse drive up the slip road and a gang of men (our prop boys) take the coffin out and lay it on the grass verge. Later, two hitch hikers were dropped off at the roundabout and starred at two men sitting in the sun on a coffin. When a Hearse arrived as if from nowhere and the men shoved the coffin, unceremoniously, on aboard the hitch hikers chose to move to another spot. Had a camera been in evidence, of course, all would have been explained but the camera crew were out of sight on the by-pass itself.

I can recall another unfortunate occasion when the fact that the camera was hidden from view caused a degree of alarm. This was many years after the Emery incident and I was by now a senior producer at BBC television training.

One of the students was filming a 'Gothic Horror' as his final exercise. We had permission to film in the picturesque grave yard of Aldenham church. The church was only a couple of miles from our base at BBC Elstree and we frequently used it as a location. We had a good reputation with the vicar for being 'responsible', but I fear we rather damaged it this time. The scene involved the lead character coming face to face with 'death'. The effects team did a great job filling the church yard with fog and the costume department came up trumps with the most convincing Angel of Death I have ever seen. A hooded, sinister humpbacked figure, complete with long finger nails and an enormous scythe. I was by the camera that morning as the student director prepared for his first shot and I remember congratulating him on managing to stage a truly terrifying image. But that is the point, I was by the camera. We hadn't banked on anyone entering the church yard that early in the morning from the little used side gate. A little old lady did just that and as she rounded the church one of the large yew trees screened off the camera crew from her view so all she saw was an eerily foggy area amongst the ancient head stones at the centre of which stood the Angel of Death himself. Her scream might well have been heard back at the studios. The situation was not helped by that fact that the actor playing death was so concerned about the lady that he rushed towards her with open arms; thank God she had a strong constitution. We made things up to her with a strong cup of unit coffee and some chocolate biscuits. Then, as a gesture of good will, Death obliged her with his autograph.

Not long after this church yard encounter Dick Emery had an encounter with the Grim Reaper, but this time it was no actor. I don't know if they exchanged autographs or not, from what I gather they didn't have enough time. Dick was having one of his many flings with a nubile young woman and, at last the years caught up with him and he suffered a massive heart attack during a romantic weekend at a London hotel.

I had been the production manager on his shows for three years and had directed two or three of them but I was not part of the production team at the time of Dick's death. I was however still closely involved, as in my 'other life 'as the composer 'Jack Point', I had written the incidental music for his TV films for the last six years. I thought it only proper that I should attend his funeral. It proved to be an experience that I would never forget. Show business is always at its' mawkish, tacky worst when it feels compelled to seem sincere and when an event also requires it to appear deeply religious the results can revolting in the extreme. There was an element of all this at Dick's funeral but, appropriately there was also a strong dose of tasteless humour. No one who attended the service at Mortlake Crematorium on that sunny January day in 1983 could have been entirely unaware of the irony of it all. Over the years Dick had often featured funerals and undertakers as part of his comedy cannon.

I met my friend the actress Pat Coombs outside the chapel as we all bustled about waiting for our cue to enter and she told me that she genuinely didn't know whether to laugh or cry. Dicks' wife was there accompanied by her mother, both dressed in black fur and looking like something out of *'The Lion the Witch and the Wardrobe'*. (I'll leave the casting to your imagination). Then, just as we lined up to follow the coffin inside, a car swept up and out stepped Dick's most recent mistress, and eventual nemesis, the dancer' Faye'. She too was wearing an expensive fur coat, probably from the same furrier as had supplied Jo and her mother, and almost certainly paid for by the same cheque book. Although about twenty five years Jo's junior the two woman looked quite similar even excepting the fur coats. Jo had platinum blonde hair and so did Faye however it was pretty evident that Faye's hair colour was a gift from nature whereas Jo's came courtesy of Proctor and Gamble. You could have cut the atmosphere with a knife, although a couple of battle axes were more immediately to hand. The startled mourners were just about recovering from Faye's dramatic arrival when there came in her wake something even less welcome; the reptilian brat pack of the British gutter press. Photographers from the arse end of journalism, the Sun, the Express, the Mirror, the Mail and the News of the World had somehow learned that both wife and girlfriend would be attending the funeral. They wanted pictures and if there was a cat fight they each wanted the most violent image with which to delight their paper's discerning readership.

And so in an atmosphere of tense expectation and an aura of unctuous humbug we all trooped into the chapel. BBC light entertainment executives, producers, production managers, assorted B and C list celebs and, elbowing each other to be in a position to grab the front pew alongside Jo, Mum and Faye.

The press pack did their best to gate crash the service but the crematorium attendants were too quick for them and swiftly shut and bolted the doors before they had a chance to gain entry. Jo and Faye exchanged occasional daggered looks but the large congregation settled down and it seemed as if the funeral had a chance of proceeding in a dignified fashion. It was not to be.

At the time of Dick Emery's funeral I had worked in television for eighteen years so I was no media virgin and I knew how aggressively the 'gentlemen of the press' could pursue a story and a photo opportunity but I had never encountered their tactics at first hand. Their behaviour that day the crematorium convinced me that journalists from the popular press could give master classes in hooliganism to the National Association of Lager Louts. The doors may have been shut in their faces but that was not going to stop the gang from trying to grab a high-earning photo.

As I have said, the service got off to a seemly start but after a very short while, camera lenses and photographers faces started to appear at the windows. Most of the chapel windows were clear glass and, though they were quite high off the ground, it was not impossible to reach them if you clambered onto an up turned bench. Many of the paparazzi were used to this sort of situation and carried tall step ladders in their cars so that within a very few minutes from the start of the service, there was no privacy in the chapel at all. All of those windows which were not stained glass had cameras peering through them and, what was far worse, the photographers started to fight amongst themselves for prime position. They elbowed each, shook their rival's ladder or just simply belted him one. The effect on the religious proceedings had to be experienced to be believed; the parson's droning incantations mixing with the crude oaths of the mob outside in a most surreal fashion.

"The Lord gave and the Lord hath taken away."

"Get off my ladder you wanker!"

"The Lord is my light and my salvation, who then shall I fear?"

"Wiggins you tosser; fuck off out of my way!"

"We brought nothing into this world and it is certain…."

At this point there was a loud crash as one of the photographers was pushed off his ladder. It was followed by a scream as hit the ground but unfortunately he was not sufficiently injured to shut him up. The resultant stream of swear words and threats of vengeance were both louder and more obscene than anything we had endured so far and several of the men in the congregation unbolted the door and went outside to try and restore order. I was glad that my place in the middle of a long pew gave me an excuse for staying put. I would have happily reinforced their efforts had I not been a lifelong coward. I'm not sure how they managed it, perhaps they said that the police had been called, but they certainly had an effect. All went quiet. Now, at last, only the sun streamed in at the windows and the still small voice of calm prevailed. However there was to be one more intervention before the end of the funeral service; but this time it was divine. When the parson reached the committal an event took place which topped everything that had gone before.

"Unto Almighty God we commend the soul of our brother departed and we commit his body to the fire."

It was amazing. At this very moment the sun ceased to shine. It was suddenly covered by a single dense black cloud. The chapel became chillingly dark and as the coffin started to vanish from our sight there rang out a single, deafening, clap of thunder.

I have often thought about that moment in later years. Dick's several wives might well have wondered if it was the Devil calling back one of his own, but his many fans probably think that it was God having a bit of fun at the expense of a comedian who had so often revelled in playing comic vicars.

Chapter 27.

Music Hath Charms.

From my earliest childhood I have always loved music. When I was three the family would regularly go to the bandstand on the embankment in our home town of Bedford, on Summer Sunday afternoons, to listen to the town band. I loved it and would often pick up a stick and stand and mimic the conductor. Somewhere in a box of fading family snap shots there is a small print of the three year old me 'conducting' which people find either cute or revoltingly precocious, depending on the state of their digestion. Anyway there could be no doubt that music delighted me as a child, it still does and I am sure it always will.

I had formal lessons on the piano, trumpet and later the French horn, but, sadly, I was never to become a very accomplished instrumentalist. I was, however, sufficiently enthusiastic to 'keep at it' into adult life and eventually found that a knowledge of and feeling for music was a huge advantage for a film maker. Later, when I discovered that, whilst I was not very good at playing it, I wasn't bad at writing it I soon realised that music could bring me in a very useful second income. But all that was in the future; at the time that I was learning to play the piano and the horn, life was full of other distractions. I had discovered the cinema. I wanted to make films and at the age of thirteen, with a borrowed Kodak 8mm movie camera that is what I started to do. For the next five years I made a film every summer which I showed to the school in the following winter term. These were not four minute comedies. They were half hour, and eventually, forty five minute, swashbucklers. It was the swashbuckling films at the cinema that I so longed to emulate, my films provided me with exactly what I wanted from life; complete escapism. School masters frowned and finger wagged as my obsession became more and more evident, but there was little they could do. I didn't waste much time writing the scripts and we made the film in the holidays. I couldn't, therefore, be accused of neglecting my school work but instinctively some of the masters knew that my mind was seldom fully occupied with the subject of the lessons. It could always escape from the drudgery of tedious reality into the wonderful world costume drama. That is where my full concentration lay and so all my studies suffered accordingly. The pity was that this neglect also infected my, then second, love: music. I had a succession of competent piano teachers and one truly great teacher for the trumpet and the horn but I hardly ever put in enough practice. So I remained mediocre. The films that I made were mediocre too, but I didn't know that at the time and what nobody knew was that a grounding in artistic mediocrity was the perfect preparation for a career in television.

One result of my daydreaming and lack of attention to detail was to result in one of the funniest performances at a supposedly serious concert that I have ever witnessed. This is what happened. In July 1965 I was in the history sixth at Bedford School. One break time near half term I was talking to my friend and class mate Martin Milman. Martin was a very good actor and I was persuading him to appear in my next great production. This was to be a romantic adventure set in the time of the English civil war. I wanted Martin to play a villainous puritan. He agreed and just before we went back to class our conversation strayed to other topics.

"Half term's coming up, can't be long before the music club concert." said Martin.

"Suppose it can't be," I agreed, "but it doesn't bother me, I haven't been asked to play."

"No neither have I." said Martin.

"Well that's bloody odd." I said and indeed it was because, though my solo horn playing would not be much of a 'miss' to the programme, Martin was an excellent flautist, grade eight with distinction, all that stuff. At that point another friend, Stephen Pringle walked past.

"Hey, Stephen, are you playing in the music club concert?"

"No, no one has mentioned it, I'm at bit miffed to be honest, it's next Sunday week, you know."

"Blimey that really is odd." Stephen was an exceptionally good pianist, he had recently played the second Brahms piano concerto at a concert given by the school orchestra and, indeed, I had opened the first movement with the sublime French horn solo, rather less than sublime as I was playing it but fortunately I hadn't put Stephen off too badly. The point about all this is that the school's big formal concerts were organised and rehearsed by the music staff whereas the Music Club concert was organised and rehearsed by the boys themselves.

"Well who the hell is running the music club these days anyway?" said Martin. He reached into his jacket pocket for a copy of the school diary. Every term one of these was issued to every boy: it contained a list of dates and times for all the events that term and a list of all the societies and the names of the people who ran them.

"Right here we are, Music Club, oh bugger..... Music Club; President M. Milman, Vice President .S Pringle, Secretary M Crisp."

"Oh blimey, well when's the concert? " I asked.

Martin consulted the diary again. "Shit, Stephen was right, it's a week on Sunday."

"And its Tuesday now," added Stephen, helpfully stating the obvious.

My first instinct was to cancel the damn concert. It has always been my instinct to find the easy way out of any problem: it has always been my strongest instinct as well as my greatest weakness. Stephen pointed out that that would be an unwise move as he knew that the Headmaster was planning to come and bring his wife along too. Now this was important, not only because the headmaster of any minor public school is looked on as one notch down from Royalty, but also because there was a huge argument festering in the staff room as to whether music was taking up too much time in the calendar of school events. The old guard of 'cold showers and rugby' was fearful that the establishment was becoming 'too wet by half with all this music and drama rot'. An endorsement from the headmaster would therefore be seen as an important victory for the arts lobby over the reactionaries.

As it turned out, it was not too difficult to put a reasonable programme together. Martin could do a couple of flute solos, I could struggle through a piece I had recently learned for grade 7 horn and Stephen had plenty of Chopin in his repertoire. Being the good sort that he was, he also agreed to serve as the concert accompanist for all who needed it. By the end of break the following day we had the event almost completely planned. Tim Jones would perform a movement from the Mozart Clarinet concerto, Peter Meiklejohn would perform the grandfather from *'Peter and the Wolf'* on his bassoon and Christopher Roseverre would play something extremely difficult, and particularly unappealing, on the oboe. The school's head boy would also be involved. He was Ian Barrett, son of a wealthy property developer. The vicious rumour among the other prefects was that Ian had been made head boy after his father had bunged the school building fund a couple of hundred grand. Ian was rather too fond of himself for my liking, but at least he was a musician. All previous heads of the school had been hearty 'rugger buggers' so I suppose we should have welcomed his appointment as a sign that the wind of change was with us. Ian played the 'cello and he wanted to play a duet for piano and 'cello by Olivier Messiaen. All very high brow.

Now, for me, Messiaen is one of those ' love him or hate him' composers. If you like music which sounds like the church organ is being played by someone wearing boxing gloves then he is just the man for you. My musical tastes are simple in the extreme and all that 'twelve tone dissonance' sounds to me like a frantic search for the king's new clothes; the sort of music that if you heard it at home on the radio and were all by yourself, with nobody around to impress, you would turn it off post haste, whilst thinking, 'Christ, what a load of old bollocks!' Still, if Ian Barrett wanted to play Messiaen, he was head boy and we were sure not going to stop him. Besides we needed his influence to kick the junior philately society out of the hall on the night we needed it for the concert. They had got in before us with their booking and they were not going to budge without some authoritarian muscle being brought to bear.

By lunch time on the Friday before the concert we were in good shape, the posters had been made and displayed and Stephen had found time to rehearse with all the soloists who needed accompanying. Of course Ian Barrett took up the lion's share of the rehearsal time as the Messiaen was of extreme technical difficulty. After two hours intense work it didn't sound much different to me but Ian was happy. I suppose that the discords that were meant to really grate sounded more grating and the discords that were supposed merely to irritate sounded more irritating. The two brief occasions when the instruments played in blessed harmony were checked against the score and proved to be misprints. It was just as Ian and Stephen were coming to the end of their rehearsal time that the door at the end of the memorial hall opened gently and a shadowy figure entered and stood at the back. Stephen looked up from the piano and mouthed to me,

"Oh my God, it's Adrian Friar." The shadowy figure came forward.

"Hello you guys, if you've finished your rehearsal I'd like to try through the pieces I am going play at the concert. I need to get used to the piano."

Now this was news to me. As far as I knew nobody had asked Adrian Friar to play at the concert and I thought I knew the reason. Adrian Friar was 'a bit odd' and in the cannon of public schoolboy etiquette being 'a bit odd' was about the worst thing you could be. You could be accepted if you were 'a bit thick' or if you were a 'bit of a sadistic bullying bastard' but to be 'odd' was to be distrusted. That, I thought, was probably why Martin hadn't ask him to play; but I was wrong, for at that moment Martin came in and greeted the odd fellah.

"Oh Adrian, at last! I've been looking for you all week, nobody seemed to know where you were."

"No I went missing for a purpose. I might tell you about it sometime." He cast a glance towards Ian, head-boy, Barrett. "But not now."

"Well I need to know what you are going to play, we will be printing the programmes tomorrow."

"I thought I might play some Liszt studies."

'Now there's a surprise,' I thought. You see, List was an integral part of Adrian Friar's oddness. He never stopped talking about Liszt and one day he, Adrian Friar, would be the world's greatest exponent of the maestro's compositions. This seemed to us all to be a fond hope. Adrian was an averagely good pianist, but nothing more. His fantasies about future triumphs on the concert platform were just a part of what made him odd. Mind you there were other things too. He was morbidly fascinated by the mummification rites of ancient Egypt. He was a pagan who dabbled in the occult and he was the only boy in the school who, at that time, confessed to smoking dope. We later discovered that the reason Martin had been unable to find him, for the last three days, was that he had taken himself off into a wood to cast a voodoo spell on Mr. Amos, the head of the music staff. Mr. Amos had told Adrian that he didn't think that he was yet ready to take grade 8 piano, so the boy planned a terrible revenge. He made a wax image of Amos, complete with some purloined hair, and with food in one satchel and black candles and pins in another, he set off to the woods, there to cast his terrible curses. No wonder he didn't want to confess that in earshot of the head boy. Looking back now, after the passing of fifty years, it is difficult to know if those curses worked or not. I know that Mr. Amos remained in post, as head of the music department of the school, for another fifteen years, so perhaps they did.

We left the hall that night to the sound of Adrian warming up with some scales. Martin was confident that we were going to present an interestingly varied programme and we were all relieved that we had managed to have save ourselves from a deal of embarrassment. It was the foolish optimism of callow youth.

The Sunday evening of the concert was warm, almost hot, after a beautiful summer's day. We opened the windows of the School's Memorial Hall and a gentle breeze entered the building like a waft of expectation. A half an hour before the concert was due to start most of the musicians were already in the library on the ground floor. The Memorial Hall, itself, was, indeed still is, on the first floor and is approached by a wide elegant stair case.

At about 7.20pm we were excited to hear the sound of quite a large group of boys running up the stairs to hall and Ian Barrett went up to get them seated and enforce some order. It turned out that they were some members of the junior philately society who had not been told about the change of venue. They were just about to leave and set off to the new location when the headmaster arrived together with his wife. Ian Barrett considered that it would look very bad for the head man to see a crowd of juniors rushing from the room so he forced them to sit down and shut up. The poor little buggers were therefore cheated of a happy evening spent sorting stamps with fellow enthusiasts. They had, instead, to sit through a concert stuffed with music, much of which was about as entertaining as a wet weekend in Frinton. Still, they swelled the ranks of the audience. After all, the concert was a club event and not an official school occasion, so no boy was compelled to attend. There were a few boys present apart from the kidnapped philatelists. They were either friends of the participants or junior instrumentalists who had come along for inspiration, or more likely, for a quiet giggle at our expense. Of course there were a few doting parents, but as many of the pupils at Bedford were boarders, there were not many of them. The Head Master's attendance had brought, in its' wake some other members of the teaching staff. A few of the sad old bachelors, whose whole life was 'the school' and who attended every event and also a few young and thrusting young masters with their young and thrusted wives. They had, doubtless, heard that the head master was going to be at the concert and so grabbed a chance to demonstrate how committed they were to the boys' out of school activities, ever hopeful that the post of house-master or head of department might result from such tactical crawling. So that was our audience. Martin and Stephen were just about to walk from the foyer area at the back of the hall to the performance space at the front when they were delayed by the late arrival of Christopher Roseverre. He struggled up the stairs carrying the family reel to reel tape recorder. It was a big one even by the standards of the time. He reached the top sweating rather heavily and then entered the hall to set it up. We were somewhat pissed off by this untimely disturbance but in the mid-1960s it was still quite a novelty to have a concert recorded, so we let Roseverre get on with it. It all took rather longer than expected as several audiences members had to vacate their seats in order for access to be gained to a wall cupboard in which the power points were concealed. Even after that there was much pissing about with cable runs and microphone stands as Roseverre installed his apparatus. I was glad that I was not on first and I certainly admired Martin and Stephen for the way they managed to stay calm and focused. Eventually, after of several of the quintessential, squawks whines, and screeches that accompany the start of any amateur recording session, our eccentric oboist gave us the thumbs up and Martin and Stephen walked, somewhat self-consciously to the front of the hall. I breathed a sigh of relief and the audience settled down to enjoy a rendition of two duets for flute and keyboard by Pergolesi. The boys done good. The applause they received was warm and genuine, and even the stamp collectors had not been as bored as they had feared that they would be. Martin returned to the back of the hall leaving Stephen at the piano to play two Chopin nocturnes. As expected, he played them well and again the audience showed its genuine appreciation. Christopher Roseverre's oboe solo was next and as I feared it's aggressively modern nature did not go down anything like as well as the previous items and the junior boys became distinctly fidgety. My turn was next and I was a bit fearful that I might split some notes. The junior boys were already restless and restlessness is often one notch away from attacks of the giggles. I hoped to God that I wouldn't suffer that humiliation. The piece that I had chosen to play was tuneful and well within my limited technical abilities, so I did my best to look confident. A quick tune up to the piano, I gave Stephen the nod and we started. It was ok, nothing to prompt hysteria amongst the ranks of the philatelists. I was getting through it all quite well when, to my astonishment there was a series of bangs and general kerfuffle near the back of the hall. I glanced up from the music and could hardly believe what I saw. Christopher, bloody, Roseverre was de-rigging his tape recorder, winding up cables collapsing the mic. stand and finally asking people to stand up so that he could open the cupboard and un-plug the damn thing. We were only two items away from the interval but he had recorded his piece and now just wanted to be off home. In some ways he may have done me a favour because I was so angry that I had no spare capacity for nerves and I got to the end of my solo on auto pilot and without any splits. However, at the time, I didn't see it that way and it was a good job that Roseverre had managed to pack up and leave before the end of my solo. Had I been able to lay hands on him and his oboe I had every intention of shoving the instrument into a place which would have required him to seek surgical intervention to effect its retrieval and, though it might have proved more difficult to achieve, I had similar plans for the fate of his tape recorder. As it was all I could do was to resume my seat at the back of the hall and quietly fume. My attention was taken by Ian Barrett. He was now in place tuning his 'cello and there was a sudden, noticeable, improvement in the behaviour of the junior boys. Barrett was, after all, head of the school so any boy would be a fool to upset him. I looked at my watch and prepared to be bored but then, to my surprise, Barrett made a short speech.

"Ladies and Gentlemen the piece I am about to play for you is by the contemporary French Composer Olivier Messiaen. It is of deeply religious significance. I would therefore request that at the end of my performance you refrain from applause and, instead, we all observe a moment of silent reflection."

"Christ, what a pretentious wanker." Martin, whispering in my ear, had read my thoughts exactly.

Barrett started to play and we all sat in respectful silence. The piece was in the frequently adopted style of ' contemporary serious composers.' It started with a series of long low pedal notes and then gradually became more rhythmic as percussive discords entered the scheme; quietly at first but becoming ever louder until the frantic bowing made it seem as if Barrett was determined to saw his cello in half; an outcome which may have proved to be popular. I can't now remember which particular Bible story was supposed to be represented by this music, it might have been the agonies of the crucifixion, Herod's slaughter of the Innocents or the beheading of John Baptist. It was one of those many depressing gospel tales from which legions of the devout have drawn comfort and cohorts of guilt ridden composers have drawn inspiration but it did cross my mind that Messiaen would very probably have written something similar for the wedding celebrations of a relative. At length the music shuddered to halt and I have to admit that it had woven a powerful spell over time and space for, though my watch confirmed that we had been listening to it for no more than fifteen minutes, it felt, to me, as if it had gone on for at least an hour and a half. The audience were entirely heedful of the 'cellist's request and he left the stage in a complete stunned silence.It was as if a prophecy had come true.

The last item before the interval was Adrian Friar playing Liszt. As he walked up the centre aisle towards the stage he looked almost serene but as he passed me I couldn't fail to notice two things: that his eyes sparkled with an evangelical fire and that the book of music, which he was carrying, was simply enormous.

Adrian sat down at the piano, adjusted the stool and flexed his fingers. He opened the book, at the first page, and started to play. The first piece was well received by the audience. After the frenzied writhing of the 'cello it came as a blessed relief. It was short, melodious, and

Adrian Friar played it well. The same was true of the second piece and the third. By the time we came to the fifth I was beginning to feel somewhat uncomfortable as I began to harbour the awful thought that Adrian Friar was proposing to play thorough the whole bloody book. By the time we reached item seven something even more disturbing was emerging .It was this. The pieces in the book had been printed in order of difficulty and that at number six they reached the limits of the pianist's technique. Item seven proved to be a watershed. The audience, by this time, had certainly had enough and gave evidence of this by much restless shifting in their chairs. Again it was the junior boys whose behaviour was the most distracting as they had, once more, become bored to the verge of the giggles. The increasing number of mistakes that were creeping into Friar's performance gave them good cause but there was also now another disquieting feature. It was becoming disturbingly obvious that every time Adrian Friar made a mistake he swore. At first this was quietly under his breath but as the mistakes got worse the volume of the swearing increased in strength and so did the vulgarity of the words that he chose. The crisis point was reached with the eighth piece in Friar's selection. This was one of those hugely demanding Liszt studies which was supposed to depict man's eternal struggle against temptation, lust and the torments of hell. Appropriately enough there were already a number of struggles taking place in the hall with the audience trying to contain its' anxiety and Adrian Friar failing to contain his language. The structure of this dramatic composition was Liszt at his most extreme. There was a repeated motif which started with ominous rumbling chords in the base .These were followed by furious arpeggios requiring the prefect synchronism of right and left hand as they raced from the bottom of the keyboard to the top in a dazzling shower of chromatics; then, once they had arrived at the very summit, there was a silence of one single beat before the striking of a chord, so gigantic in its stretch and so vibrant in its harmony it seemed impossible for it to have been played by one single pianist. There is then the briefest of pauses before the whole sequence starts over again in a different key and with even more startling harmonies. That I hope is a fair description of the music as Liszt conceived it. Any resemblance between what we heard that evening and the composer's original intention was, sadly, entirely coincidental and the image of a dog partaking of its' fist meal of day came forcefully to mind.

Adrian could just about mange the low rumblings so the mistakes were few and the swear words mild and *'sotto voce'*. The difficult ascending arpeggios were less fortunate, and many of them degenerated into a dissonant scramble and the swearing associated with them got commensurately louder and more objectionable, often referring to those parts of the body which are seldom spoken of in polite society. It was the fortissimo huge chord that completed each phrase that came off worst. Hardly a note that the pianist played had any connection with the composer's intentions; the sound was terrible and the language truly appalling. The overall effect was something like this:-

Keyboard: Low rumbling chords including the occasional mistake.

Vocal Accompaniment ad.lib Mezzo piano.

"Damn, Blast, Sod it."

Keyboard: Scrambling arpeggios badly executed and full of mistakes.

Vocal Accompaniment ad lib Mezzo Forte.

"Bollocks and Bum 'oles."

Keyboard: Deafening, awful chord, including hardly any notes as written by the composer.

Vocal Accompaniment ad lib. Fortissimo

"FUCK!"

It must be understood that the construction of the piece required this challenging sequence of sounds to repeated over and over again in a variety of keys and, whilst Adrian Friar's technical ability had assuredly met its' Waterloo, his prowess as a purveyor of oaths was seemingly limitless. The F word was replaced by the C word then followed the F sharp and C sharp words. After that he availed himself of street slang from the United States as he accused the piano of indulging in sexual relations with its mother. Then he became almost Shakespearian as he shouted the old English words for a variety of sexually transmitted diseases from which he believed the piano to be suffering.

The audience's reaction to all this was one of dumb amazement. At the very first whisperings of bad language there was a natural tendency to giggle, especially amongst the younger boys but as Friar's obscenities became wilder and louder, the fulminating presence of the Headmaster cowered everybody present into a shocked silence. We all knew that if we seemed to be amused by such an outrageous display of profanity, we would find ourselves in almost as much trouble as the deranged pianist himself. Fortunately I was sitting right at the back of the hall and, though I was shaking with laughter, I managed to keep silent by forcing my handkerchief into my mouth. I looked around at some of the other senior boys and saw that many of them were biting their lips and some had tears of hysteria flowing down their cheeks. The Headmaster's face told a different story. This was a man who suffered from blood pressure problems and, at the most relaxed of times, was of a ruddy complexion. Now, as he confronted a situation the like of which was completely outside his long experience, he seemed pole-axed into inactivity. He was trembling. He had gone purple and then he turned almost black when a particularly awful chord elicited a devastatingly filthy oath from the deranged boy the grand piano. A meaningful look was exchanged between the Headmaster and his Head Boy and, as the man reached into his waistcoat pocket for some life-preserving pills the boy, accompanied by another perfect, and approached the performer.

Adrian Friar was completely oblivious to his approaching nemesis and the rumbling chords, the buggered- up arpeggios, and the cacophonous chords continued to reverberate around the hall. He even continued when Ian Barrett, approaching from behind, shut music book. Friar did however react when the other prefect tried to close the piano lid. He simply punched the boy on the nose, then he carried on playing. This action, however, caused other representatives of the establishment within the audience to mobilise and three masters now joined the affray which was taking place around the Bechstein. It must be said that Adrian Friar did not surrender without an heroic struggle. He didn't stop playing until his jacket was pulled down off his shoulders, thus pinioning his arms to his side. Then his adversaries were able to pick up the piano stool, with Adrian still sitting on it, and carry him off, like some demented boy pharaoh. The two senior boys carried the stool; one master had his hand clamped over Adrian's mouth whilst the other two held his legs to prevent anyone from receiving a kick Even so Adrian Friar continued to jerk and sway as if still mentally struggling towards the climax of the musical composition which had so fearfully possessed him.

That manhandling of a musician in the advanced stages of artistic frustration was the last time that I saw Adrian Friar. We later learned, from Ian Barrett that as Adrian had already sat his final examinations the Headmaster decided that it would be best if he was sent home early, before the end of his last term. It was rumoured that the letter to his parents explained that Adrian was displaying signs of nervous exhaustion and needed a period of quiet rest. The head master also strongly advised that the boy should be discouraged from practising the piano for more than twenty minutes a day and should confine his repertoire to nocturnes and lullabies.

Chapter 28.

Unexpected Events.

The unusual performance at the music club concert took place in early July 1965. I left the school at the end of that summer term and joined the BBC as a trainee assistant film editor in November of the same year. It was certainly an adventure to have the centre of my universe change from the authoritarian self-righteousness of Bedford School to the shabby eccentric bustle of Ealing Film Studios. They had been built in the 1930s and bought by the BBC in the early 1950s to provide a home for the corporation's expanding film department. When I first saw the studio lot it still contained several bits and pieces left over from the glory days of 'Ealing Films'. The street for *'The Lady Killers'* was still there, as were the prison gates for the last fateful scene of *'Kind Hearts and Coronets'*. The lot was small by the standards of the major British Studios, mainly because Ealing Studios were land locked in the leafy, somewhat snooty, suburb of West Ealing. With Ealing Green at the front of it and Walpole Park behind it there was no room for the studio to expand and consequently the plot given over to 'the lot' (the area on which to build exterior sets) was minimal.

A lot with a couple of streets of buildings of indeterminate period is a huge asset for any studio. The buildings on the Ealing lot looked like a part of Islington or Hackney. As these parts of London were built in the 1830s, and are still standing, their architecture is ideal for film lot design. Park a couple of handsome cabs in the street and you are in the 19th century, park a Bull-nose Morris; you are in the 1920s or a Ford Cortina and the action is set in the 1960s. The production designer of the Ealing Studios' lot' knew his business.

The reason why a good 'lot' is a huge advantage for any studio is that it allows action to be filmed that would be fraught with difficulty if staged on real streets. Things like bank robberies, traffic jams, gun fights or riots. In fact, even simple dialogue sequences are more easily achieved under the controlled circumstances of the studio lot; as my experiences with Dick Emery proved, filming in public places can prove a time consuming nightmare. A simple thing, such as a car parked in the back ground of the shot, can become a problem if the owner of the vehicle decides to drive off. Suddenly there is no continuity of 'back ground'. Studios lots certainly have their uses; even the one at Ealing, which was beginning to look rather tatty by the mid-1960s.

The first time I saw studio lot in use was for an episode of 'Doctor Who'. The series was in it's infancy in those days. No one would have dreamed that it would ever become an international cult. They certainly wouldn't if they had witnessed the action of the scene I watched on that Spring day in 1966. The Daleks had invaded the earth and crowds of terrified Londoners were fleeing from the deadly extra-terrestrials. Well, that was what the writer had imagined in the script. The production, however, was creating the event with every expense spared. A dozen uninterested extras were reluctantly buggering about whilst supposedly being chased by three Daleks. I say 'supposedly' as the Daleks couldn't go very fast because they kept tipping over. The deadly robots had been designed for use on the smooth floor of a television studio so the uneven road surface of the studio lot was to prove their undoing. I learnt an important truth that day; one of the best defences against a Dalek attack would be to live at the end of a cobbled street.

About six months later I had another encounter with the good Doctor's adversaries. The lot was once more being used, but this time his enemies were the Cybermen. As I walked towards the studio canteen that morning two figures walked past me. A Cyberman, with a fag hanging out of his mouth, was accompanied by a lady, who for reasons known only to fans of the show, was bright green; green costume, green face and wild green hair. She had accessorised with a silver aerial sticking out of the top of her head. As they passed me I heard her say,

"Cynthia's having one of her frightful coffee mornings next Friday. I suppose we'd better go." Somehow I felt strangely reassured.

That afternoon, as I walked past the lot on my way to pick up some cans from film despatch, I paused to watch the Cybermen destroy London. They had an intergalactic nuclear device. This looked, for all the world, like a tea chest covered in Bacofoil and the nuclear explosion, when it came, was also distinctly underwhelming; a pantomime flash was followed by the toppling of some cardboard boxes. One could only hope that the cunning use of camera angle and slow motion cinematography would work wonders, but it seemed unlikely. I believe that the episode that I saw being filmed that day is one of the celebrated lost early episodes of '*Doctor Who'* and I imagine that the director is not very anxious for it ever to be found.

It is certainly true that sometimes the simplest photographic tricks can be used to great effect but you cannot always depend on the fact. During our training period we had a lecture from the head of the visual effects department. He was determined to show how ingenious and innovative his team could be, especially when working to a tight budget. To prove his point he brought with him a film clip for a forthcoming Sci. Fi. space series. He told us that to make the space ship he had painted two old domestic hair driers silver and then glued them together. The strange looking object was then hung on a wire in front of a star-cloth back drop. Then, cunningly lit and filmed in slow motion, it was pulled across the screen by a length of fishing line. When he ran the film we were amazed. Even though we had been told the secret, what we saw looked exactly like two old hair driers being pulled across the screen by a wire.

Not long after the attack of the Cybermen I was reminded of Mr. Amos, the Bedford School director of music, who had upset Adrian Friar so badly. Mr. Amos was very keen that all orchestral players should learn to read a full symphonic score and this ability was now about to provide me with an interesting break from the routine of the cutting rooms.

The music and arts department were making a documentary about the composer Sir Michael Tippett. There would be the inevitable, tedious, interview but the main body of the film would consist of the great man conducting a performance of his concerto for orchestra. The sound recordist for the project had asked if he could have someone in his team who read a score as this would be helpful, both for the initial recording and also for marking up the tape for filming to playback. The standard method of filming orchestral performances is to film a master shot for both sound and vision and then have the musicians mime to their own performance when the time comes for close ups and shots of the various instrumental sections. This is the only way that the tempo, tuning and sound balance can be maintained as the editor cuts from shot to shot. It was surprising that nobody in the sound department could read a score. Had they asked Radio 3 there would have been dozens of keen young techies up to the task, but this was film department and honour demanded that the work was kept strictly 'in house'.

I suppose it must have been as a result of jungle drums and canteen gossip that the recordist for this film got to learn that there was an assistant film editor who could read a full score; anyway he did, and a week later I was heading off to Gloucestershire for five days location filming.

The standard practice when filming on location was to find a cheap bed and breakfast which charged less than the BBC's overnight allowance and then pocket the difference, but this proved impossible for the Michael Tippett film because there was a Music Festival taking place in town and the only hotel with any spare rooms was the prestigious King's Head in Cirencester. Many of the crew grumbled like mad about having to pay full whack, but not me. Five days in a luxury hotel, on expenses, was a novelty and a treat for a lad from the cutting rooms.

To be honest, I don't remember much about the filming that week. However I do remember a feeling of blind panic when I was handed the score that I would be required to read. It was so full of notes as to be almost impenetrable. They were the sort of chords and scurrying scales that would probably have delighted Adrian Friar, but the sight of them filled me with alarm. In the event I needn't have worried because setting up for the filming took an age and

I had plenty of time to get familiar with the great work. Our cameraman was David Trossock, who was very much of the old school of film cameramen. That is to say he was slow as a wet week. He put enough arc lights into the concert hall to illuminate Wembley Stadium and then complained that the orchestra all looked sweaty. Even so, his slow pace meant that by the time he was ready for the first take of a master shot I, too, was ready to cue the recordist with my 'Trumpet fanfare in four bars time' or my 'Change of key, 'cello solo next.'

As we were recording directly to quarter inch tape, with no possibility of a re- mix, such information helped the recordist to subtly adjust the balance, as the performance proceeded. In the event we did OK. There were no retakes required for sound and I was able to relax a little and to feel that I was earning my keep.

However the most memorable event that week did not take place in the concert hall, it happened in the hotel dining room on the last night of our stay.

The shoot had gone well, there was only a few remaining shots to take on the Friday morning before we all headed for home, and the director suggested that we should meet for a final celebration meal. We would pay for the food out of our expenses but the production would pick up the drinks tab. This was a generous gesture, because the one thing you could never claim for on expenses was alcohol.

The dining room at the King's Head was very much in the tradition of old coaching Inns. The elegance was fading but the pretentions were still of a high order. Like so many expensive restaurants at that period it very much depended on the fact that very few of clientele would recognise a gourmet experience, even if it got up from the plate and shook hands with them. In those days it seemed that disappointment with the food was to be expected.

The ambience of the room was discreet and 'high class', the menu expensive; it would be simply asking too much for the food itself to be anything special. This was the era when the dessert trolley was considered the height of culinary sophistication. However, at the age of 19, I had seldom eaten in such a smart place and it all seemed wonderful to me. Even when the cohort of waiters gave the impression that they had much better things to do than to bring you a menu that seemed only right and proper. It was a restaurant with a distinct hierarchy. The ordinary waiters wore black and white, in the old French tradition, but the senior staff wore red tail coats engendering a strong image of the hunt, which local aristocrats may well have found endearing. Unfortunately this sense of hierarchy extended from the waiters to their customers and if you were under 45, quiet and polite, your chances of getting half decent service was zilch.

As we took our seats at the reserved table I was, therefore, grateful that leading our party was the cameraman David Trossock. David was in his mid-fifties and very much the ex-army officer. He had been in the army Kine Corps, or film unit, in civilian speak. He certainly knew how to handle these waiter Johnnies and I was relieved to be under his command for the evening. As the director had decided to sit with Sir Michael Tippett at a discreet alcove table for two, Mr. Trossock sat at the head of our large table surrounded by his crew. I can remember the impressive re-pro Jacobean chair in which he sat and the tapestry that hung on the wall behind him. The whole impression was redolent of pageantry. Trossock snapped his fingers and an elderly waiter shuffled forward with a menu.

"Now listen to me chaps, oh sorry Val", he nodded in the direction of the only female in our party, Val the production secretary. "Well then, listen to me ladies and gentlemen. The only way to avoid disaster at a meal like this is to keep the order simple. I've looked at the menu and, frankly, the only thing likely to be any good is the steak, as to starters well, the best chance is for prawn cocktail, whitebait or the soup. Agreed? Good then I'll order for all of us."

To my surprise nobody objected to our cameraman's plan. They had doubtless experienced similar restaurants at previous 'production meals.

"Right hands up," continued the commanding voice.

"Prawn cocktails two, White bait five, soup one, got that waiter?"

"Now the steaks, Rare three, medium four, well done one. Good all done and dusted now I'll peruse the wine list, if you please, thank you waiter."

"Thank you sir, the wine waiter will attend you shortly."

"Very well, please make sure that he does."

And there we were, order placed. I noticed that no one had yet taken a menu to the director and Sir Michael in their discreet corner.

About two minutes later the wine waiter arrived beside David Trossock. He was one of the red coated variety and less easily intimidated.

"The wine list sir." Before taking hold of it, Trossock donned a pair of large horn rimmed spectacles. He obviously believed that the wine list deserved more careful attention than the food.

"Would Sir be requiring any help Sir?" the waiter spoke with more than a hint of patronage.

"You'll be doing well if your cellar is half as good as the one that I have at home."

Some put down, I thought. Then I remembered that David Trossock was known for his love of good wine. There was a studio legend that he had been phoned one night by an anxious director. The phone had been answered by Mrs Trossock who politely but firmly informed the caller that Mr. Trossock could not possibly be disturbed as he was 'taking his claret'. So, yes, he was a bit pompous and he was a bit boring, but he wasn't a bully. He was courteous to his crew and certainly not the worst cameraman a director might be allocated. He was simply not a man to be easily pissed about and that was proving to be much to our advantage. The director and Sir Michael were still casting hungry glances towards any waiter who happened to pass by.

My whitebait didn't taste of anything much. They tasted of pepper, if you put pepper on them and of lemon if you squeezed on some lemon, but they were hot and crispy; not so bad I suppose. The Steaks were generally very successful. The local butcher must have been a good one and we all agreed that steak had been a wise choice. The wine, too, was excellent. As the production was paying for it, David Trossock saw no reason to economise in either quality or quantity. As was to be expected, he chose a bottle of claret; well, several in fact.

As the sweet trolley was trundling in our direction I pointed out to Val, that as far as I could see our esteemed director and his honoured guest were still waiting to order. She had been seated with her back to their alcove and so was unaware of the fact. She left our table to have a word with the head waiter. When he realised that his staff had been ignoring a knight of the realm he scurried away in an extravagance of mortification and shortly afterwards I could hardly see the director's table for the number of obsequious minions flurrying around it.

The sweet trolley was not very exciting. A trifle that was making a farewell tour prior to retirement, a fruit salad fresh as the day that they had opened the tin, some profiteroles that looked like Yorkshire puddings in disguise and a 'home made' black forest gateau', which it probably was if your home was on an industrial estate outside Birmingham. I decided on ice-cream which I reckoned would be a safe bet. David Trossock, however was by now in expansive mood. Perhaps the claret was taking effect, but anyway he threw caution and economy to the winds and chose Crêpes Suzette. The waiter looked almost impressed and then hurried over to the director's table where he whispered to one of the many staff which had been lately assigned to serve Sir Michael. This person was presumably the Chef des Crêpes as shortly afterwards he came over to us pushing the crêpe trolley. I don't think that I had ever seen crêpes being made at the table before and I was interested in all the paraphernalia involved. The shiny silver spirit stove, the bright copper frying pan, the sliced oranges, vanilla sugar and bottles of Cognac, Cointreau and Calvados. It was rather disappointing that the pancakes, on a plate on the lower shelf, had been pre-made; but it still promised to be an interesting spectacle. The trolley had, by now, arrived beside Mr. Trossock.

"The crêpes are for you sir?"

David Trossock nodded and tried to look both authoritative and casual at the same time.

The flame of the sprit lamp lit with a pop and some butter was put into the copper pan. There then followed an awful lot of, what seemed to me to be, camping about. Pancakes were placed in the pan and sugared, then orange juice was added and finally brandy was poured in and heated. Someone explained to me that the brandy would only light when it was warm. When the waiter did light it, I must say the flames were quite impressive. There were some mild gasps of delight from people at near-by tables and even a ripple of applause. All was going well, the waiter had already made two crepes and, sensing that he was the centre of attention, he became increasingly demonstrative. He particularly seemed to relish the bit where he splashed extra brandy into the flaming pan. He raised the bottle to a considerable height above the flames and tipped in the spirit in the manner of a conjuror. He was able to accomplish this because the bottle was fitted with a special stopper which only let a measured quantity out at any one time.

It was as he was completing the third and final crepe, that disaster struck. David Trossock already had two excellent pancakes on the plate before him when the waiter pushed the trolley even closer for a final flourish. The final pancake was sizzling and delicious aromas of caramel, oranges and Cognac wafted around the room. The maître des crêpes ignited his final master piece and the flames burst out brightly in the pan. Then, as if to ensure perfection and to display generosity he raised the bottle for one final splash of brandy. This time his gesturing was just that bit too energetic, just a whisker too extravagantly theatrical. The stopper fell out and a whole bleedin' bottle - full hit the flames. There was a huge flash, a bang and a dense mushroom cloud of smoke rose to the ceiling. If you have ever been unwise enough to chuck petrol onto a bonfire you will have some idea of what we experienced, but remember, our bonfire explosion was happening in the confines of a restaurant. This time there were no gasps of delight or affected applause but, instead, a piercing scream reverberated around the room. There was awful crash as the waiter fell over and a worse one as the crêpe trolley fell on top of him. This was followed by a hoarse cries of pain and profanity from underneath the trolley. As the smoke cleared, the scene of devastation was terrible to behold; but no one at our table took very much notice of the waiter's plight because of the explosion's even more dreadful consequence.

David Trossock had disappeared. Like some genie in a Palladium Pantomime he had vanished into thin air. The only sign of his recent presence were two uneaten crepes on his plate, both now edged with carbon, and a silhouetted outline singed onto the tapestry behind his chair. This was a chilling reminder of the great man's erstwhile persona and I remember wondering if the tapestry, like the chair, was a reproduction because, if it had once been valuable, it certainly wasn't anymore.

In those more innocent days little was known about PCDT (Post Crêpe Disaster Trauma). Nowadays at least some one present would have known what to do and rushed out to find an armful of soft toys with which to mark the spot. All we could think to do was sit there, aghast. The room fell silent, save for the ersatz ticking of the reproduction long case clock. Then, as the shock was beginning to subside, our table started to shake and tilt in a most spectral fashion. We looked towards David Trossock's smouldering place setting. There was a moan, then a grunt, then a blackened hand appeared from beneath the table to be followed by another and then, at last, by David Trossock's head. His glasses were askew, his thinning hair was standing on end; he had lost his confidence, his dignity and his eyebrows. He was not entirely black, more piebald, but he was surrounded by veil of curling smoke. In short he looked, not so much as if he had been pulled through a hedge backwards, but more as if he had fallen down the chimney, forwards. The terrible thing was that I found it very hard not to laugh and I couldn't help thinking that the Cybermens' nuclear explosion had been pathetic by comparison.

Our director rushed across from his table to discover if his camera man had been badly hurt. He was much relieved that it was only a case of cuts, bruises and minor burns. He was very concerned. The shots he had planned for the following morning might well have been jeopardised.

Val and the assistant cameraman helped David back to his room, the rest of us retired to the bar. The director returned to his table to wait for his first course to be served.

Chapter 29.

<u>Down the Drain.</u>

It was a disturbing phone call. My friend Andy Musset, who worked in the music library, near Broadcasting House, had come back from a short holiday to discover that some meddling fool had given the BBC's entire collection of military band arrangements to the Brigade of Guards. Had this decision been made a few years earlier nobody would have known nor cared. The BBC dismissed its In-house Concert Band in 1953 and the vast library of music which had been purchased for it now lay mouldering in the cellars of Yalding House. Andy Musset joined the BBC at about the same as I did. He was a graduate of the Royal College of Music, so the BBC music library presented an opportunity to join the corporation and perhaps, one day, become a music producer. Indeed this did come to pass and Andy went on to produce many inventively novel programmes for Radio 3. But in 1967 we were still both newcomers to the great institution. We had met as a result of a section of the BBC Club, the staff association which, in those days, had all sorts of leisure facilities. We were both members of the Ariel Symphony Orchestra, which was orchestral section of the BBC Club. For a couple of happy years this ensemble survived well enough, but then, like so many amateur orchestras, it collapsed for lack of sufficient string players. It was Andy who had the idea to form a BBC Club Concert Band. Good wind players are much more plentiful and reliable than string players, especially if there is good pub nearby for a drink after rehearsals. One of the senior music librarians had told Andy about the existence of the military band library but, as nobody had used it for fifteen years its whereabouts was uncertain. It was somewhere in the basement of Yalding house. The basement was cavernous with lots of dusty passages leading to locked, dank rooms, the forgotten library would take some finding but, if the idea for a new wind band was going to take off, it would need some music to play. Andy started a search. His original idea was to take time out of his lunch hour to poke around in the basement but this had to be abandoned because he would return to his desk covered in dust and cobwebs. He therefore decided to organise a weekend foray into the cellars. A group of musician friends, suitably dressed in old clothes would meet on a Saturday and work the whole weekend, if necessary, until the lost treasure was discovered. With four or five of us on the task it didn't take that long. At about noon on the first day we came to a door at the end of a long corridor which looked suitably forgotten and forlorn, It was padlocked but, as Andy was a member of the library staff he had been able to draw a huge set of rusting keys which were supposed to be the ones for the basement rooms. The keys themselves had taken some finding. They had been stuffed at the back of a cupboard years before. Several keys nearly fitted but at last one worked and we opened the door.

It would be tempting to use clichés like 'Aladdin's cave, or to compare our find with Howard Carter as he first beheld Tutankhamen's treasure. Our find was less spectacular but important, nonetheless. Three thousand huge brown paper envelope bags containing just about everything that had ever been published for a wind band between 1890 and 1953. It was not very appealing to look at, but the potential that it held was mind boggling.

The bags themselves were thick with dust. Mice, maybe rats, had eaten away the corners of some of them, but the parts inside the envelopes were still in reasonable order. We were thrilled by our discovery.

For the next several weekends we met to clean up the store, dust down the bags and replace those that had suffered rodent attack. It was dirty work but, of course, well worth it and the dust provided us with the perfect excuse to have a few refreshing pints at the end of each session. We were all wind players, after all.

And that is how the BBC Club Concert Band got started. Andy got permission from his boss for us to use the library and for two happy seasons we made full use of it for rehearsals and concerts. The original group expanded too, and we were able to attract some very talented instrumentalists.

Then it happened. Fresh back from holiday Andy walked the now familiar corridor to our precious store of music, opened the door and found it completely empty! Some steaming pillock had given it to the Brigade of Guards, without reference to anyone.

My first reaction to the news was one of devastation, shortly followed by rage. Classic signs of bereavement, as I was learn in later life. There was one big difference, however. Unlike the death of a love one, our situation was not irreversible. We knew where the music was. It had been taken to Chelsea Barracks. It was going to be difficult and embarrassing but we were going to have to get at least some of it back. If we wanted our band to continue, there was no other choice.

About a week later Andy and I were driving to Chelsea Barracks to borrow some music back from the former BBC library. Andy's boss, the head of the music library, had come back from a three month attachment to a production department to discover that the man who he had left in charge during his absence had wreaked havoc. All sorts of barmy changes had been made, of which the disposal of the military band music was but a part. This 'new man' was one of that destructive breed of mad men who, at that time, were only just beginning to appear in management jobs. The sort of people who delight in enforcing new systems without any consideration of why and how the established methods evolved. There are various terms in the world of business management for such people, the one I prefer is 'wankers'. How else would you describe a librarian who thinks that a room in the basement will be more cost efficient when it is empty than when it is filled with 3000 items of irreplaceable music?

Fortunately the returning head was sympathetic to our cause but he had to be tactful. He couldn't just write to the director of music at Chelsea Barracks saying, 'Sorry but I left my department in the hands of a Dick Head'. A degree of face saving had to be invented. A letter was written saying something about the library being a' long term loan' and that from time to time the BBC would require the use of certain items from it. There was a curt reply from' the military' but at least Andy and I had a premise on which to make a visit to the Barracks and retrieve sufficient items for our next two concerts.

To say that we were treated courteously when we arrived for our appointment would be an exaggeration. A deputation of conscientious objectors would probably have been made more welcome. A sergeant met us at the gates, with much stamping of boots faffing about with clipboards and then told us to follow him to the director of music's office. He then stomped off across the Barrack yard and we followed, trying to look casual and confident.

I could sense that he really wanted to yell, 'Keep in step you 'orrible little gits.' It was all rather intimidating, but then, it was meant to be. When we reached the great man's office the sergeant knocked on the door and did his best to march us in. The sight of the officer who sat behind the desk did little to inspire us with confidence.

'Crumpled' would be the first word that came to mind when I looked at the Director of Music; 'Sad' would probably have been the second. He looked old for an army officer and must have been close to retirement. As we entered he seemed to be much involved with his paper work, but that was probably simply to demonstrate what a busy man he was. There was a cigarette burning in the overflowing ash tray on his desk but we would have known he was a heavy smoker anyway. Not only were his fingers stained with nicotine, his moustache was too. He was a bulky man but yet his uniform fitted rather loosely, suggesting that he had shrunk since he was last kitted out. He was red in the face with steely blue eyes that were now rather watery. All in all I don't think he would have passed as A1 fit for active service. He looked at us with an expression of irritation.

"Well then what do you want?"

We explained the reason for our visit.

"The bloody music has only been here five minutes and you already want some of it back? Seems to me the people at your end don't know if it's Christmas or breakfast time."

Although we agreed with him wholeheartedly, we thought it politic to simply mumble some apologies about as unforeseen need for some of the music. We knew enough about the military mind to know that we wouldn't get very far with him if we were to slag off our superiors, however much they deserved it.

"Oh well you better get on with it I suppose. Take them up to the music store sergeant, oh and you'll need this to show the guard at the gate." He scribbled a note on piece of yellowing official paper.

"We'll leave a note of what we take," said Andy, ever the librarian.

"Can if you like," replied Colonel Nicotine,"I doubt if there is much there that we haven't got six copies of already."

"That's great," I thought, "they don't even want the stuff and we're desperate for it. What a balls up."

The Sergeant's stamping march was, by now, really getting on my nerves. There was simply no point in it. We were not recruits and so we were not impressed by it; to us it just seemed ridiculous. I suppose stamping and swinging his arms was what he did whenever he wanted to look important, no matter what the circumstance. I wondered how he would behave in a brothel.

The Sergeant stomped along corridors and up stair cases; we followed on behind glancing around to take in the grim bare brick reality of the Barrack's interior. At last he showed us into a large hall that looked as though it might once have been used as a gym. There before us, in sad muddled heaps, were the bags of music which we had, until recently, looked on as our own. Towards the back of the room was a corporal who seemed to be trying to make some sort of sense out the chaos. The Sergeant snapped out an introduction.

"This is Corporal Jennings, he might be able to help." He turned smartly and was gone.

Again we found ourselves recounting our sad tale but, this time, it seemed that we had found a sympathetic ear. Corporal Jennings was part of the Brigade of Guards Music library staff, so this sort of put him on our side. At least he could appreciate our situation.

"As you've probably guessed," he said. "that officer you saw is an idiot and the sergeant is both an idiot and a tosser. When the news came about the BBC library I wanted to organise some of my lads to make the collection, but no, they had to do it their way and send a load of brainless squaddies. As a result all the music has been shuffled up and it will take an age to get it back into catalogue order. Still it proves the point: if you want something fucked up good and proper just send in the guards."

After an hour's serious searching and with the help of the good Corporal Jennings we managed to find most of what we were looking for. About eight items eluded us but we found suitable substitutes and then struggled to carry them back down to the front gate. Bags of music are no light weight and twelve each was as much as we could manage. Once we were at the gate we once again came to the notice of the dreaded sergeant. I asked if I could bring my car into the yard load up by the door to the library block and save us having to carry the parts all the way across the barrack yard to the gates.

"No bloody chance!" came the unhelpful, if not unexpected reply. We struggled on with our load to the gates and then I left Andy 'on guard' while I went round the corner to pick up my car. It was an old Morris Oxford Estate, with a 'drop down' tail gate. I was back at the gates in less than five minutes, but of course there was nowhere to park. To be honest, by this time, I had had enough of being buggered about and so I parked directly in front of the gates. We were only going to be there for a couple of minutes, after all. But, of course, we weren't. Why is it that when you are tense, tired and vulnerable fate decides to take a hand to make matters even worse? That is what happened when I unlocked the tail gate boot of the car so we could start loading up. It had never happened before, and I made bloody sure that it never happened again, but on that one critical occasion, the keys fell out of the lock. This would have been of no matter had I not been parked near a drain in the gutter. The keys bounced lightly, as they hit the ground and then took a graceful dive down the drain. I looked on in blank disbelief.

It was Andy who kept his head. 'When all around him (namely the bloody Sergeant) were losing their's and blaming it on you,'(or, in this case, me.) Amid much unhelpful ranting of "Get that bloody car shifted right now." from guess who? Andy explained that, whilst nobody was keener to get the car shifted than he was, the simple fact was that the keys had gone down the drain and that there was not a lot we could do until we got them back. Then to my amazement he added. "But don't worry, I know how we can get them back." I could hardly believe my ears. I was thinking that the keys were lost for all eternity, but Andy knew better.

"Chelsea and Kensington Borough Cleaning depot is just around the corner, they'll be able to retrieve the keys, and they got a special gadget, just for that purpose." And with that we headed off.

"Were you making that up about a gadget to get keys out of drains?" I asked anxiously, as we hurried to the depot. "I always thought that when something fell down a drain it went directly into the sewer. I imagined that my keys would be half way out to sea by now."

"I used to think so too," Andy replied. "Until my Dad dropped his keys down a drain. It's true that below the grating there is the pipe that connects to the sewer but beneath that pipe there is a sort of large bucket so heavy things fall down into that. What the road cleaner guys do is pull up that bucket and poke around in the muck."

"Sounds lovely." I said.

We turned the corner and there before us stood the Borough Kensington and Chelsea Cleansing Depot. It was one of the strangest buildings that I had ever seen. It was huge and Victorian Gothic. It might have been built as a series of exhibition halls or, perhaps, as grand covered market, but whatever it had been, its glory days were surely past. It was built on the side of a short length of Canal which linked it directly to the Thames. That would have been very practical for delivery purposes in days of the hall's illustrious past. Now, in modern and enlightened times this connection to Thames made it possible for the cleaning department to load barges full to the gunnels with stinking garbage, take them out into Thames Estuary and dump their rotting cargo into the water.

At the very front of the Depot there was a glazed cubicle that looked as if it might have once been a box office, so maybe the exhibition hall theory was the right one. We walked up to it and were glad to see that it was occupied. At least we could make immediate human contact. The day was turning out to be full of the unexpected and the man in this Victorian cubicle was no exception. He looked as if he had worked there since the building first opened. In my memory I see him writing in a big ledger with a quill pen and though this must be a false memory it, never-the-less captures the essence of that moment. He was a very Dickensian looking little man, with gold, *demi lune*, spectacles. Again, I would like to say that they were *pince- nez*, but that image, too, must be my memory embroidering the encounter. Suffice it to say that had his name been Mr. Pickwick it would have come as no surprise; his dress, his demeanour, even his patterns of speech were all from a bygone world. The window at the front of the 'box office' slid up with a rattle.

"Good afternoon to you gentlemen, may I be of assistance?"

"I certainly hope so, sir." I said. I went on to describe our predicament. I couldn't help noticing that when I mentioned that we were from the BBC Mr. Pickwick sat up in his chair and brushed some dandruff form his lapel.

"Well that is all most unfortunate sir, but rest assured, you have come to right place. I will put you in touch with my colleague, Leading Sweeper Harris."

I must say that it had never occurred to me before that there was a hierarchy amongst the ranks of road sweepers but now that I realised that there was, I was glad that we were to be attended by a leader in the field; or would that be the street ?

"Now I am afraid," our anachronistic new acquaintance continued, "I'm afraid that I cannot connect you with Leading Sweeper Harris by phone, his office don't have one. The quickest solution to your problem would, therefore be for you to go to his office yourself. I will give you a note instructing him to give you every assistance."

"That really is very kind, thank you."

"Not at all sir, only too glad to help." He scribbled a note on impressively headed paper.

"Now listen carefully and I will tell you how to find the right office. You see those doors over there?" We could hardly miss them. They were huge, once magnificent pieces of mahogany complete with brass door furniture, now sadly dulled by neglect.

"Go through those doors and you will be in the grand hall. Follow the marked walk way to the other side of the hall and go through the door there. You will then be in the small chamber. Turn left and walk along the length of the wall until you come to the second door. Go through that door and you will be in a vestibule, ahead of you will be three doors. Leading Sweeper Harris' office is the middle door. Just knock and enter. Now have you got that?

"I think so; thank you again." and we set off on another phase of, what was becoming, a journey into the surreal.

If you remember the film *'The Wizard of Oz'* you were probably impressed when, twenty minutes into the story, Dorothy goes through a door and the image turns from black and white into intense Technicolor. It was rather like that when Andy and I walked through those huge doors at the rubbish depot, but in our case the world changed from colour into black and white. It was one of the most bizarre scenes I have ever witnessed. The 'Grand Hall' had certainly once been very grand. Ornate wrought iron columns with finely chiselled stone bases reached upwards to support the huge glass roof. Near the top some evidence of the original magnificence of the hall remained; the gilded finials and the roof beams painted with flower motifs, were still intact. At floor level the contrast was staggering. Huge piles of rubbish bags were everywhere. Great walls of stinking garbage built to height of ten or twelve feet. We had no trouble in finding the 'marked walk way' as there was no other way we could navigate through this ocean of filth. Just occasionally a break in walls of bin bags gave us a glimpse through to the side of the hall which opened onto the canal. There were the barges, stuffed full of more filth and shortly to be performing their civic duty by dumping it all in the Estuary. The experience was breath taking, both visually and literally, because the stink was overpowering. Half way across the hall we both in-stinctively paused for a moment. Common sense told us to get to the exit as fast as possible yet something about that cathedral of corruption was strangely compelling. It was such a perverse use of a once beautiful, structure. We seemed to be the only people in the hall and all was very quiet, yet like all large empty buildings, it wasn't com-pletely silent. Every now and then there came a distant in-explicable bang which sent echoes around the tiled walls. We pressed on.

The 'small chamber' came as a blessed relief because it didn't stink so much. It was used for storing the larger items of junk, metal bed frames, old sofas, bicycles and the like. We followed our instructions, found the second door and entered the vestibule.

We felt sure we had found the right place because lined up before us were eight road sweeper barrows, complete with brooms and bins. Close to them, on the opposite wall, were three doors. In the office behind the middle door we very much hoped to find Leading Sweeper Harris and an end to our difficulties. We paused again.

"Oh well here goes," I said to Andy. I knocked and walked straight in. Then, in an instant, I walked straight out again. The reason for this was because of what I glimpsed during my few seconds in that office. There were two old men in the room, one of whom was presumably the Leading Sweeper. Nothing unexpected about that; the reason for my swift exit was that I had discovered them in a less than decorous circumstance. The anodyne euphemisms of present day social workers would express what I had seen as' two men of mature years behaving inappropriately. The unvarnished truth is that I had witnessed two disgusting old men with their trousers down. One was stretched across a desk and the other was bunging him one up the bum. Which of these two was Leading Sweeper Harris I neither knew nor cared; retreat seemed to be the only option. I stuttered out an explanation of what I had seen to Andy.

"Are you sure?"

"Of course I'm sure. My imagination is not sufficiently vivid as to dream that up."

"No of course not, sorry; but what the Hell do we do now?"

"God knows."

"The trouble is we really need him to help us."

"Yes I know."

"Tell you what, let's wait about five minutes and then both go in. I don't see what else we can do."

"Ok but this time you go in first."

It seemed a long wait but after five minutes we steeled ourselves and each other to a deep breath, which was not the wisest of actions considering the over whelming stench of the place. We walked smartly to the door and knocked.

"Please enter." came a reedy voice from within. We did so.

A magical transformation had occurred. Leading Sweeper Harris sat at the larger of two desks and his colleague, I hesitate to say the 'under sweeper', sat at another. They were both seemingly totally absorbed in paperwork. I realised that we were being invited to consign my recent sordid vision to oblivion and I was only too happy to play along. We introduced ourselves, handed over the note from the front office and recounted the tedious tale of the keys.

"Fear not sir, I will drop everything and attend to you immediately." Leading Sweeper Harris was both anxious and unctuous to please. I knew that this was the price of our conspiracy of silence, and I couldn't have cared less. I reckoned that we could certainly bank on first class service from Leading Sweeper Harris and his team as I already knew of their capacity to drop everything.

"I would suggest that you return to your vehicle, sir. Sweeper Prendergast and I will attend you there directly. We merely have to gather together our equipment." A second double entendre crossed my mind but I simply smiled my thanks and we headed off back to Barracks.

We arrived back to find that, our friend, the sergeant, had not been idle. A car parking space had become available right by the gates and he had ordered a group of his recruits to shift the vehicle into it. I had left the car unlocked, of course, because the keys were down the drain.

"Oh so you're back, well a right bleedin' lot of work you've caused us."

"I can't help thinking sergeant that had you let us into the yard to pick up the music in the first place we would have all been saved a deal of trouble." I was surprised to hear myself. I am seldom so direct when dealing with authority figures but stresses brought about by the events of the day were beginning to tell on my nerves. Before the sergeant could come back with a riposte from his phrase book of standard army insults a council van pulled up alongside us. Leading Sweeper Harris and his partner got out.

"Good morning once more sir." came the greeting. His tone might have been just a touch too ingratiating but it was certainly more pleasant than the sergeant's.

"Now then Sir, down which grating did your keys fall?"

"Down this bleedin' grating 'ere." chipped in the sergeant, before I could draw breath.

"This one, right outside the bleedin' barrack gates."

"Well there's no need to be aggressive sergeant, with any luck this shouldn't take long. Ah here comes Sweeper Prendergast with some apparatus." The Leading Sweeper's mild put down to the sergeant was encouraging and for the first time that day I got the feeling that things just might turn out alright.

"Will you try the magnet first Mr. Harris?" asked the dutiful assistant sweeper.

"I think not, Prendergast. There has been a lot of rain lately and experience tell me that there will be too much sludge in the vessel for the magnet to work efficiently. Besides these gentlemen are busy people so let's get them on their way as quickly as possible." We were obviously getting a gold plated service.

"Very well Mr. Harris. I will fetch the vessel retractors at once.' Prendergast returned to the van I felt sure the artificially formal conversation between the two cleansing operatives was especially for our benefit. Harris put on a pair of protective gloves and, with his feet planted either side of the grating, and with a grunt, he lifted the heavy piece of metal from its place. Prendergast was back now, and this time he carried several fearsome looking metal devices. Several long rods with hooks at the end, a huge ladle, again with a very long handle, and a sort of grabbing device. He also had a sieve under his arm. With the exception of the sieve none of the items he carried would have looked out of place in a torture chamber and I did wonder for a moment if these two council stalwarts had ever had occasion to use the devices for inappropriate purposes of their own devising.

The procedure was very efficiently effected. It was deft, swift, and absolutely disgusting.

Leading Sweeper Harris lowered two of the hooked steel rods into the depths of the drain and worked them about until they had engaged in rings at the side of 'the vessel'. Then he had Prendergast lifted it out. It was like an oversized bucket about eighteen inches across and two feet deep. It was full to the brim with stinking black gunge.

"Now we have the vessel safely out let's see what we can find," said Harris, with the air of a surgeon at an anatomy class. He gave a nod to Prendergast and, with a practiced twist of the rods, they tipped the entire revolting contents on to pavement.

"Just what the bloody hell do you think you're doing?" The sergeant was apoplectic.

"I would stand back if I were you, we're not quite finished yet." Harris was quiet yet firm with his advice but the sergeant took no notice and blustered forward. What the sergeant planned to do or say we shall never know because at that moment Harris gave the bottom of the vessel a bang and another huge quantity of muck fell out, splashing about as it hit the pavement and covering the sergeant's boots, gaiters, and lower trousers with great dollops of putrid black slime.

"Bloody Norah!"

"I did warn you."

"Just you wait, just you bloody well wait!" with that threat the sergeant hurried off into the gate house.

I have to admit the rotting filth which now covered a large area of the pavement was not a thing of beauty. Amongst the oily black pool of putrefaction there were a few items that had not completely lost their identity. Most notable of these was a large dead rat but there were other items too, including a dog's collar and a bottom set of false teeth. These last presumably the result of a night on the tiles which had ended as a night face down in the gutter.

"The Probe please Prendergast." Leading Sweeper Harris was becoming tense as he sensed a result. A shorter rod was handed over and Harris used it to stir the festering mess.

"Ah ha!" He had found some keys, but they weren't mine. More poking and stirring which released several awful wafts of powerful pongs. There were several old coins, a cigarette lighter and then, at last, my keys!

"There we are sir, these are yours I imagine." The clue for Leading Sweeper Harris was my Morris Motors key ring.

"Thank you very much, I really didn't think that I would ever see them again."

"Only too happy to be of assistance sir." Harris and Prendergast lowered the vessel back down the drain and then together they replaced the cast iron grating. We didn't shake hands, but I thanked them once again and I slipped Harris a fiver. As they walked back to their van the sergeant reappeared. He had cleaned himself up a bit and still had a towel in his hands. He must have been watching us from the gatehouse wash room. He nearly knocked me over as he rushed past to challenge the Leading Sweeper.

"And where the bloody 'ell do you think you are going?"

"Our work here is done Sergeant, my colleague and I are therefore returning to base."

It was becoming obvious that Harris had little time for the sergeant.

"You can't go yet. What about all this shit on the pavement?"

"What about it?"

"You can't just bugger off and leave it there. The pavement in front of these gates is Crown property, in case you didn't know?"

"Yes I did know, as a matter of fact and that is why I know that it is not the council's responsibility to clear up the mess. Good morning to you Sergeant."

Andy and I exchanged a glance, it was time to go and to go quickly.

The traffic was not too bad that afternoon and as I drove us towards Broadcasting House I began to relax.

"Well that was all very interesting." said Andy.

"It sure was."

"And we've got enough music to last a while."

"I know." I replied, "but I doubt if we will ever be able to get any more."

"Oh I think we'll be ok." said Andy.' "I had a chat with that corporal in the library when you were carrying the first load down to the yard. He said next time we should just get straight on to him and he'll look out everything we need, even drop round to Broadcasting House."

"My God what a hero."

"Yes that's what I thought but he said he would be grateful for the excuse to get out of barracks. By the way, how much did you give Leading Sweeper Harris?"

"A fiver"

"Blimey, that's a good tip."

"I gave him another tip as well."

"What?"

"I told him to fit a bolt to his office door."

Chapter 30.

<u>From Pillar to Post.</u>

I left the BBC on my 49th birthday, which was May 12th 1996. I had been with the corporation for nearly thirty one years. It didn't come as a great shock as, under the 'new broom' tactics of director general John Birt, anybody with a record of long service, and who therefore could remember what the BBC was supposed to deliver, was considered a threat. It only recently occurred to me that I joined the BBC during the tenure of one of the best Director Generals that it ever had, and left during the incumbency of one of the very worst. In that respect, at least, my career had a certain symmetry.

In 1965 Hugh Carlton Greene, was at the helm and the corporation was a confident and respected institution. When I left, in 1996, it was riven with self-doubt, obsequiously obliging to every deceitful politician and the victim of every half arsed, management efficiency scheme that could be foisted on to it by charlatans. The staff was saddened, indeed often infuriated, by this, but seldom surprised. What else could you expect from a man whose first notable celebrity in the post of Director General was the exposure of his attempts at tax avoidance?

The list of determined asset-stripping destruction that took place under John Birt is too depressing to examine in any great detail but suffice it to say that 33,000 music reference books were flogged off on the second hand market. The design reference library, one of the finest in the world, was junked and the' Radio Times Hulton Picture Library' was sold off for a fraction of its value. While the BBC still owned that library, a picture of practically any person or event past or present was available to the programme maker at no cost whatsoever. As soon as it was sold off there was a £50 charge for any picture supplied for research and a charge of £200 for any picture actually included in the programme. The people who had the good sense to buy this invaluable resource soon became rich men.

The concept of the 'internal market', which was so loved by disciples of Thatcherism, had already started to destroy the National Health Service, but this in no way deterred the new guard BBC *Gauleiters* from grasping it with both talons. It is true that this primrose path had first been trodden by Birt's immediate predecessor Michael Checkland. He had been an accountant with the BBC before attaining the post of DG and so came to the job with all the programme making sensitivity of a duty vet in an abattoir. One of his most memorable achievements was to introduce a costing system whereby it was cheaper for a producer to go out and buy a CD required for a programme than to borrow it from the BBC record library, who would already have at least six copies available for loan.

Of course, none of these far reaching 'cost saving' new policies could be brought in without paying obscenely large fees to outside management consultancy firms. This always struck me as particularly ironic as the senior management had awarded itself huge pay increases on the grounds that it was having to take a plethora of difficult logistical decisions; yet, in the event, none were ever taken without first bringing in the consultants, and subsequently paying through the nose. The important thing was that no one could be blamed, every daft policy could be passed off as someone else's idea, so it was money well spent; that is if you know that you are useless and are anxious to protect your pension.

It was galling for an old film fanatic like me to see the BBC, in the 1980s, rushing towards the same drain as that down which MGM had descended in the mid-1970s. Again it was the accountants who gained control and convinced the board of management that MGM could not afford to make films any more. Seeing that film production was the firm's only reason to exist, you might think that someone would have questioned the wisdom of this advice; but no one did. The accountants won the day and, on their infallible advice MGM gave up film making. They sold off their studios, equipment, costumes, props and even the rights to their huge library of feature films for a fraction of their true value and they went into the hotel business. They then went bankrupt shortly after that, but, with bankruptcy, had at last found an area in which their accountants had some expertise.

I am not so naive as to think that the BBC was faultless in the 1960s, but the differences between its management style in 1966 as compared to 1996 were enormous. The most obvious difference was the huge gap between the pay of a senior producer and the pay of the Director General. In 1966 the DG earned about three times more than a senior producer but by 1996 this had risen to about ten times more and this despite a huge increase in cohorts of faceless managerial assistants immediately below the Director General himself. There were more and more 'suits' on large salaries attending meetings and sending vitally important memos to each other couched in the language of management-speak, which nobody understood, including themselves.

I think the most significant event, for me, came when the BBC decided to sell the Ealing Film Studios to the BBRK scenery construction firm. Ealing had been the home of the BBC film department since the corporation bought it in 1955 and its' sale was indicative of the imminent demise of the BBC's, once distinguished, film department. The fact that immediately the sale had gone through, the BBC decided to rent the studios back again, caused a slight raising of suspicious eyebrows, though we were all assured that the fact that the new boss of BBRK was the departing head of BBC Finance had nothing whatever to do with the implementation, of the deal. Three years later, after the BBC had paid out a very considerable amount in rent, it transpired that the corporation had never received the purchase price from BBRK and so had been paying rent on a studio which it still legally owned. This was perhaps the jewel in the crown of the new management team's financial probity. The BBC of old may have been hidebound and self-satisfied but it was basically honest and respectful of license payer's money. It was also liberal, often fearless and always supportive of the talent of its employees. It provided secure employment in the world of the arts and journalism, both of which were notoriously treacherous as providers of a regular income. Sure, the traditional BBC had its share of eccentrics and incompetents but that was a small price to pay for the safe harbour for creativity that only the BBC could offer. Independent Television started broadcasting in September 1955 and expanded dramatically in the 1960s. Despite the fact that ITV offered salaries far in excess of anything that the BBC could afford there was not a stampede towards the new employer. Some people left, of course, but many, at the top of their craft, remained because they realised that only the BBC offered them the right to fail, and, strangely, that right is the one essential for truly innovative programme making.

It was the gradual decline of the long term 'staff contract' that eroded all that. When producers are on short term contracts, a broadcaster seldom has to resort to censorship because the desire for a contract renewal will insure that the producer plays safe. Unsurprisingly, the use of short term contracts and hence 'censorship by mortgage' first took hold of the BBC's News and current affairs departments, but it gradually spread throughout the Corporation.

The BBC was the first broadcasting company in the world and was therefore the first to feel the pressure of bullying government. It was only four years old at the time of the general strike, in 1926, but the fact that the strike had dramatically reduced the numbers of newspapers in circulation suddenly focused all ears on the News from the BBC. John Reith, the first Director General, came under heavy pressure from the government of the day to censor any item that might seem to explain the reasons for the strike. He was even told to deny the Archbishop of Canterbury broadcast time, in case the church delivered any words of comfort to the striking workers. It was as a result of this confrontation that the BBC's concept of balance and unbiased reporting emerged to challenge its' critics: but one man's 'balance' is another man's bias and, consequently, every right wing government since 1922 has thought that the BBC was a den of left wing loonies and every left wing government has been convinced that it was an enclave of right-wing elitists. You need strong, principled men at the top to cope with that sort of paranoia and, sadly, since 1922, there have been few of them at the top of the BBC.

When I was a film editor for the late night news programme *'24 Hours'* a reporter would often come up with a story which exposed corruption in high places. If the report looked like being a real bombshell the programme editor would ask for a member of the BBC's legal department to view the film before it was transmitted. I was often delighted by just how daring these media savvy lawyers were prepared to be. Having watched the film they would usually ask the reporter but one simple question,

"Can you prove all this?" and if the answer was, 'Yes.' the lawyer would say,

"OK, go ahead and transmit it."

Then the programme editor would ask,

"But surely they will sue?"

"Of course they will, but if we can prove it's true they will lose, so bloody well let them sue."

"Oh dear, I really don't think I can risk that, I think we'd better drop the item."

Time after time I witnessed that sort of gutlessness from programme editors; it did wonders for my nascent cynicism.

Strange to relate, the only time I ever worked on a show which was to feel the full, unpleasant weight of Downing Street's Thought Police was not when I was working in Current Affairs but, rather, when I was the production manager on the last series of *'Steptoe and Son.'* There was an episode in which Harold Steptoe hoped to seduce his new girlfriend, Marcia Wiggly, by showing her his newly purchased water bed. There were several scenes of comic seduction in which the actors rushed at each other with cries of,

"Oh Harold, Harold, squeeze me Harold!"

"Marcia, Marcia, I want you Marcia!"

It hadn't occurred to anyone on the production that the newspapers had recently been full of rumours about an affair between the Prime Minster of the day (Harold Wilson) and his personal secretary, (Marcia Falkender). On reflection I think that it probably had occurred to the writers, Alan Simpson and Ray Galton; it was just the sort of joke they would have relished.

The day after the transmission all hell broke loose. The Prime Minister's Office phoned the BBC, convinced that there was a conspiracy, at the heart of the corporation to pour scorn on the leader of Her Majesty's Government.

We were told that making fun of two love birds called Harold and Marcia was practically treason, given the delicate state of the Premier's love life. Heads would roll. The Head of Light Entertainment was summoned to give an explanation, the Producer of the show, a dear man called Dougie Argent, was summoned, I was summoned, anybody who might have had anything to do with the outrage was questioned until it dawned on some senior civil servant that it was very much a case of 'If the cap fits, wear it.' and that it might save a lot of needless embarrassment if the whole matter was quietly dropped. It nevertheless contributed to Harold Wilson's growing conviction that he was being persecuted by BBC. His overreaction also contributed to the growing fear, in the cabinet, that the great man was suffering the early stages of dementia. After all the ' Harold 'in *'Steptoe and Son'* was a sad looser with delusions of grandeur and his girlfriend, Marcia, was a grasping tart on the make. Other than the coincidence of the names what possible resemblance could there be between those two and the other couple?

When I think back to my time at the BBC I can never escape the fact that the best time that I ever had was in my first year. It was during the spring and summer of 1966. I was a trainee and I had been forgotten about by the system. As a trainee assistant film editor you spent your first month having lectures in a class room at the Ealing Studios and then you spent the next eleven months being attached to a different cutting room every four weeks. You moved from arts documentaries, to sport; from drama to news and current affairs. The idea was for each trainee to encounter as many different programmes and techniques as possible. Generally the idea worked very well in that you got to know what programmes and people you would try to avoid like the plague when the great day came and you convinced the appointments board that you had learned enough to be employed as a full assistant editor. This peripatetic year was by its' very nature rather unsettling. You arrived at a strange cutting room on a Monday morning to meet with an editor and his or her assistant, who were more or less welcoming, and then you hung around waiting for them to find something for you to do that you wouldn't be likely to mess up. Obviously the success of these 'attachments' depended very much on the generosity and patience of the editing team to whom you were allocated and also on the point in their schedule at which you joined them. If you arrived at a time when they were in a state of panic with a transmission date staring them in the face, and with a mountain of film still requiring to be cut, a trainee's best plan was to sit quietly in a corner and try not to get in the way. On the other hand, should you have joined your 'home for the month' at the time when the editor was just starting to cut a new programme, then there was a much better chance that some time would be found to teach you some of the mysteries of the craft. In many ways the worst thing about the system was that just as you had got settled in to the ways of a particular editor, it was time to move on. The one thing I dreaded was to be attached to one of those high pressure 'cutting edge' programmes on which everybody was expected to sacrifice life and soul in order for the programme to meet its impossible deadlines and shock the nation, once a week, with some sensational social revelation. The editing teams on these programmes seemed to have given up all claim to a social life and just accepted the fact that they would be required to work long days and all weekends for months at a time. Of course, the overtime was an attraction, but I think that the adrenaline trip that such pressure induces also became a factor; people who worked on shows like that became addicted to the pressure.

One such programme, in the mid-sixties, was *'Man Alive'*; a fifty minute documentary series which, every week, tried to shock or to wring the withers of the Nation with some depressing tale or other. The executive producer was an ex Daily Mirror journalist called Desmond Wilcox. Sharp witted, sharp suited, and reptilian, Wilcox was anxious to convince everybody, and especially himself, that he was a great programme maker. The Mirror had taught him that sleaze spelt success and he brought this maxim with him to television.

A typical subject for a *'Man Alive'* film would be people who had just been told they would be dead in a couple of months. They, of course, would be encouraged to tell the world how it felt. Well, it probably felt much as I did when I was told that my next assignment was going to be *'Man Alive'*.

Like all the other buttock clenching, hard hitting and impossibly scheduled programmes, *'Man Alive'* was based at the Lime Grove Studios. It was a rambling, scruffy dump of a place and I hated it from the word go. I remember that on my first day as a trainee on *'Man Alive'* The Editor, his assistant and I went to a viewing theatre to check the show print for the next evening's transmission. We were met there by the great Desmond Wilcox himself.

John, the editor, tried to introduce me. Wilcox took no notice at all. We sat down and the viewing began. A parade of distressingly unfortunate characters appeared before us, all of them in the last stages of a terminal illness. The thing I most remember about the film was that during one particularly harrowing interview Desmond Wilcox turned to his editor and said,

"Do you know I had to burn off two thousand feet of film before that bloody woman would actually break down and cry?"

If Wilcox had hoped that such a heartless remark would result in gasps of horror from the editing team he was to be sadly disappointed. Even at the age of 19 I realised that Wilcox was simply hoping to perpetuate his image of the tough unshockable journalist whose nerves of steel had been forged in the refining fires of Fleet Street. So we didn't react. We just sat there thinking, "What a pathetic turd."

Back in the cutting room, after the viewing, Colin, the assistant editor, showed me how to mark up the film for transmission and then showed me the tortuous route to the telecine area from where the film would be transmitted. He was a pleasant enough guy. He warned me not to get stressed when things got tough in the cutting room. If people yelled and screamed at each other that was just par for the course. He told me that this week wouldn't be too bad as we were starting on a new film but that after that I should be prepared for very long days and for working at the weekends too. That evening I set off back to my bed-sit in Ealing, with my heart in my boots.

The next couple of days were, as Colin had predicted, not too bad. There were no appearances from the dreaded Wilcox and we got on with sorting out the rushes for the new film. The editor John was a quiet man but kind and helpful. It seemed to me that he looked quite ill. Colin told me that John's nerves had been shattered by working on the programme but that he had large debts; so the over-time was very welcome. In an effort to save every penny John would not eat in the canteen. His wife made him sandwiches every day and he ate those in the cutting room. Colin said that you could always tell John had had a row with his wife because, if he had, she made him carrot sandwiches. John hated carrot sandwiches. During the short time I was with them I couldn't help but notice that John's economies regarding the canteen in no way seemed to extend to bar. I was amazed at just how many pints he could sink at lunch time and yet still remain capable of standing, let alone editing, in the afternoon. According to Colin, this was all on account of John's 'bad nerves'.

By the Thursday of my first week attached to *'Man Alive'* I was becoming reconciled to my fate. I reckoned that both John and Colin were decent, skilled, pros from whom I could probably learn a great deal. Maybe there would be long days ahead but I would just have to put up with it. At least I knew that I had the next weekend off, so I arranged to go back home to my parents in Bedford, meet my old friends there for a Saturday night pub crawl and enjoy one of Mum's Sunday roasts. Then, at about eleven 'o clock on that fourth morning came the bombshell. I had just returned to the cutting room after taking something or other to film dispatch when Colin told me that the editing office at Ealing film studios had called and wanted me to phone them back urgently. I didn't like the sound of that at all. I couldn't bloody believe the news. I was to leave *'Man Alive'* straight away and report to the film department of Television Enterprises at Woodstock Grove. They had a major panic on and needed extra staff urgently. So that was next weekend up the spout and every other week end for the foreseeable future I imagined. John and Colin both said that they were sorry to lose me, we had the makings of a team. I tried to persuade John to phone back and say he really needed me to stay but he was not a man to ever question the management. Besides I think my usefulness was more a figment of my imagination than an actual fact. I went to the canteen for a sustaining coffee then trembling with a mixture of nervousness and rage I headed to the opposite end of Shepherd's Bush Green to find the BBC building in Woodstock Grove.

Of the varied portfolio of London premises owned by the BBC at that time, Woodstock Grove was certainly the most bizarre. It stood at the end of the road from which it took its' name and was built across the road to form a *cul de sac*. With large forbidding wooden gates, it very much resembled a prison, especially as there was a smaller 'pass door', for pedestrians, cut into the right- hand large gate. In the mid-sixties that area of Shepherd's Bush was pretty rough, so, for me, walking that day down Woodstock

Grove, towards that unlovely building, was depressing as hell. Stepping through the pass gate brought me into a courtyard. The positioning of the windows in buildings, which formed a quadrangle looking down onto this yard, gave the impression that the architect was probably a madman. They seemed to be randomly scattered across the facades with no matching line or symmetry However I didn't bother myself with this conundrum for long because very shortly after entering the confines of Woodstock Grove, I became aware of its' most memorable feature. This was an all pervading and sickening pong. I later learned that the stink emanated from the design department's fibre glass work shop which occupied one whole side of the building. Here any piece of scenic moulding, statue or other special 'prop' could be made to order and, in those balmy days, before the rise and rise of health safety, nobody knew, nor cared, that the fumes from the process were carcinogenic.

I found the film dispatch office on the ground floor and asked for directions. The man to whom I was supposed to report was called Neil Fowler. The lad in dispatch was helpful.

"Oh I'll give him a ring and tell him your here, he'll probably come down and meet you."

"Oh no, I'm sure I'll be able to find his office myself."

"I doubt it, this place is maze, floors at one end of the building higher than those at the other, Corridors with bridges in them to join up the levels. You'd better wait."

"Why ever was it built like that?"

"I dunno, never really thought about it."

"But then you never really think about anything much do you Danny?" a new voice had joined our conversation. I assumed it must be Neil Fowler; I was wrong.

"Hello are you Mike?"

"Yes."

"I'm Ray, Neil's assistant, follow me mate. See yer Danny."

We left film dispatch, crossed the yard and set off up a winding stair case. Ray chatted as we went.

"Danny's a nice lad, a bit of a dreamer. He wants to be a writer. I tease him about it quite a bit but he's right about this place, it is a maze."

We had reached the second floor and headed off along a corridor which sloped upwards quite steeply.

"Ray?"

"Yes mate."

"Do you know why this building is so odd?"

"Oh yes mate it was built as a munitions factory during World War One, my auntie used to work here in those days. All the odd spaces and levels were to accommodate the machinery. The BBC bought it cheap, not surprised; neither will you be when you've been here a while.' He laughed rather mirthlessly and my spirits sunk to an even lower ebb.

We reached the end of the corridor and then went down several steps to end up at the same level as that on which we had set out. As we walked I formulated a plan. I was going to insist that I had the forthcoming weekend off. A family wedding, or better still a funeral or maybe a relative in hospital? Anyway some convincing yarn that could bring tears to the eyes of a marble statue. Whatever, I was not going to work the coming weekend.

The corridor we were on suddenly divided .To the left it continued, on the level, past some office doors; to the right there was a sort of bridge. We took it and it brought us up to another level and another corridor.

"Nearly there." said Ray.

"Thank God for that." I muttered.

At last we arrived at door which had a large frosted glass panel in the middle, presumably an attempt to let a bit more light into the dingy corridor. Ray opened the door and directed me in ahead of him. He made a formal intro-duction.

"Ere we are Guv, this is Mike."

A cheerful man, with a very red face, looked up from the motoring magazine that he was reading. "Hello Mike, mate, I'm Neil. Welcome to Woodstock Grove."

I shook hands with my new boss and took in as much detail as I could about the man and the room. Neil Fowler, I guessed was about fifty. He had wavy grey hair and was wearing a, once smart, suit. He looked as if he could appear quite elegant if he made the effort but somehow 'effort' didn't seem a likely part of his persona. He was of average height and build and, as I have already remarked, he had the ruddy complexion of a man who was no stranger to the demon drink.

"So you're a trainee assistant editor, how are you liking it?"

"Oh I like it very much, I'll just be glad when the training period is over and I can settle somewhere for a while."

"Yes, I bet, well we're glad to have you with us, we've got as bit of a crisis, you see."

"Yes the office mentioned that when I was told to come here." I plucked up all my courage and rather blurted out. "Sorry to ask, but will I have to work many weekends?"

Ray burst out laughing and I felt foolish. At that moment the door opened again another assistant came in with a load of paper work. He handed the bundle of forms to Neil.

"This lot should be with us next week Guv."

"Ok thanks Reg, put them on the desk. Oh, by the way this is Mike, who is taking over from Edna, Mike this is Reg."

"Pleased to meet you Mike."

"Thanks Reg." I was just wondering who on earth Edna was, and what her job entailed, when Ray chipped into the conversation

"Mike was wondering if he would have to work many weekends."

"Oh I see." said Reg, "that's why you were laughing. Will you tell him or shall I?"

"Best let him find out for himself, Reg. We don't want to depress the poor lad on his first day here."

I started to feel a bit sick; perhaps this would be the time to play my 'sick relative in hospital' card? Neil started to shuffle through some of the forms that Reg had just delivered and spoke to me, as he did so.

"Mike you will quickly learn that Ray and Reg are a couple of jokers and bleeding lazy with it. That is why they like it here. Just so you know, we never work weekends and we don't hang around much after four o'clock on Fridays either."

"Oh, well that's great, but I thought you had a panic on?"

"Well I had to tell them that at Ealing, otherwise they would never have sent us anyone to replace Edna, and then we would have had a panic on, but now you're here it will be fine. Come with me and I'll show you where you will be working.'"

I followed Neil down another maze of corridors and, as he explained to me what my new job was to be, I couldn't quite believe what he told me. The department of which he was in charge ordered film recordings of BBC television programmes for sale abroad. Quality control was an important factor, so before any programme was sent out if had to be viewed and assessed to make sure that it was technically satisfactory. Edna, the woman who had gone off sick, was their senior programme viewer but she had developed eye strain. The other viewer, a man called Ken Fleet, insisted that he could not be expected to cope alone.

So that was it! My job would be to sit in a comfortable viewing theatre all day and watch film recordings of television programmes.

Chapter 31.

<u>Train Spotting.</u>

The more Neil explained to me about my job as a 'programme viewer' the more incredible I thought it to be. I was to have my own viewing theatre, complete with a dedicated projectionist, and my task was to view programmes and fill in a report form to evaluate the quality of the recording. Top quality prints were sent to Canada, Australia and the USA; second rate prints to India and Jamaica and prints that were plain bloody dreadful to places like Nigeria and Botswana. The reason behind this was not one of racism but rather of economics. The African countries paid very poor rates and often didn't bother to pay at all. Perhaps they might have done if we had ever sent them better prints, but we never did.

I spent my first day working alongside the other viewer, a man called Ken Fleet. He was quite short and wore an old fashioned suit. From the very first he seemed to me to be slightly crazed. The most noticeable thing about him was that he had hair growing out of his large, flat nose. I don't mean out of his nostrils but out of the nose itself .The hair was black and curly; why he didn't shave it off, God only knows?

Once he had taught me how to fill in the report forms, and had and given me some idea of what faults to look out for, he started to bang on about how under-valued the job was and how difficult it could be.

"Some people in the front office think that this is cushy job, boy, but I tell you this, boy, sometimes when I arrive in the morning that film rack over there is stuffed to brim with programmes, boy, and when that happens, boy, I'm telling you boy, It's View, View, View!"

I nodded my head earnestly as I decided he was definitely nuts.

At first Ken Fleet seemed to perceive me as some sort of threat and was constantly saying that he wouldn't tolerate low standards and that it was a 'real man's job'. How watching television programmes all day could ever be con-sidered quintessentially masculine I was unable to imag-ine, but I as long as I frequently said I needed a break, be-cause I was becoming exhausted, he seemed reassured. When he discovered that we had very different tastes and that I had no interest in sports programmes we became good colleagues. It was a quickly agreed that Ken would view all the sports shows and I would specialise in music and arts. Comedy and Variety shows would be split be-tween us, but Ken would have first choice. Suddenly all was well with the world. Ken Fleet continued to call me 'Boy' all the time I worked with him but, after a while, it sounded less aggressive. It was always patronising but, if it kept him sweet, I could put up with that.

I had two other colleagues in the' viewing team'. Ludi and Alan who were the projectionists. The two viewing theatres were quite small and stood side by side so that one projectionist could have easily served them both but this was the BBC in 1966, so one theatre, one projectionist was the rule.

It happened that on my first day only one projectionist was working; this was Ludi. She was a matronly Austrian woman and seemed anxious to please. She explained that the other projectionist Alan suffered from ill health and frequently needed time off to visit various clinics. She drew me into to corner to whisper that as a consequence of one of his illnesses Alan had lost all his hair and that he wore a wig. This, I should understand, was a tragedy for a young man and I had to promise Ludi that when I eventually did actually meet Alan I would pretend not to notice his adornment. I had a lot to think about as I headed home that night but one thing seemed certain, Ludi was a kindly soul.

That night I phoned home from the pay phone in the hall of my Ealing bed-sit. I was able to pass on the good news that I would definitely be able to come back for the weekend and indeed for every weekend in the foreseeable future. I enjoyed the most relaxed night's sleep that I had had in ages and set off bright early for my new job the next morning. I arrived at the viewing theatre at 9.25; five minutes ahead of time. Ludi arrived a 10 and Ken at 10.15. We then all went to the canteen for coffee. This was my first indication of the schedule of the average working day at television enterprises, which was this: Arrive about 10am and have coffee, watch a programme from 10.30 until 11.25(approx.). Have another coffee. Watch another programme. Lunch from 12.30 until 2. Watch three more programmes in the afternoon with a break for tea around a quarter to four. About 5.15 head for home. However as my first day was a Friday the hours were slightly different and we knocked off at 4.30. Ludi told me that the projectors were always maintained first thing on Monday mornings so there would be no point in my arriving much before 10.30. I thought that I had better confirm this with Neil before I left. I needed to deliver my report forms to him anyway. When I got to his office everybody had gone but there was a note for me on his desk. It read, 'Dear Mike, I hope you enjoyed your first day. Please leave your forms on my desk. I should have told you that the projectors are maintained on Monday mornings so don't bother to come in before 10.30. Thanks for everything, have a good weekend regards Neil.' As I set off to St Pancras station I was probably one of the happiest young men in London. I was working with a friendly bunch which consisted of the most work-shy gang of idlers that I was ever to encounter in all my time at the BBC. It suited me down to the ground; I had seldom been happier.

The fact that it was OK to arrive and hour late for work the following Monday was also a real advantage. It meant that I could catch a later train from Bedford to London and miss the worst of the rush hour, and the ticket was cheaper too. I can remember being able to get a seat on the tube train, which was a novelty and, once again, thinking how lucky I was to be going to a job that I would really enjoy.

As I walked confidently up Woodstock Grove, that morning, I recalled that, only four days previously, I had slunk towards those same wooden gates like a condemned prisoner and I now felt guilty that I had not trusted in my Guardian Angel.

I looked in at film dispatch and said a cheerful 'good morning!' to Danny, then I set out on the convoluted route to my viewing theatre. I only went wrong once but the mistake took me right past the tea bar so I was able to get a coffee and a bun to set me up for the hard graft of a full day's viewing. As I approached the theatres I could hear someone bustling about in the projection room. Sure enough, when I opened the door, there was a man fussing around the projector that served Ken Fleet's room. I surmised that this therefore must be Alan and I remembered Ludi's warning. The man was bent over in order to clean the projector's gate so, at first, I could not see his head. What I could see was bad enough, he was wearing an electric blue suit with orange socks and light suede shoes with thick crepe soles. It was the type of outfit that might have been worn by a 'second banana 'comic in a burlesque show. The sound of the door made the man pause and turn round to see who had entered. As I looked on amazed I required every last ounce of self-control to heed Ludi's warning and not to laugh out loud. I knew at once that this was certainly Alan and I had never seen anything like it in my life. The wig, the syrup, toup or Irish, call it what you like, was simply dreadful. Images of curled up furry animals asleep, of hearth -rugs or even coconut door mats came flooding into my mind. The one thing that this particular peruke failed to do was to convince anyone within a distance of 100 yards that its wearer was not bald. Mind you the wig did fulfil one useful purpose in that it distracted an onlooker's attention from away from Alan's truly dreadful false teeth. Whether the disease, to which Ludi had alluded and which had caused Alan to lose all his hair, was the cause I knew not, but it was startlingly evident that, unadorned, the man who stood before me was not only hairless but toothless as well. I had no doubt that it was the NHS that had supplied the wig and the gnashers and that a 'one size fits all' philosophy had been taken to the ultimate with both. At that time the thinking was that false teeth should be perfectly white and perfectly even with the result that they always looked perfectly dreadful. Analogies with pantomime horses and moon-lit grave yards, though hardly original, were, none the less, entirely apposite.

You must understand that the rather lengthy description above snapped into my brain at a glance and that I had to do my very best not to let my thoughts be too evident to my new colleague. This was not made any easier by the fact that Ludi had given me to understand that Alan was a thrusting young blood who had been tragically stricken in his prime by some nameless affliction. It seemed to me that he was quite simply a bald old git with terrible false teeth; however I had a strong presentiment that it would not be long before I would hear the whole sorry tale related by the man himself.

"Good Morning, I'm Mike. I'm filling in for Edna."

"Hello there Mike, my name's Alan Flotsam. I'm the projectionist for Mr. Fleet." There was a distinct implication in that statement that Alan had no intention of lifting a finger to help me in any way at all.

"Oh yes I know, Ken has told me a lot about you." I thought that referring to 'Mr. Fleet' by his first name might prompt Alan Flotsam to loosen up a bit. It worked after a fashion.

"Oh yes I suppose he would have done, I've not had an easy life, you know?" I paused for a moment before I answered him because I feared that whatever I said the result would be the same. I was going to get the full ghastly history of Alan's challenging medical condition. Fortunately fate intervened. The room started to shake and the windows to rattle.

Before that moment I hadn't realised that a railway line passed so close to the east side of the building, right past the window of the projection booth, in fact. It had been one of the many useful routes that had crossed London before the Second World War, but by the mid-1960s it had been closed to passengers and was used only for moving rolling stock between main line stations.

"My God that's loud." I said. "Do we get many of them a day?"

"Oh no, only two or three a week, if that. It's just used as a service line, but the Royal Train goes by sometimes, it must be stored somewhere around here. My mother was thrilled when I told her that. I live with my mother, you know. I keep a camera in my locker and I've promised Mummy that one day I'll get her a good photo of the Royal carriages. She'll be thrilled if I manage it.'

The fact that Alan still lived with his mother didn't really come as surprise, neither did the lady's rather limited expectations about what Alan might be able to 'manage'. Putting his wig on straight seemed to be one challenge too many. Ludi arrived and I breathed a sigh of relief. She glanced across to the film rack.

"Oh there's quite a lot in today then, would you like to make a start Mike?"

"Well its 10.40 already, so I think we'd better."

"Oh no we must wait for Mr. Fleet." said Alan. "He is the senior; he must have first choice of what to view."

"Oh we've already settled that." I said with a touch of authority. "Fortunately Ken's tastes are very different from mine; he wants to watch all the sport programmes, which is fine by me. He doesn't much care for serious plays and can't stand classical music. I like both of those, so if there is a play on that shelf to be viewed or a concert, then let's start with that, Ludi."

An awkward moment was averted by the sound of another approaching train. Alan suddenly started to tremble with anticipation and he rushed to his locker to grab hold of his camera. Ludi, meanwhile dashed to the window and raised the Venetian blind .Their actions had the appearance of a well-rehearsed routine. Ludi looked across to Alan as he faffed about with his Pentax.

"Hurry up Alan, I think it's the Royal train."

"I'm coming, I'm coming! Sod it I can't see a thing in the finder. What the hell's wrong with it?"

"You've got the lens cap on."

"Oh yes, bugger!"

The train sped past the window.

"Was it the Royal?"

"Yes."

The door opened and Ken fleet made his entrance. "Good morning all. That was the Royal train wasn't it? Did you get your picture at last, Alan?" Alan shot Ludi and me a mean-ingful glance. "Yes thanks, Mr. Fleet, I think I got a good one." he lied.

Chapter 32.

<u>Goodbye To All That.</u>

My time as a programme viewer for television enterprises was speeding past all too quickly. As I have said, trainee attachments were only ever supposed to last for a month, so towards the end of my third week at Woodstock Grove I became increasingly fearful of the dreaded phone call that would post me to some other job where I would automatically revert to the role of dog's body. Had I been burning to advance my career, to work on the high pressure programmes and be seen to be able to cope with the intense demands of impossible schedules, then I would have wanted to leave the sleepy backwater of Neil Fowler's cosy empire post haste. But I have never felt there was much point in working any harder than absolutely necessary, especially in the world of television where one notch up from the bare minimum would often be hailed as the work of a driven genius. I reached the end of my fourth week and no call came, so I decided to ask Neil Fowler what I should do. He asked me if I was happy in my odd new job and, when I said that I was, his advice was both wise and typical. He told me to do nothing. I had obviously been overlooked by 'the system'. The mistake would probably not be spotted until it was time for trainee assistant editors to be given their trial postings as full assistants. When that time came he promised to give me a glowing report and also to recommend me to one of his editor friends. Someone for whom it would be good to work and who would make sure that I was fully prepared for the final exam at the end of the training period. I gratefully accepted his offer.

For the immediate future I would remain in the job which I still considered to be the best in London.

As it turned out my time as a programme viewer was far from wasted. I got to learn a lot about the technical faults of film prints. I could tell if the problem was simply with the print or more seriously with the negative. I also gained an insight into the extraordinary mistakes of which the film laboratories were occasionally capable. The sound for reel two being printed on the picture of reel three or even the sound printed in reverse so that it was only comprehensible when the picture ran backwards. Of course I also learned a great deal about the whole contemporary output of BBC television and which of those programmes were in the most popular with foreign buyers. The overriding impression that remains with me to this day is how technically crude many of the shows actually were. The 60s may well have been a creative golden age of television but, my God, some of the shows were as rough as an old boot. The ambient level of background noise in the television studios of the period was always intrusive. So Anna Karenina's boudoir throbbed to the hum of the studio extractor fans and Jane Eyre's sleep was disturbed quite as much by the clunk of cameramen changing lenses as it was by the mad woman in her attic. Indeed it was not entirely unknown for cameras to collide with each other as they rushed from set to set. The majority of programmes, at that time, were broadcast 'live'. A programme was recorded, on film as it was transmitted, in order to be able to repeat it and to be able to sell it to other overseas broadcasters. Therefore a number of the plays that I viewed occasionally contained cock-ups of an extraordinary nature. For example, in an episode of *'Hereward the Wake'* an actor knocked over a candle and set fire to a bear skin rug. The quick thinking director cut out of the scene early to allow the growing conflagration to be dealt with; but the set for the next scene was right next door to the one with the fire. In the story this new scene was supposedly located in France, the other side of the channel from the inflammable bear. The illusion of action in a distant land was somewhat spoiled by the dense smoke which drifted across the new scene and the sounds of fire extinguishers in full flood. In the BBC's version of *'The Hunch-back of Notre Dame'* an even more disastrous event occurred. The King of the vagabonds was showing a novice brigand how to steal a purse. A large mannequin dummy, dressed as a jester and covered in jingle bells, was suspended from a beam. The idea was that an accomplished cut-purse could remove the purse attached to the dummy's belt without making the slightest tinkle. If the novice failed in this task he would be beaten but, out of roughish fairness, the King of the Vagabonds would demonstrate the required skill. As this was always going to be a tricky feat to pull off on live television one might possibly question the decision to cast Wilfred Lawson in the role of the Vagabond King. He certainly looked the part; but Mr. Lawson's capacity for booze was legendary. Come the transmission he was as pissed as a newt. His attempt to silently cut the purse from the bell dummy was, therefore, less than successful, He not only fell off the table on which he was standing, he brought the whole damned dummy crashing to the floor. Once again the director swiftly cut to the next scene but, once again the viewers at home were to be distracted by thumps and tinkles on the sound track combined with, less than decorous, oaths from Mr. Lawson as he struggled to escape from under the weight of his clangourous adversary.

It was incidents such as these that prompted directors to start to do retakes. The show might have been transmitted live but there was no reason for the repeat to contain the same awful mistakes. Immediately after transmission all that was needed was to re-do the scene that had messed up. As the programme had been recorded on film the re-take could easily be cut in by a film editor. It wasn't long before the penny dropped and most directors realised that a far better method of production would be to abandon live broadcasts of drama and simply record them in the first instance. Any mistakes could then be resolved and edited before transmission. Studio time was thus freed from the shackles of live broadcast and the overall polish of the productions was much improved. This system worked well; a whole department of film editors was formed to work on telerecordings and, for as long as television remained in black and white, the picture quality of 35mm film recordings was acceptable.

As I have said, it was telerecordings made for sale abroad that I was checking in my cosy viewing theatre in Woodstock Grove. The most recent productions had been edited, as I have described but programmes were still for sale which had been made in the days of live broadcast so I witnessed a lot of bizarre 'on screen' events. These frequently involved the end credits. The technology was crude, the list of names was made in white letters attached to a long strip of black paper wound onto a roller. This was then mounted in a frame and pulled upwards by a second, electrically driven, roller at the top. A camera focused on the roller and this image was usually superimposed onto final scene. Had these roller gadgets been better made and more reliable then all might have been well, but they weren't. They hardly ever ran at the same speed twice, they often jammed, and, worst still, because of a weak levelling screw, they sometimes fell over sideways during their run. This induced an aura of tat to, otherwise sophisticated, productions as credits suddenly collapsed and shot across the screen at a drunken angle You can still sometimes see such credits if you search' You Tube' for vintage T.V. programmes

Very early in my time as a programme viewer the boss, Neil Fowler, had advised me not to reject too many prints. There was always some country, somewhere which would accept even the duffest of copies. So it was that I continued to view my daily quota of telerecordings and simply marked my forms as good quality, medium or bad. If the credits suffered from the running up the screen on the piss syndrome, I would add a comment like, 'Amazing end credits!' This was true but did not read as if there was anything wrong with the programme. It wasn't long before I realised that if nothing was ever rejected there was really no point in the work at all but that didn't worry me; it was still a great job.

The weeks passed, Ken Fleet continued to come in late every morning with tales of what a night he had had on the town and what a 'real man's life he lead. I think he was a repressed homosexual but then, so was I, so I pretended to be enthralled by his fictitious tales of heavy drinking bouts with his mates and of his heterosexual conquests. Occasionally he would say something genuinely surprising. There was a story in the news about a policeman being beaten up by a teenage thug.

"Do you know what I'd do if I saw a policeman being duffed over by a lout, boy? I'll tell you what I'd do, boy, I'd get stuck in and help him."

"The policeman you mean?"

"No, boy, I'd help the lout."

I reckoned that Ken Fleet was certainly a man with an odd past. For all his ultra conservative veneer and Brylcreemed hair he harboured some very anti-social tendencies.

The daily routine was, by now, well established. Every morning I would arrive punctually at 9.30 and go straight to the canteen for breakfast. As long as I could be in my theatre before 10.00, I could avoid Ken Fleet's arrival and his compulsive recounting of fantasies about his 'real man's life'. Ludi always got in on time and would have a film laced up and ready for me when I came in from breakfast. Alan usually got in at about the same time and messed about with his camera just in case the Royal Train went past. He had still not yet managed to take the picture which he had promised his elderly mother. Recently there had been a change in his appearance. He had taken to wearing large fedora-style hats. One tea break, when Alan was out of the room, Ludi told me the reason for this new image. Alan had overheard the land lord of his local pub discussing some of his regular customers with a friend. Alan was sitting behind a pillar, out of sight of 'mine host' and was appalled to hear mention of the 'camp old git with a dead cat on his head.' Alan left the pub that night having made two important decisions. He would find another local and he would buy a large hat.

Twice, while I was working for Neil, he asked us all to stop what we were doing for the day and help to clear some space in the film vaults. This was boring, rather dirty work but it had to be done, now and then, to make room for new stock. Some programmes, which had not sold as well as had been hoped were cluttering up the shelves and needed to be sent for recycling. The image in black and white films is made up of grains of silver nitrate and it is not very difficult to retrieve the pure silver from the celluloid film base. Hence the economic sense for getting rid of old, unsold, black and white film negatives and prints. The fact which the management overlooked was that the programmes which TV Enterprises sold were 16mm film recordings. This meant that anyone who had a 16mm sound projector could show them at home. It is true that by the mid-1960s most home movie enthusiasts used 8mm, but remember, the guys and gals who were ordered to clear out the vaults, worked in the profession and, therefore, many of them did have 16mm projectors at home. As a result many of the prints which were destined for the recycling skip ended up being spirited away and stored in attics, under beds, and in garages. The significance of this only occurred to me many years later when archive programmes that had been officially 'lost forever' started to miraculously appear and be digitally re-mastered. How did that missing Dr Who episode ever get to end up in a loft in Acton?' some naive jerk of a media correspondent would ask on a radio feature. The answer is simple. In the 1960s Reg used to rent a flat in that house and that is where he stored the telerecordings that he had filched during a vault clearing session.

Even some programmes which were recorded on video tape and then subsequently wiped managed to survive by the same freak chance. This was because they had often been transferred into to a film recording for sale overseas. In the early days of video tape only the richest companies could afford to buy the new video equipment and so the poorer stations still wanted the programmes to be available on film. Film recordings therefore continued to be made for a while. As long as television remained in black and white recordings on film served a purpose. It was the advent of colour that finally spelt doom for the curious process of tele-recording. The technique of filming a television screen which, however cunningly modified the camera might be, was the basic crude system for tele-recording simply didn't work well enough in colour. The results were nearly always ghastly and garish.

A couple of days after the second vault clearing secession Alan arrived for work in a very excited frame of mind. He was wearing yet another new hat, one result of the two resolutions he had taken after hearing himself ridiculed in his local. Of course the hats he had chosen to hide his wig were all ill advised. This one was black with an orange band around it, presumably to match in with his favourite socks. It did little for him because, whilst it did hide the wig it somehow managed to emphasise the teeth. Ken, Ludi and I all assured him that it was a great hat. There was no way that we were going to cause a rift, by being honest. We would leave that to the regulars in his new boozer, he could learn the truth from them, for he had changed pubs, just as he said he would, as part two of his resolution. Indeed, it was as a chance encounter in his new watering hole that was causing all his excitement as he rushed into the projection room that morning.

"I just can't believe my luck, I've met this amazing man in 'The Queen's Head.'"

At first I thought that Alan had found the light of his life and was so head over heels in love that he had become reckless and determined to 'come out.' The truth was less dramatic, but it was portentous all the same.

Alan had got into conversation with an elderly railway worker called Wilf and Wilf had access to all the rolling stock movements along the line that ran past Wood Stock Grove. Alan's days of waiting on tenterhooks for a chance passing of the Royal Train were over. For the price of a few drinks Wilf would divulge this classified information and the next time the Royal Train ran past our windows Alan would be ready and waiting.

"It's Mum's birthday at the end of the month and it would be great if I could give a framed photo of the train. She's always wanted one, I've told you that before, but now I've got a good chance of taking a really good picture. Oh she'll be thrilled!"

I found this hard to believe but Alan was convinced and it would have been churlish to dampen his enthusiasm.

"How much notice can this chap Wilf let you have?" Ken Fleet was casting himself in the role of project manager.

"A couple of days he reckons."

"Is his info any good?"

"I wondered that too, but we can test him out. He said that a load of goods wagons will pass by at 11.15 tomorrow. If they do, then I think we can trust him."

Alan's problem, in the past, had always been that with the clatter of the projectors and the noise from the loud speakers in the viewing theatres an approaching train often went unnoticed until the last minute. Advance information would enable him to be prepared and ready for action.

The next morning we all got in early and Ken and I worked out our viewing schedule so that neither of the theatres were running at 11.10. We then all sat and waited. Sure enough at 11 12 we could hear an approaching train and at 11.15, on the dot, a dirty old engine pulling a load of goods wagons passed under our windows.

"There we are then," said Alan," Good old Wilf .Now all we have to do is to wait until he tips us off about the Royal Train."

"Maybe," said Ken, "But I think we should be more organised than that."

"How do you mean?"

"Well the Royal Train doesn't come past very often, so I think we should plan a rehearsal. Alan, find out from Wilf when the next train is due to pass, any train, it doesn't matter. We've all got cameras and we should bring them in and practice taking shots. We can find out the best places to stand, we can even open the windows. You and Ludi will take pictures from the projection room and Mike and I can raise the blinds in his viewing theatre so we can photograph from there. Don't worry, you'll have the best spot, but we will provide back up, ok?"

So that was the agreed plan and two days later, when the next goods train rattled past, we were ready for our dummy run. Alan stood on a chair so that he could lean out of the top of the first projection room window. Ludi, who had the best camera of any of us, stood on the floor by the open second window. Ken and I were in position by the window of my viewing theatre. The Venetian blind had remained undisturbed for about a hundred years so we got showered in thick dust when we raised it, but we stuck to our task.

"In this life we have to make sacrifices sometimes, you know Boy?"

"Oh yes Ken, sure we do." I had an idea that Ken Fleet was intent on adding this thrilling encounter with a dangerous Venetian blind to the story book fantasies of his 'Man's Life'.

The scruffy old goods train rattled past a couple of minutes ahead of schedule but we were ready for it and each of took about six pictures. It was a useful rehearsal; shutter speeds focus and exposures were all noted and we also determined if we needed to adjust were we stood. Ludi thought she would have been better placed further to the left; Ken and I should have stood further apart and Alan said he would have been able to lean out of the window better had he been on a step ladder instead of a chair. We had learned a lot and now eagerly awaited our big day.

We had to wait another ten days before Wilf delivered the news that the royal train was likely to pass us at 14:30hrs the following Monday. He could not be 100% sure as the train was never mentioned by name on his schedules, for security reasons. However a 'special' was listed and Wilf felt pretty sure that special, in this case, meant Royal.

There was a distinct feeling of suppressed excitement in the viewing area that Monday morning. Alan was all fingers and thumbs when it came to lacing the projector and he claimed to have hardly slept a wink. Ludi went into mother hen mode and brought us all so many cups of coffee that by mid-day we were all seriously over-caffeinated. Ken Fleet 'went military' and kept droning on about the need for us to be a disciplined unit. I did my best to take it all seriously and, anyway, I was genuinely keen that we should get Alan's mad old Mum the picture she wanted. We took an early lunch and Alan went to collect the step ladder which he had arranged to borrow from house services. By 14:10 we were in place and primed for action. Ken explained that it was better for us to be ready too early than to have to panic at the last minute. He had a talent for stating the bloody obvious; but then at 14.15, as if to prove him right, we heard the distant approach of a train.

"Ok everyone this is it, final check of cameras, take your positions and good luck." This was Ken in the full flood of fantasy.

"Here she comes," screeched Alan in a sort of high pitched falsetto. Then Ludi said,

"Well that can't be it, surely?"

"The only thing that is special about that is the fact it is even dirtier than the usual goods train." said Alan from the grim depths of disappointment. We were all deflated. There was an anticlimactic pause.

"What's the time?" asked Ken, "Is the tea bar still open?'

"Yes," said Ludi it's only twenty five past.

"Well I don't know about you lot, but I'm going for a tea."

"Hang on a minute," said Alan.

"No, I'm going now." said Ken.

"No I mean shut up and listen!"

"Alan's right," said Ludi, "there's another train coming."

"And it's nearly half past two." I added excitedly." Ken Fleet rushed to the window shouting as he went, 'Positions!"

"It's gleaming in the sunshine," said Alan. "This has to be it." He shot up his ladder so fast that he nearly fell out of the window but Ludi pulled him back and we were all in place when the shiny red and gold carriages glided past.

"I've got a good one," Alan shouted, as he leant even further out of window, "And another."

"Me too." said Ken, "How about you Ludi?"

"Three I hope."

"Ok, Mike?'"

'"Yes Ken, two good ones I think."

"Oh Hooray Hurrah!" Alan shouted as he came back down to earth. Ludi looked over to him and nearly dropped her camera.

"Oh Alan, oh dear me Alan, I think you had better sit down, love."

"Whatever for?" he said.

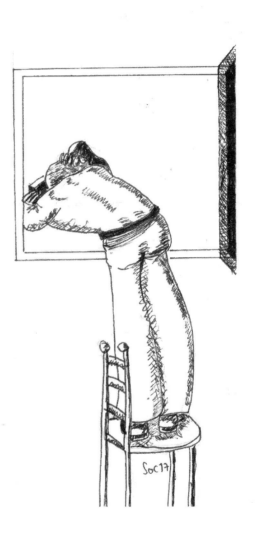

511

When the pictures were developed many of them were very good but we agreed that it was one of Alan's photos that would make the best present for his Mum. This wasn't because it was especially better than any of the rest but he had taken his first. On all the pictures, taken a few seconds later by the rest of us, there was a strange object clearly visible on the roof of her Majesty's private carriage.

It was Alan's wig.

A couple of weeks after the drama of the Royal Train Neil received the phone call from Ealing, the one I had been dreading. It was time for trainee assistant editors to be placed as acting full assistants in the run up to the final tests at the end of the year. I knew that my job at Woodstock Grove could not go on forever but I was still sad to learn the news. Neil was good as his word and fixed it for me to work with a really kind and experienced old editor from whom I learned a hell of a lot and whose teaching helped me pass my end of year exam with no trouble.

As I left Woodstock Grove on my last Friday I knew that I would never experience such an easy going time again and I resolved that for however long I continued to work for the BBC there was one goal I had to fulfil, one maxim that would guide my every career decision;

"It's only television and it's better than working."

THE END

28081322R10282

Printed in Great Britain
by Amazon